A
Pilgrim's
Almanac

DISCLAIMER

The author, fully aware of the crimes which the Chou rulers of China (1122-256 B.C.) considered to be so damaging that no defense was possible and punishment was a swift death, makes the following statement:

The feast days, dates and facts in this book are not guaranteed by the author or the publisher. While every effort has been made to provide you, the reader, with an accurate almanac of important and interesting events, neither the author nor the publisher can swear under oath to the absolute correctness of these entries. Scholars across the world differ on the precise dates of some historical events which occurred before the modern age of keeping records.

The greatest crimes according to the Chou rulers were: "To bewilder and perplex the multitude, whether by wearing strange clothes, playing unusual music, inventing new tools and machines or **spreading false information about the days and seasons**." The author has worked under the principle that it is better to celebrate a feast with a 90% chance of its accuracy than not to celebrate it at all.

A Pilgrim's Almanac

Reflections for Each Day of the Year

A book of feast days and holy days,
holidays and festivals,
of seasons, astronomical occurrences,
interesting and humorous events and strange phenomena;
birthdays of the famous and the infamous,
of the forgotten but creative people
who have helped shape our daily lives;
dates of important and wondrous inventions;
words of wisdom from ancient and modern sages;
special events not to be forgotten;
important historical dates from the future
which both give hope and cause concern;
sacred observances and observances of all kinds

and

reflective readings and short parables
intended to season your life, inspire your spirit
and awaken your soul.

Edward Hays

Forest of Peace
Publishing

Suppliers for the Spiritual Pilgrim

Other Books by the Author:
(available through the publisher or your favorite bookstore)

Prayers and Rituals

Psalms for Zero Gravity
Prayers for a Planetary Pilgrim
Prayers for the Domestic Church
Prayers for the Servants of God

Parables and Stories

The Gospel of Gabriel
The Quest for the Flaming Pearl
St. George and the Dragon
The Magic Lantern
The Ethiopian Tattoo Shop
Twelve and One-Half Keys
Sundancer
The Christmas Eve Storyteller

Contemporary Spirituality

The Old Hermit's Almanac
The Lenten Labyrinth
Holy Fools & Mad Hatters
Pray All Ways
Secular Sanctity
In Pursuit of the Great White Rabbit
The Ascent of the Mountain of God
Feathers on the Wind

A Pilgrim's Almanac

copyright © 1989, by Edward M. Hays

Library of Congress Catalog Card Number: 89-91470
ISBN: 0-939516-12-8

published by
Forest of Peace Publishing, Inc.
PO Box 269
Leavenworth, KS 66048-0269   USA
1-800-659-3227

printed by
Hall Commercial Printing
Topeka, KS 66608-0007

1st printing: October 1989
2nd printing: March 1990
3rd printing: May 1992

4th printing: January 1994
5th printing: December 199
6th printing: September 1ʳ

cover art and illustrations by
Edward Hays

DEDICATED TO

a fellow pilgrim, friend and
companion in community life for twelve years

Thomas Skorupa

who has edited this book
as well as my other writings
with such creative skill and love

SPECIAL GRATITUDE TO

Thomas Turkle   as managing editor, for his invaluable suggestions and input.

Paula Duke   for her careful proofreading and editing of this book.

Thomas Jacobs   for his assistance with the layout.

Steve Hall   for his assistance as the printer—and to the fine staff at Hall Directory, Inc. of Topeka, Kansas.

David DeRusseau   as art consultant.

Father Bill Maher   who encouraged me several years ago to write a column for *The Leaven*, the Kansas City, Kansas Archdiocesan newspaper. The essays in this book are taken from the collection of those previously published columns.

and to my companions in the community of Shantivanam for their encouragement, suggestions and assistance in the publication of this pilgrim's almanac.

TABLE OF CONTENTS

HOW TO USE THIS PILGRIM'S ALMANAC

There will be a natural temptation to read in advance or to flip through this pilgrim's almanac to find reflections which interest you. While that can be fun, be aware as well that this almanac is intended for daily use and reflection. To use it to its full advantage, you will sometimes need to hold back the child within you who is eager to open presents before Christmas, and read the reflection only for the present day. Then use the reflection for the day as a seed to carry with you, making it your daily meditation. Expand its personal meaning as you go about your daily activities.

The reader will find that certain dates not only have a historical or spiritual event to celebrate but also a reflective saying by the person or about the event that is being commemorated. Besides the brief daily reflections there are also 149 longer readings, parables and prayers inserted among the 366 almanac entries. These latter reflections expand some of the daily thoughts or offer a counterpoint view, or at times they highlight the season of the year that is being celebrated.

PILGRIM FEAST DAYS

The Gregorian Calendar is used by most countries for government and business, but other calendars are used in some cultures to keep their sacred celebrations. Most religious feast days of Jewish, Moslem, Hindu, Buddhist and other religions are determined by lunar cycles. As a result, while some of these celebrations are referred to, they are not generally listed among the dates in this almanac which is designed to be used for daily prayer every year. This is also true for the Christian sacred seasons of Advent, Lent and Easter and the feasts of Ascension and Pentecost. There are, however, some Lenten, Advent and Easter reflections in the main body of the text, as they fall within the central range of dates which these movable seasons span. For additional readings (there are sixteen in all) on the Christian annual pilgrim feasts, please consult the concluding section of this almanac. You may also wish to join in celebration with those of non-Christian religions who do not use the Gregorian Calendar for their sacred days by each year obtaining a calendar which indicates these festivals.

PREFACE FOR A PILGRIM'S ALMANAC

VIEWING YOURSELF AS A PILGRIM

If you look closely at the two pilgrims shown on the cover of this book, you will see that both of them are wearing the mark of a scallop shell, a medieval sign of being a pilgrim. This practice began when those on a pilgrimage to the shrine of St. James of Compostella in Spain used this symbol to identify themselves as pilgrims. It has been carried over to modern times in unnoticed or unlikely ways, such as the Shell Oil Company employing the scallop shell as a symbol of providing service to travelers. It would serve you to inwardly carry this symbol with you as you read this pilgrim's almanac to help you remember that you are a pilgrim on the Way.

You are such a pilgrim in at least three ways. Firstly, in the broadest sense, from the womb to the grave you are on a holy journey. As your life unfolds, you pass through the holy lands of infancy, childhood, adulthood and retirement, finally coming to the last sacred shrine, your death. To make such a journey holy requires the celebration of personal historical events and memorable encounters.

Secondly, since you have come from God and are journeying back again to our Sacred Source, you are also on a prayerful pilgrimage that has its own unique sacred shrines. These are sacramental times of transition such as baptism and marriage. They also include encounters with holy guides, seasons of suffering, significant personal deaths and rebirths as well as the holy experiences of love and friendship. Your experience of this pilgrimage is enhanced as you remember the purpose of your journey by celebrating the feast days of saints, holy heroes and heroines and the various holy days of your religious calendar.

Thirdly, as an earthling, you are traveling in space at this very moment at a speed of 67,000 miles per hour on the ancient pilgrimage of Earth's 365 day journey around our daystar, the sun. At the same time as that pilgrimage is taking place, you, along with the sun and the planets of our solar system, are traveling at 633,000 miles an hour in a circular journey around our galaxy. This is a lengthy pilgrimage which takes our solar family 230 million years to make one complete circle around the center of the Milky Way. And as a resident of that galaxy, with its more than 200 billion stars, you are also traveling at 1.4 million miles an hour on a mystic pilgrimage toward the constellation Hydra and beyond. Truly, each one of us is a cosmic pilgrim.

May this pilgrim's almanac assist you in remembering and reverencing these sacred journeys and in celebrating the festivals, feast days and holidays of the past, present and future. And may you begin your journey through this book as processions and pilgrimages began in olden days, with the blessing *Procedamus in pace*, "Let us proceed in peace."

January

1   **New Year's Day**. In ancient times and cultures the new year was a great feast of rebirth. The old year had died and a new one was born. It was a time for the rebirth of all things. Make this holiday truly a fresh new beginning. And in this coming year, invest yourself in this activity as often as possible. The sacred seasons of Lent and Advent provide other festivals for freshness and rebirth. Begin this new year by being new in as many ways as possible.

SOMETHING WORTH THE WEAR OF WINNING

A new year is more than a change of calendars; it's a new beginning—or at least it can be for those who are willing to seize the opportunity. The English writer and poet Hilaire Belloc once wrote,

> From quiet hours and first beginning,
> out to the undiscovered ends,
> there's nothing worth the wear of winning,
> but laughter and the love of friends.

Striving to win is not wrong unless we are wearing ourselves out attempting to win the wrong things. In America we have the custom of celebrating New Year's Day by watching bowl games, a ritual of competition and the fight to win. Belloc advises us to strive rather to be victorious in winning the goal of "laughter and the love of friends." What better advice at the beginning of the new year to help us examine our priorities.

True friendship is a rare gift to win in our all-too-busy world, our lives overloaded with obligations and work. For friendship takes time and effort, requires creativity as well as that mortal sin of the assembly line, the ability to "waste time." Unless we are willing to waste our precious hours being in the company of a good friend, seeking nothing but the pleasure of another's company, we shall miss one of life's rarest gifts.

In olden days friendship was easier, for people spent most of their lives in the same village or neighborhood. Today our work causes us to frequently move from place to place, and with so much greater ease in mobility, it is commonplace to have a large number of acquaintances but few friends. While we often use the word "friend" even for people we have known for only a short time, it should imply a deep and profound sort of communion. Among certain tribes in Africa, when two friends ended a relationship, it required a formal ritual of divorce by the whole tribe. As in so many other matters, primitive peoples often had a deeper understanding of the realities of life than do we.

In reading the Gospels, it is clear that Jesus had both a profound respect for and personal knowledge of friendship. His use of the word implies the sort of bond which primitive peoples considered as sacred and secure as marriage.

This new year can be a fresh beginning, or it can be nothing more than an overlapping and extension of the past, where the only thing that changes is the page on our calendar. In these first new days of a new year, what better resolution could we make than to deepen our existing friendships into relationships of communion that are truly holy.

Feast of Baby New Year. The image of a diapered baby wearing a banner with the number of the year has its origin in fourteenth century German culture. But the New Year symbol of a baby is an ancient one, going back to the Egyptians and Romans who carried an infant in a basket in their New Year parades. How can your new year really be a sign of new life rather than just a dull continuation of the past year?

2

Birthday of J.R.R. Tolkien in 1892. This creative storyteller of great adventures said, "All that is gold does not glitter. All those who wander are not lost." As the new year begins, you might ask, "Am I heroically wandering on a true quest, or am I lost?" There's a bit of folk wisdom that says, "Those who know where they are going today aren't going anywhere!"

3

Short People Day. General Tom Thumb's birthday, 1838. Standing three feet, four inches tall and weighing seventy pounds, he was a star of P.T. Barnum's shows. Having performed before Queen Victoria and heads of state, he teaches us that size has nothing to do with talent or greatness. His enterprising spirit suggests how we can maximize our seemingly small talents.

4

THE VIRTUE OF BEING ENTERPRISING

We have used only a few days in this new year with its over three hundred and sixty new, fresh days. While the year is still young, we still have time to determine any changes in how we wish to live it. Can we address the issues of our lives, the conflicts and the challenges of our relationships, with greater creativity and with a spirit of initiative? An old Moslem parable may help us in this regard.

Once upon a time there was a very clever but non-religious man. Worship and prayer were not a pattern in his life. Now it happened that a serious problem entered his life, and having exhausted all his efforts to better the situation, he began to pray to God. In his prayer he made a vow that if God would resolve the problem, he would sell his beautiful home and give all the proceeds to the poor. God heard his prayer and granted him a favorable response. But as the man looked at his palatial house and saw how much money would go to the poor from its sale, he had second thoughts about his vow. Now the man also owned a cat, and a clever idea came to him about how to work around the vow he had made. He offered his home for sale at the price of one silver piece, but with the home came the cat which cost ten thousand silver pieces!

This story echoes the theme of the parable of Jesus about the unjust servant who was discovered stealing from his master (Lk. 16: 1-8). Knowing what was to happen, he began to cut in half the bills that were owed to his master so that he would find a new home with his master's creditors. Jesus congratulated the unjust servant for his initiative and said that the children of the world are more enterprising than the children of God.

Both of these parables reveal a truth that non-religious people tend to show more initiative and creativity than religious people. A quick glance at society reveals how much time, energy and work—and how much risk—are involved in the pursuit of purely material matters. And if we look at the effort and creativity we put into our prayer and worship, we might find it to pale in comparison. Our search for the mystery of the Kingdom is usually marked more by habit, routine and passivity than by the spirit of enterprise. Indeed, we can easily become "Pilgrims of the Rut."

The word "enterprising" implies a readiness to experiment and be involved with what might be risky and difficult. We tend to take few risks in our lives. Prayer can easily become as routine as brushing your teeth. When we play it too safe, all life becomes more automatic and less interesting. The parable of Jesus in Luke's Gospel is a good one to read at the beginning of a new year because it challenges us to make all of our life enterprising: our marriages, our homes, our relationships, our prayer, our worship, the finding of time for silence and solitude and the pursuit of our spiritual life.

This first week of the new year is still not too late to make an invigorating resolution to become more enterprising. If we could only approach our prayer life and our personal relationships with the same zeal, creativity and initiative that others employ in their pursuit of making money, think of what might happen!

5 **Twelfth Night, Eve of the Feast of the Magi**, an ancient feast of parties and celebrations. Go outside tonight and feast your eyes on the stars which spangle in the skies. Spend a minute or two in adoration of the marvel of those distant suns, aware of the vast space that separates them. The closest star to our daystar, the sun, is Alpha Centauri which is only twenty-five trillion miles away.

6 **Epiphany, the Twelfth Day of Christmas**. The feast of stars which honors the great star that led the Magi to the Christ child. Traditional feast to bring peace and a blessing to your home. Also a day to ponder the larger home in which you live, our galaxy, which is located in that vast and awesome neighborhood of the universe. Step outside this evening and look up at the over 200 billion stars that blaze in beauty in our galaxy alone. The splendor of it should cause you to pray as did the Magi, in adoration of God.

The Birthday of Life on Planet Earth. Life begins in the sea, 3.5 billion years ago. Single-celled organisms begin to form more complex, multi-cellular life forms. Celebrate, today, the great and long struggle-dance by which divine seeds of life grow into their radiant fullness.

7

A NEW NEW YEAR'S GREETING

We are already one full week into this new year, and we have already begun to wonder whether this is really going to be a happy new year. While our problems tend to increase like our federal taxes, as we add up our holiday debts and look at our credit card bills, we might seriously question how happy this year of our lives will be.

The Chinese celebrate their New Year in February at the new moon. I don't know how they express New Year's greetings, but Confucius, a saintly Chinese sage, had an expression that holds the secret to how our new year can be both good and happy. Confucius said, "The gem cannot be polished without friction, nor any person perfected without trials."

Since the goal of our lives is to be perfect (at least Jesus challenged us to be perfect as is our heavenly parent), it would seem fitting to propose a new New Year's greeting: "May you have a Troubled New Year!" Yet the very sound of such a greeting hurts the heart. We all have enough troubles now: who wants a whole year full of them?

No one of sane mind would ask for troubles, but we know that the days of this new year will have their fill of minor and major problems, troubles and trials. If the gem of the God-seed within each of us is to be made brighter and more beautiful by these problems, we will need to recall the words of another holy man, St. Francis de Sales. He said, "Do not look forward to what may happen tomorrow; the same everlasting Father who cares for you today will take care of you tomorrow, and every day. Either God will shield you from suffering, or God will give you unfailing strength to bear it. Be at peace, then, and put aside all anxious thoughts and imaginations."

A realistic view of the coming weeks and months tells us that we will have times of trial. But we should recall the counsel of saintly Francis de Sales to "put aside all anxious thoughts" and to "be at peace." One way to be at peace as we hear the newest trial ringing our doorbell is to remember as well the words of Confucius: "The gem cannot be polished without friction...without trials."

Each time you respond to a difficulty using the compass of the Gospels— meeting hate with love, greeting anger with peace and holding the pain of others with compassion—that hidden gem within your heart grows brighter and brighter. If we truly understand the purpose of these brief years of life given to us, we might actually find a new year to be happy *because* it would be full of polishing opportunities.

So perhaps the best greeting for the new year is to wish you "A _____ New Year" and let you fill in the blank with what your heart tells you is the best adjective.

---

8   **Celebration of Galileo Galilei** who died on this day in 1642. He theorized that the earth revolves around the sun. He was condemned for his teachings and threatened with excommunication if he did not retract his theory. The common belief was that the world is flat, and Scripture was used to prove that the earth is the center of the universe. The Church feared that if what had been taught for centuries were proven wrong, common people would lose faith in her other teachings. Do we as well fear something new simply because it is contrary to what we have long been taught? (See also the entry under February 9.)

---

9   **The First Free Balloon Flight in America**. In 1793 Jean Pierre Blanchard makes the initial human-navigated air balloon flight with President George Washington in attendance. Blanchard and one passenger, a small black dog, travel fifteen miles in forty-six minutes. Whom do you take along on your great adventures?

THE MUSICIAN

Once, long long ago, a musician well-known for the beauty and sweetness of his songs was asked to play for the royal audience. The king was so pleased with the performance that he made the musician part of the royal court. His highness loved one particular melody so much that he had the musician play it over and over, several times each day. It went well for the musician who now had everything he needed, and fame and prestige as well.

After a time, however, the musician grew weary of repeating the melody and no longer played it with the same zest and passion as he once did. This disturbed the king, because his favorite song now lacked much of its original vibrancy. So, in order to rekindle the musician's interest in the song, the king ordered that someone who had never heard the melody be brought to the palace from the market each day. Now, when the musician saw someone who had never heard his song before, it inspired him to play the piece with renewed vitality. This solution restored the melody to its original beauty, and so the king was again pleased.

But after some time, the king needed to seek the counsel of his advisors, for finding a new audience each day was not an easy task. After listening to the wise advice of all the court's sages, the king decided that the musician should be blinded! The musician was drugged into a sleep and his eyes put out so that he never knew what had happened. And he never saw a human form again. From that time on the blind musician would continually sit before the king. And whenever the king wanted to hear his favorite melody, he would say, "O musician, here comes someone new, a person who has never heard you play before.'' And the musician would play his song with the utmost skill and spiritedness, as if for the first time.

And the meaning of this new year's parable? I leave that for you to determine. For in the words of an Eastern sage: ''When you go to the market to buy fruit from the green grocer, you do not ask him to chew it for you!''

Feast of Music. Music is produced by humans for the first time in what is now France in 25,000 B.C. Considering the fact that the twentieth century person has lost touch with the primal pastime of playing a musical instrument because of radio, musical recordings and television, make some music today or sing a song. May this Feast of Music help you recapture part of your forgotten human resources.

10

Feast of St. Theodosius the Archmonk who lived for a time in a cave said to have been the resting place for the Magi on their way to Bethlehem. He died at the age of 106 in 529 A.D. This is a feast for creating the inner spaciousness to receive all the guests and pilgrims you meet today—as well as the Divine Guest.

11

UKULELES IN THE PEW

While commonly associated with Hawaiian music, the ukulele didn't originate in those sun-kissed islands but rather in Portugal where it was known as the machete. It was brought to Hawaii in the late 1800's by a British army officer named Edward Putvis who was an avid player of the machete. Putvis was a short man and, it seems, very active. He would constantly jump around while playing his machete, and so the Hawaiians gave him the nickname "ukulele," from *uku*, "flea," and *lele*, "jumping." And when the islanders began to construct the small four-stringed guitar themselves, they named it after Edward Putvis.

It is understandable that we who belong to an always on-the-go culture would adopt a hyperactive holiness. It is also not accidental that in this generation the old-fashioned porch swing has disappeared along with the front porch. We don't have time to sit and swing, and we find it difficult to sit still— unless we're in front of a television tube. Sunday services and times of prayer find us like ukuleles, jumping fleas, who fidget and fuss if forced to sit still, especially when it seems that nothing is happening.

Recent years have seen the appearance of prayer forms and liturgies that appeal to ukuleles. They invest the ritual and prayer with lots of clapping, hand waving and foot-tapping music and large doses of movement, hugging, exchanging greetings and holding hands. Many people think that a "good" liturgy is a ukulele service, where one isn't forced to sit in stillness. Worship is a mirror of life, just as life is supposed to be a mirror of worship. But while ukulele prayer may be enjoyable, it's unfortunate when it's the only prayer promoted, simply because we all live like ukuleles today.

We lack the kind of prayer and worship that calls us back to that very human and holy art of being able to sit still. Among the most beautiful prayers in Scripture is the line from Psalm 45: "Be still and know that I am God."

While good liturgical celebration should involve the body as well as the heart and while we all need creative expression and are led into prayer by opportunities to proclaim our fellowship and joyfulness, we also need silence and stillness if we are to know God fully and directly.

Hyperactive holiness and prayer only feed our twentieth century addiction to anxious activity. The pace of our lives invites us back to slower times, to rocking chairs and front porch swings—to sitting still. The porch swing is an excellent spiritual master which can teach us how to know the presence of God. But we don't have to wait till spring comes along when we can go outside to enjoy a swing, we can daily sit quietly in our prayer corner, making ourselves available to the Divine Guest and allowing ourselves to be gently rocked in the divine rest.

Mindful of Edward Putvis' ukulele nickname, "jumping flea," perhaps we should take a cue from our pets. To help find enjoyment in the quiet prayer of sitting still, perhaps we could all wear flea collars!

12
Remembrance Day of George Fox, founder of the Quakers, on the eve of his death day in 1691. Be in communion today with the Quakers, for whom silent prayer is central in communal worship, as you pray your silent prayer.

13
Birthday of Alfred Fuller in 1885. His idea of the traveling salesman, "the Fuller Brush Man," became famous as the pattern for door-to-door selling. If you are bothered today by a salesperson at your front door or on the telephone, greet him or her with a "Happy Alfred Fuller Day!"

A NEW YEAR KNOTTED ROPE

Among the many legends of ancient Greece is the story of Gordius who was chosen to be King of Phrygia. Gordius had a prized wagon that he dedicated to Jupiter. So ingeniously did he fasten the yolk of the wagon to a beam with a rope woven of bark that no one could untie it. The rope and its Gordian knot became famous.

When Alexander the Great was shown the knot, he was also told the prophesy that accompanied it: "Whoever unties this knot will reign over the whole East." Alexander looked at the rope with its complicated knot and said, "Well then, it is thus that I perform the task," and he drew his sword and cut the rope in two!

It is from Alexander's legendary and radical solution to the impossible task that we have the expression, "to cut the Gordian knot." This saying implies that one gets out of a difficulty with one decisive step, resolving the problem swiftly by force or the sword. How frequently do parents—or anyone in a position of power—use Alexander's method for solving problems. "You're fired!" or "I won't discuss it, go to your room!" are Alexandrian solutions in our lives.

And how easily are we "tied up in knots," as we attempt to resolve difficulties in our lives. Instead of striving to untie the knots within us, we often pull back in resentment, anger and rejection. The efforts of both parties to resolve a problem without compassion, each holding tightly to his or her own point of view, only pulls the rope tighter as knots are simultaneously formed in our stomachs.

What prevents us from acting with compassion? Is it the fires of anger and resentment? If so, what ignites these fires of passion? Whenever we are obstructed by another, we are easily reminded of times in our childhood when our mother or big brother blocked our infantile desires. Fathers, teachers and a whole cast of characters from the past have left knots in the ropes of our lives. It is in times when our will is impeded for one reason or another that we experience the most clear-cut blockages or knots in the usual flow of things. These knots readily awaken our awareness to the hidden knots which have been there since childhood. Injury remembers injuries, the hurts of days past, and such a chain reaction causes us to pull back from a situation—and from any compassionate response—only to further tighten the knot.

In the feast we have just celebrated, Epiphany, the Christ Child was adored by kings because he was recognized as the King of Kings. In Jesus' way was found the answer to the ancient riddle of the Gordian knot, and the prophecy, "Whoever unties the knot will reign over the whole East," was indeed fulfilled. But Jesus resolved it not with the sword or by force but with compassion and love.

If we wish to follow in Jesus' footsteps, we must first untie our own hidden knots. When that is done, we will be surprised at how easily love flows through us. We will find that with such an unknotted heart, any problem at hand will effortlessly untie itself if we are patient.

As this new year begins, we might find it easier to resolve the conflicts of this year by keeping a knotted rope over the kitchen window or on our desk. It could be a rope of about twelve inches long, but with several knots tied in it. Such a symbol would remind us at the appearance of a difficulty to take a moment to untie the knots in our heart before attempting to resolve the knotty problem. Such a rope symbol might help make the wish of the angels on high at Christmas, "Peace on earth," a living reality for us in this new year.

Festival of the Helping Hand. Meditate today on that African proverb: "Not to aid one in distress is to kill him or her in your heart." Can we give flesh in this new year to the hope of the angel's song at Christmas for "Peace on earth"?

14

Birthday of Dr. Martin Luther King in 1929. A leader in the civil rights movement in the 1960's, Dr. King organized nonviolent marches that opened the way for demonstrations for equal rights and justice by all sorts of groups, from students to farmers. This brief quote sums up much of his vision: "I believe that unarmed truth and unconditional love will have the final word in reality."

15

COLD SHOULDER, ANYONE?

Whenever we give someone "the cold shoulder," we treat that person with disdain and a chilly contempt. We might do so for various reasons. Perhaps we believe they are spreading gossip about us, they may have offended us in some way or we may consider them beneath us in social standing, intelligence, how they act or even how they look. In our personal relationships, in marriage or friendship, we might give others the "cold shoulder" because they failed to meet our expectations, arrived late for an appointment or were the cause of suffering. But whether we give the "cold shoulder" or receive it, we are always a victim.

The expression probably entered our language in the days of knighthood. When a knight appeared at a castle in those more romantic times, he was treated with great respect and honor. Usually upon his arrival he was given a hot and sumptuous meal. But a commoner or stranger who came to the door was lucky to receive a plate of cold meat. Mutton was a common food, and since the shoulder was one of the tougher parts of the lamb, a piece of cold shoulder was given only to the poorest of the commoners.

When we give people the "cold shoulder," we treat them as if they were strangers, and therefore not deserving of our warm and loving attention. "But," you may ask, "what if they deserve it? What if they are the cause of their own chilly reception?"

Jesus, in painting his graphic image of the Final Judgment, spoke of those whom we turn away: "I was hungry and you gave me no food..." (Mt. 25: 35). He went on to say, "and as often as you neglected to do it to one of these least ones, you neglected to do it to me" (Mt. 25: 45). When we refuse to love others—family, friends, lovers or strangers—in an unconditional way, withholding our love from them and neglecting them, regardless of the reason, we also do it to Christ.

The unspoken message in giving someone close to us a "cold shoulder" is, "Feel like a stranger? Well, you've hurt me. So *do* something about it; restore our relationship." But such communication is both unhealthy and unchristian. It requires humility to speak directly to the other and point out what it is that causes us distress. Humility is needed because frequently the problem is petty, and we hesitate to say that a minor issue has caused us to be upset. But honest and humble communication is the royal road to reconciliation—and the most Christlike.

If we believe in the words of Jesus, that he is present in even the least members of our society, then we must realize that he can also be present in the most important: our husbands and wives, neighbors, friends or lovers. If wandering knights of old were treated with respect and honor, how should we treat the wandering Knight of Nazareth? And should it matter whether the Prince of Peace wears the disguise of someone we know and love or when he comes as a stranger?

16
Prohibition Begins in the United States in 1929. The war against alcohol, like all wars, is doomed to failure. A good day to "live and learn." Have we learned a lesson from our mistakes about how social evils can best be corrected?

17
Feast of St. Anthony of the Desert who died in 355. During his solitude in the desert he endured dramatic psychic and spiritual struggles. Besides

being the founder of the monastic lifestyle, he is the patron saint of domestic animals, such as dogs and cats. Have a party for your pet today in honor of St. Anthony.

Festival of Rereading Your Christmas Cards. Before you store them or throw them away, take time to once again read the messages of love and friendship that you received during the Christmas season.

18

A NEW FEAST DAY NEEDED

Our calendars are short at least one much needed feast day. We need a new feast between Christmas and Valentine's Day, a feast of memories. And perhaps we could name this new holy day the feast of Our Lady of Memories. The Gospel reading at dawn on Christmas day concludes by saying, "Mary treasured all these things (the events of the first Christmas) and reflected on them in her heart" (Lk. 2: 19). Reflection is an important part of the prayer of gratitude that is so essential to living happy as well as holy lives.

By mid-January we have boxed away the Christmas decorations, storing them in the basement or attic until next December. As our minds turn to the daily problems of making a living and paying our bills, the marketplace is already busily gearing up with bright Valentine's Day decorations. Christmas is all but forgotten. So much happens in so short a time—the gifts from friends and family, the greeting cards with notes of affection from persons we love and the rich liturgies of our faith that overflow with beauty at this sacred season of the year. How easily we allow daily demands and the urgings of the advertising world to turn our attention to a new occasion for buying things to erase all the memories of beauty, to overshadow the treasures of our Christmas past. We need a new holy day, an occasion to remember.

How about using today as such a feast? We could take time right now to sit back, close our eyes and "treasure all those things" that happened to us this past Christmas. One by one we could recall the gifts that were given to us, aware that each one of them was the container for the real treasure, a gift of love. We should take some time on this personal feast of memories to recall the expressions of love and friendship from those who sent us greetings at Christmas, some of whom we hear from only at this time of the year. And perhaps next year we could plan ahead for such a feast day, setting aside our special Christmas cards to be reread, treasured and reflected upon once again a couple of weeks after New Year's Day.

We could also slowly and prayerfully reread the beautiful readings from the liturgies of Christmas and New Year's to reflect on these unending sources of insight. Each year, the story of the birth of Christ can open new possibilities if we only take time to sit with the story and let it speak to us. A feast like Our Lady of Memories might spark a habit of remembering, of retasting past treasures of our lives in the midst of being swept along in the parade of passing events. When we allow ourselves to be nourished by such reflection, we plant the seeds of happiness in life. Such remembrance requires that we take time to light the lamps of our hearts so that we can delight in the hidden treasures there.

As we step out of the fast pace of passing events, we can pray, "Hail Mary, full of memories, help us to remember." And after such a prayerful pause, renewed by the recovery of our hidden treasures, our hearts alive with gratitude, we will find ourselves to be much happier and, as Mary of Nazareth knew so well, much holier.

19

Good Memory Day. A day to improve your memory. A good memory is but a by-product of being fully present to the present moment. Practice, today, performing as many acts as possible with full attention fixed upon what you are doing.

20

First Lunatic Asylums appear in Europe in 1533. George Bernard Shaw once said, "Earth is the planet to which all the other planets send their insane."

21

Death of Vladimir Lenin, leader of the U.S.S.R., on this day in 1924. Shortly after he took power he is known to have said, "Without a doubt, an oppressed multitude had to be liberated. But our method only provoked further oppressions and atrocious massacres. My living nightmare is to find myself lost in an ocean of red with the blood of innumerable victims. It is too late now to alter the past, but what was needed to save Russia were ten St. Francis of Assisis."

ILLEGAL CRUCIFIXES

I shuddered when I heard that in Tokyo novelty shops you can purchase switchblade knives disguised as crucifixes! That a sacred sign should become a disguise for a lethal weapon is truly a tragedy. But it happens frequently, and not only in Tokyo novelty shops. How often have preachers used the crucifix of Christ to induce guilt in us? "**Your** sins caused the death of Christ!" Swish, the blade of guilt cuts to our soul, slicing right past the love of Christ which calls us to greater love. How often has the crucifix been used to intimidate us into obeying God? In past ages, how often was the crucifix held up before women burned at the stake as witches? How often has it been raised before armies to encourage "holy wars" and to justify murderous deeds of discrimination?

A switchblade can wound deeply. The cross of Christ has the same power, but it is not a "hidden" weapon. Christ and the other spiritual masters of history have all told us that we cannot achieve holiness and wholeness without great personal sacrifice, without suffering and struggle. The crucifix symbolically calls us to cut deeply into our selfishness and our false inclinations so that our true selves can be freed. But we usually reject the cutting away and the pain that accompanies it. We want an easy way to perfection.

We do not want love to demand constant self-denial, the daily stripping away of the ego. We want our personal and religious commitments to require no effort, no pain. Yet, hidden in every crucifix is a potential knife that points the way to holiness. At one time, many homes had a crucifix on the wall. They are not as easy to find these days; perhaps their presence in our homes is too powerful a sign. And when we do see a cross, do we dare to live out its message of sacrifice by slicing away at our selfishness?

Perhaps those switchblades in Tokyo are really not so tragic after all. Knives are seldom signs of the Kingdom; but Jesus spoke of his heavenly Father as a vine dresser who trims away from the good vines with a pruning knife in order that they may bear an even greater harvest. Crucifixes with or without switchblades inside them all speak of this mystery.

Feast of St. Vincent, the patron of wine growers, who died in 304. Legend says that if the sun shines today there will be a good crop of grapes this year. May the sun shine today on your "harvest" in life. Also a good day to pray for what you need to produce a "good yield." **22**

One Tooth Rhee Day. This is a Korean feast that commemorates the mythical inventor of the custom of having every bureaucrat wear four hats so that contradictory sets of instructions can be given to workers. Take time today to honor your local "confusionist" bureaucrat. **23**

Gold Discovered in California, 1848. As Francois de la Rochefoucald said, "Before we set our hearts too much upon anything, let us examine how happy they are who already possess it." **24**

First Child Born in Space in the year 2050. A girl is born to a Russian father and an American mother who are settlers on an Earth-orbiting space colony. The infant girl is baptized according to new space rituals, which take zero gravity into account, and is given the name Gaia. **25**

EYE OPENER PRAYER

Only a month ago we were all involved in the wonder of giving and receiving gifts. But one month later, our gifts have generally become possessions of which we take little notice. That's the way it is with gifts—they soon lose their wonder and become commonplace. In *Pilgrim at Tinker Creek*, Annie Dillard tells of a twenty-two-year-old woman who had been blind since birth. But through the skill of a brilliant surgeon, she was given the gift of sight. When her bandages were removed and she opened her eyes, what she saw was too marvelous. She shut them immediately and refused to open them for two weeks! When she finally had the courage to open her eyes again, she could only repeat over and over, "Oh God, how beautiful, how beautiful."

Our greatest gifts are those which, at this very moment, we are unaware that we possess! Our most priceless gifts are so common that we take them for granted until sickness or accident suddenly awakens us by repossessing them. It is often only by their absence that we become fully aware of their value. The litany of such overlooked gifts is a long one: sight, hearing, taste, smell, good health, the use of hands and feet, even the ability to have a good night's sleep. These are gifts we should never allow to become ignored or commonplace.

The admonition "Don't forget" can be expressed positively by saying, "Be forever grateful." Constant gratitude for common things is *un*common, but it is the ideal prayer which allows each of us to live life as a perpetual Christmas, a feast of treasures. Prayers of gratitude are the perfect response to the Divine Source of gifts. In such prayers of gratitude is hidden the expression that most delights the heart of the gift-giver—the knowledge that the receiver greatly enjoys the gift.

The paradox is that unless we make room in our crowded lives for prayers of thanks, we usually fail to be truly conscious of the wonder and enjoyment of our eyes and nose, hands and feet, for being able to walk freely or dance around the kitchen. How easily we forget that such common possessions are always gifts.

Prayer is the great eye opener that holds the magic of making us mystics. A mystic is simply one who experiences God poured forth in every moment. When ending our daily period of prayer, perhaps at the conclusion of a time of silent centering prayer, we should open our eyes with the same wonder as that twenty-two-year-old woman. If we do, we will be stunned at what we see, at the marvel of the everyday beauty that surrounds us. And the fitting "amen" to our prayer could be the continual chant of the mystic: "Oh God, how beautiful, how beautiful."

26 **Birthday of Our Daystar, the Sun**. You wouldn't be able to put five billion candles on the cake, but that's the age today of our wondrous daystar. Give thanks today for the sun's hard work of converting, by a thermonuclear reaction, 4.5 million tons of hydrogen into energy every second! Let this feast be an occasion for wonder, an occasion to feast your eyes on all the sun-touched gifts of creation in your life.

27 **Birthday of Wolfgang Amadeus Mozart** on this day in 1756. Extremely gifted and precocious, he began performing at the age of three and started to compose music by age five. He died on December 5, 1791 in the city of Vienna. His burial place is unknown, but his shrine is in the hearts of all who love beautiful music.

Also, the **Feast of St. John Chrysostom**, Bishop of Constantinople, born in 345 in Antioch. John once said, "Feeding the hungry is a greater work than raising the dead."

28 **Remembrance of Fyodor Dostoyevsky**, Russian author, who died on this day in 1881. In *The Brothers Karamazov* he wrote, "If the devil doesn't exist, but man has created him, he has created him in his own image and likeness." Is what we see as evil in others only a mirror of our own likeness which we refuse to acknowledge to ourselves?

THE PASSWORD

Jesus, speaking to his disciples, said, "Unless your holiness surpasses that of the Scribes and the Pharisees who keep the external laws, you will not enter the Kingdom of God'' (Mt. 5: 20). Some scholars believe that Jesus was himself a Pharisee, the sect of his day which desired greater perfection and holiness. Jesus, however, saw that his fellow Pharisees (if indeed he was a member of that group) were too caught up in the external observance of the Law of Moses as the way to holiness. So the gentle rabbi from Nazareth called those who followed him to greater holiness, to more perfection than that of law-abiding people.

To seek something **more** than mere obedience to the commandments on Mt. Sinai was indeed the next giant step in the growth of human consciousness. When God gave them to Moses, those laws were truly revolutionary for their time. For example, the law of honoring one's aged parents demanded that people of that era re-evaluate how they customarily treated the aged among them. There was a time, not that long ago, when the aged were encouraged to step aside from the caravan when they could no longer keep up with the tribe. The law of Sinai called for a radical concern for all people, regardless of their age, usefulness or material value.

Several thousand years after Sinai, Jesus called his disciples to take the next giant step beyond the commandments. The new law of love sums up all of the old law; at the same time it pushes the disciple to stretch his or her heart out to the limits. For if our holiness is to surpass that of those who merely keep the external law as perfectly as they can, then we will have to be **more** than good people. We will have to be **more** than kind or polite. We will have to be **more** than just and **more** than respectful of others.

Before we receive the Holy Eucharist, we pray a prayer that echoes the words of the centurion whose servant was ill. At Communion we pray, "Lord, I am not worthy that you should come to me, but only say the word and my soul shall be healed." What word heals our brokenness, our failings and sins that block our ability to be in communion as we go to Communion? What if, at that moment, we spoke the word "more" silently within our hearts, as if saying to ourselves, "While my life to this point has been less than a wholehearted love for you, O God, I promise to do more. I pledge myself to be more loving, more patient, more understanding." "More" is an evolutionary call to rise above the ordinary to the extraordinary.

The gate that leads to the Kingdom is most difficult to enter, for it is well hidden and guarded. Those who know the password, however, will have no problem making the gates of the Kingdom swing open. And what is such a password? As you may have already guessed, it is the word **MORE**.

Feast of First Land Exploration. The Eusthenopteron, a lobe-finned fish who could walk from pool to pool, leaves the ocean for land 370 million years ago. Celebrate, today, the significant evolutionary steps in history and in your personal life.

29

Mahatma Gandhi Assassinated on this date in 1948 in New Delhi. A day to remember all who give their lives for the cause of peace and nonviolence. May these valiant ones challenge us today to do something heroic, regardless of how small the act.

30

PEACE MONGERS

The writings of the gifted and witty English author G.K. Chesterton often reflect his deep faith and his commitment to the cause of peace. For instance, he once said, "It is incorrect to speak of war breaking out; war is the constant state of things. It is more correct to speak of peace breaking out."

Whenever war breaks out somewhere in our world it is news, and yet it's not really news. It seems that several small wars are constantly in progress across the earth. Certainly G.K. Chesterton had a point: war does seem to be the constant state of things.

When you and I attempt to start peace, even if it is only between ourselves and a neighbor or co-worker, we should know that we are involved in an unusual undertaking. Since war is the ongoing activity of the children of the earth, most of us are more skilled at war-making than peacemaking.

If we are warriors by nature, then the call of Jesus to be peacemakers is indeed an evolutionary call. Perhaps it is as radical as the command "Stand up!" was to our ancient ancestors who moved about on all fours. Standing erect was painful and difficult, and so most of them dropped back to their four-legged posture. Thank goodness for us that a few had the courage to endure the struggle of standing up straight!

Likewise, the goal of peace on earth will not come easily or without some personal pain. But the effort to make peace in our homes, in our personal relationships and at work, puts flesh and bones on our prayers for peace. If we are unwilling to work to help peace break out in our homes and in our lives, then why should we be surprised that our prayers for peace seem to go unheard by God?

The next time you put on a pair of shoes or go for a walk, say a small "thank you" to our ancient ancestors who heard the voice of God calling them to be different and responded to that divine call. And the next time you find yourself in the middle of a dirty little war, listen to your heart and you will hear the call to be a peacemaker. As you continuously respond to that call with your personal choice for peace instead of war, two things will happen. Not only will God be greatly pleased, but people far in the future, centuries and centuries from now, will thank you—even though they don't know your name.

31 **The Norse Feast of Soldag**. In the northern parts of our planet in the middle of winter, the sun doesn't shine at all. As it begins to appear at the end of January, villagers in Norway celebrate this "Sun Day." By your smiles and warm greetings you can make this a day when the sun shines for all those persons you encounter.

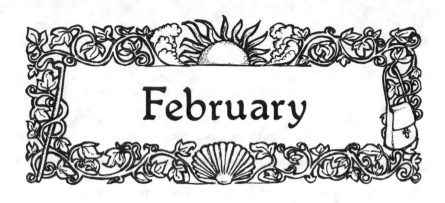

February

Awareness Day. As the famous ground hog prepares to come forth from hibernation, we should as well. The Zen master Taisen Deshimaru gives us today's lesson: "Behavior influences consciousness...our attitude here and now influences the entire environment: our words, actions...they all influence what happens around us and inside us. The actions of every instant, every day, must be right...every gesture is important."

1

A TABLE TOP SACRAMENTAL

Baby boys are customarily dressed in blue and baby girls in pink. The color of a baby's clothing is still largely a matter of tradition, and like many other traditions, we are often unaware of its original purpose. This is true for the custom or superstition that is used after accidentally spilling some salt. Tradition says that you should take some of the salt in your right hand and throw it over your left shoulder—a quaint practice when performed without thought about its purpose.

In fact, the origin of that tradition goes back to the Romans who considered spilling salt a bad omen. They thought that possible misfortune might be averted by taking a pinch of the spilled salt and throwing it over your left shoulder. If you look closely at Leonardo da Vinci's famous painting of the Last Supper, you will see that a saltshaker has been knocked over by the arm of Judas Iscariot. It is a visual hint of the evil which was to follow that meal.

Salt was employed in sacred rituals among the Greeks, Romans and Jews. It was used for sacrifice and was also a symbol of purity and incorruptibility. When I was a young priest, it was part of the ritual of Baptism to place a pinch of salt on the tongue of the infant. And Holy Water is saltwater, since part of its purification involves putting a pinch of salt into the water as it is blessed. It was not uncommon, long ago, to also place salt in a coffin to protect the person from evil, because it was believed that Satan hated salt.

Today we are urged to reduce the amount of salt in out diets, and many processed foods brag about being "salt free." Jesus, on the other hand, told his followers that they would be the "salt of the earth." One can wonder if our contemporary society is becoming "salt-free" in more ways than one!

The next time you reach for a saltshaker, instead of thinking about your health, see it as an opportunity for a mini ritual that can remind you of your vocation. Sprinkle some salt in your hand, take a pinch and place it on your tongue or even toss it over your left shoulder. And as you perform this brief ritual act, ask yourself, "Am I truly an agent of purification, a salty shield of protection from evil for my family and community? Do I season the lives of those with whom I live and work with peace, joy and hope?"

2

Feast of the Presentation of Jesus in the Temple, previously known as the Feast of the Purification. A day to celebrate the Light of the World by taking seriously your vocation to also be light and salt to the world.

Also, the folk feast of **Ground Hog Day**. A day for a playful eagerness for winter to end.

3

Feast of St. Blaise, Bishop of Sebaste in Armenia, patron of sore throats, martyred in 316. The power of prayer and faith in healing the body is greatly underestimated. Today, pray for an increase of faith in the power of your prayers.

UNTAPPED ENERGY SOURCE

Back in the years 30 or 40 B.E. (before Einstein) all rocks were just rocks. Today we know that certain rocks, like uranium, have almost unlimited energy hidden in them. And if Einstein's theory is correct, all matter can yield inconceivable energy if we only learn how to release it.

In many ways the same is true of prayer. On the surface prayer appears as devoid of power as rocks did in those ages before Einstein. Some people say: "Prayer is just a pious occupation; if you want to get something accomplished, then act!" For others, prayer is simply a last resort: "Well, all we can do now is pray!"

A leading cardiologist, Dr. Randy Byrd, conducted an intensive study on 393 coronary patients at San Francisco General Hospital and reported on it in the *Medical Tribune*. He arranged for people to pray for 192 of the patients but not for the 201 others. Those patients who were prayed for suffered fewer complications. For example, only three required antibiotics, compared to sixteen of those not prayed for. And only six suffered pulmonary edema, while twelve of the others did. Byrd concluded in his report, "Based on this study, I believe that prayer is effective and beneficial."

Those recruited to pray were Catholics, Protestants and Jews. They were given the names and conditions of the persons for whom they were to pray. But they were not told how to pray! While prayer remains a mystery, we might conclude that the more we know and care about the person for whom we are praying, the more effective the prayer will be.

Such scientific studies as Dr. Byrd's reveal only the tip of the iceberg about the untapped power residing in our times of prayer. There is a need for much "exploration" into that power and much "experimentation" in the practice of prayer. We should pray not as a last resort but as the first thing we do, even before attempting other solutions. Perhaps someday science may affirm without a shadow of a doubt what people since primitive times have believed: there is power, great power, awesome power, in prayer.

The Great Comet Appears (known today as Halley's Comet) in 1531, causing great fear and all sorts of superstition to sweep over Europe. That which we do not understand can either evoke superstition or wonder.

4

The Invention of the Chimney in England (it may have appeared earlier in Switzerland) in 1185. With this new invention it was no longer necessary to sleep around a common fire pit. It allowed for separate rooms which could each be heated by its own fireplace and chimney. Clergy denounced the invention because it made it possible to sleep naked, if desired. People were reminded that "the family that sleeps together, stays together." It was seen as the first breakdown in common family life.

5

Divine Gift Day. As you pray today, reflect on these words from the "gospel" of India, the *Bhagavad Gita*, "Whatever you do—the food you eat, the worship you perform, the help you give, even your sufferings— make it an offering to me." The same message was spoken by St. Paul to the Corinthians: "Whatever you eat, whatever you drink, whatever you do at all, do it for the glory of God" (1 Cor. 10: 31). Expand the boundaries of your daily activities to embrace the truth of those words, and you will see that there is nothing which cannot be an offering that gives glory to God.

6

ESKIMO HANDS HAVE HOLES

Go outside in early February in the Midwest without gloves on, and quite likely it will feel as though you have Eskimo hands. But there is another way of understanding the term **Eskimo hands** other than having living icicles for fingers.

Among the artists of the primitive Eskimos there was a curious and charming custom. When creating human figures, an Eskimo artist often carved large holes in the figure's hands. The pierced hands of the hunter were intended to signify that part of the game that was caught was allowed to fall through to the rest of creation. Hunters, and all others, were to share a portion of all the gifts that came to them.

More than a reminder of the cold and ice of winter, Eskimo culture was and is known for the art of hospitality. Those who wish to understand the spirit of hospitality and to practice this ageless sacred art can find much to learn in the tradition of the Eskimos. Whenever we share our home, our food or drink with a guest, we are allowing part of the good things that have come to us to be passed on to others. This sharing of bounty becomes a very natural expression when we see that all that comes to us in life is a gift. We do not earn or merit gifts; they are tokens of love. As we look around at the multitude of good things that we have been given and then look at the degree of generosity in our lives, we need to ask whether we truly have Eskimo hands.

We can ask this question not only at times of formal hospitality but whenever we are presented with opportunities to share. Do we look upon our natural physical gifts, our intelligence, education, good fortune and success as personal possessions? If we think we have earned them, we will close our fists tightly and cling to what we have. But if we can see them as gifts given by a generous and loving God, then we can pray for the gift of pierced hands; we can ask to have Eskimo hands.

The ecological wisdom of the Indians of the Far North sprang from their belief that all life is an interdependent web. Nothing or no one was seen as totally independent of others. The hunter as well as the hunted were all perceived as part of an interwoven network of life. That sense of communion was at the root of their artistic symbolism of pierced hands. We are very familiar with Christian art's image of the Risen Christ with pierced hands. They are not only nail holes but also generosity portholes. At the Last Supper, Jesus gave his friends, and all the rest of the sacred web of the world, not part of his gifts and talents but his whole self. Each time we graciously allow parts of any gift we have been given to fall through our hands, that gift to others redeems them, those we love and all the earth.

The next time you approach the altar to receive Holy Communion, the Gift of Gifts, reflect on these words. When you open your hands so that the minister of the Eucharist can place the Body of Christ there, look carefully at your hands. Do they have large holes in them? Are they, like the hands of Christ, pierced? Only Eskimo hands are truly worthy to receive the gift of the Body and Blood of Christ.

---

7   **Birthday of St. Thomas More**, Lord Chancellor of England, in 1478. For refusing to recognize the divorce of Henry VIII, he was beheaded in 1534. The martyr More wrote in *Of Jewels and Wealth*, "They wonder much to hear that gold, which is in itself so useless a thing, should be everywhere so much esteemed, that even men for whom it was made, and by whom it has its value, should be thought of less than it is." A day to consider what we consider of value.

---

8   **Birthday of Jules Verne**, author of *Twenty Thousand Leagues under the Sea*, in 1828. His imagination anticipated the invention of the submarine, light bulbs, electric clocks and today's space exploration. Festival day of wild imagination, the womb of tomorrow's inventions.

---

9   **Celebration of Eratosthenes**, Greek mathematician, philosopher, poet and astronomer. Two hundred years before the birth of Christ, he was the first to discover that the world was round! Director of the famous library at Alexandria in Egypt, he also correctly measured the size of our planet. At that library was a book by Aristarchus of Samos, who said that Earth is one of the planets which orbits the sun. The feast of Eratosthenes is an occasion to ponder why wisdom is so slow to be accepted as truth.

OF MICE AND ELEPHANTS

A noted astronomer of the seventeenth century, Sir Paul Neal, triumphantly announced that he had discovered an elephant on the moon. His discovery soon became the central topic of public conversation. But then upon re-examination, it was discovered that a tiny mouse had crawled between the lenses of Sir Neal's telescope! His error is as common as the common cold and should touch a tender—if humorous—spot in each of our hearts.

The beginning of February in the Midwest can easily give rise to cabin fever. We are forced to live mostly indoors and close together because of the snow and bitterly cold weather. One result of cabin fever is that one's normal emotional ebb and flow can take on tidal wave proportions. One can easily fall victim to the Sir Paul Neal Error, mistaking small problems for elephantine dilemmas. Cabin fever is not the only cause of such misjudgment; being overworked, tired or under too much pressure also possesses the power to transform mice into elephants.

Mice-sized events that have the potential to become inflated to elephant-like dimensions come in many different forms: a small careless word, a critical remark, an unwisely chosen bit of humor, half an hour's tardiness, milk spilled on the dinner table, not being invited to this or that—such normally unimportant events, when seen through the lens of stress or tiredness, can easily become significant causes for anger and a host of potentially harmful emotions. But to know when an elephant is truly an elephant is not an easy matter.

Whenever we, like Sir Paul Neal, find an elephant in an unusual place, we should proceed cautiously and not be too quick to pronounce it as fact. When hurt by a hasty word or upset by a small mistake, take a minute or two before reacting; step back to view the "great sin" from every possible angle instead of seeing it only through a lens of excessive sensitivity. And if it's discovered that the elephant is really only a mouse, be free enough to have a good laugh at yourself. It is amazing how the magic spell of laughter not only causes elephants to shrink to the size of mice, but also chases the mice away!

Elephantine events that "get under your skin" also are put into proper proportion when they are exposed to daylight. When we trust the other person and feel that we can express ourselves honestly, we can say, "I know that this could be a Sir Paul Neal's elephant, but I felt that... ." Careful and caring communication usually reduces the event to its proper size and frees us from having to react with hurt or anger.

We cannot laugh at the mistake of Sir Paul Neal without also laughing at ourselves, since we all at one time or another, perhaps even today, may find an elephant on our moon!

Festival of Feeling Small. Take time today to reflect on the fact that our planet Earth is 93 million miles away from the sun, our daystar. Pluto, the most distant member of our solar family, is 3.7 billion miles away. But if you could hold our entire solar system in the palm of your hand, the size

10

of our own galaxy, within which the solar system exists, would be like that of the entire continental United States! Feeling small is another way to be filled with awe.

11 **Celebration of Head Colds and Buttons**. Napoleon in his invasion of Russia in the bitterly cold winter of 1812 ordered that bone buttons be sewn on the coat sleeves of his soldiers to prevent them from wiping their noses on them. While only two or three buttons remain on the sleeves of men's coats today, this celebration gives us cause to reflect on how easily the original purpose of some things can be obscured.

12 **Birthday of Abraham Lincoln**, 1809. At a ceremony on the day after the end of the Civil War, Lincoln asked the band to play "Dixie," the anthem of the South during the war. Forgiveness toward one's enemies must be total if it is to be true forgiveness.

A HEART TRANSPLANT

Within the past few years we have seen some remarkable heart transplants. Human beings have been given baboon hearts, calf hearts and mechanical hearts. These miracles of modern medicine remind us of a fundamental human longing. Wanting a real heart was the eternal wish of the Tin Man in the classic story *The Wizard of Oz*. The poor Tin Man had no heart and was willing to travel down the perilous *yellow brick road* to ask the Wizard for a real heart. With Valentine's Day upon us, hearts of all sizes and colors can be seen at every turn. This holiday of love awakens each of us to the possibility of a heart transplant. The question is, what kind of heart do you really want: a baboon heart or perhaps a bulletproof, non-breakable, mechanical heart, guaranteed not to feel the need of love? Or can you risk the vulnerability of a heart that loves in a supernatural way?

Once upon a time when the world was very young, two brothers shared a field and a mill. Each night they divided equally the grain they had ground together during the day. One brother lived alone; the other had a wife and many children. Now the single brother thought to himself, "It really isn't fair that we divide the grain evenly: I have only myself to care for, and my brother has many mouths to feed." So each night he secretly took some of his grain to his brother's granary.

But the married brother said to himself, "It really isn't fair that we divide the grain evenly: I have children to care for me in my old age, but my brother will have no one." So every night he secretly took some of his grain to his brother's granary. As you may have guessed, both of the brothers found their supply of grain mysteriously replenished each morning.

Then one night they finally met each other halfway between the two houses and suddenly realized what had been happening all those years. They embraced with great affection as the truth dawned upon them. Legend has it that God saw their meeting and proclaimed, "This is a holy place, a place of love, and here it is that my temple shall be built." And so it was that the first temple was constructed on that site.

Both of the brothers in the parable had the kind of heart we need. It is not a natural human heart but a heart that loves with the love of God. If we love only with our natural hearts, we will not be able to give without expecting a return, nor will we be able to give back kindness for injury. It's only natural to resent an offense and to react in anger, but we are called to a higher consciousness, to a higher love. And to do that, we all need heart transplants—or at least remodeling.

May all the valentines, red hearts and decorations of this delightful February holiday call us to the kind of love that would make temples sprout up everywhere.

Where's Your Heart Day. Frederic Chopin, Polish composer, great genius of piano music, was born in the winter of 1810. When he died in 1849, his body was buried in Paris. But his heart, at his special request, was buried in the wall of the Church of the Holy Cross in Warsaw. At your death where do you want your heart to be?

13

Feast of St. Valentine, patron of lovers and sweethearts. Send valentines today of love-filled thoughts and feelings to all your friends and loved ones. Fill your heart with images of them and wrap them in love and affection.

14

HEART MAIL

In 1922, William Allen White, the renowned editor of the Emporia, Kansas *Gazette*, wrote, "...the business of life will go forward only if men can speak in whatever way is given them to utter what their hearts hold—by voice, by post card, by letter" This call to express what is in our hearts by card or letter is most appropriate as we celebrate the feast of Valentine's Day.

Valentines are indeed expressions of what is in our hearts, and each year we take time to declare these feelings of love and admiration. But valentines are not the only kind of "heart" mail. We have a need today to express more frequently what we tend to take for granted.

One aspect of satisfied people is that they tend to be silent! They never seem to comment on the good they see around them. When people are contented with the events of their lives, they generally feel no need to express their pleasure in writing. If we see streets and parks well cared for, seldom would we write the local paper to commend the workers. But if there's litter in the park or snow isn't removed from the streets, a flood of indignant mail will appear. Disgruntled people tend to grunt—to express their disapproval by voice or letter! They are prone to turn to pen and paper as if it were second nature. The same phenomenon is apparent in the Church. I lack solid evidence for this claim, but I would wager that a bishop receives nine letters of complaint to every letter of compliment about what goes on in the diocese. But because the satisfied are silent, the voice of the few becomes powerful.

Valentine's Day reminds us that we can become ministers of a most needed sacrament. While it is usually bishops who administer the Sacrament of Confirmation, each of us can become a minister of *affirmation*. All that is required to administer this sacrament is love and the willingness to take time to express, "by voice, post card or letter..." as William Allen White would say, what we feel in our hearts.

15 **Old Roman Feast of Lupercalia** honoring the god Pan. Avoid winter cabin fever and have a wild feast in the spirit of the god of wildness and the wilderness.

In Japan, the **Feast of the Birth of Buddha**, "the Awakened One," in, according to the best estimates, the year 563 B.C. Buddha's birthday is observed according to the lunar calendar in China and other countries of the Far East.

16 **Papal Decree Day**. In 600 Pope Gregory the Great issued a decree mandating that the proper response to a person sneezing is "God bless you." The blessing was to be a prayer for the person who sneezed, replacing the old expression, "Congratulations." The reason for the decree was a pestilence that was raging in Italy, one symptom of which was severe sneezing. Many died shortly after such an attack. In these months of head colds and the flu, let us bless one another with prayerful wishes for good health.

17 **Wonder Dusting Day**. Today dust off your furniture and books with the knowledge that you are dealing with very ancient dust. It is possible that some of the dust in your home is 4.6 billion years old! Each year four million tons of dust from outer space falls on our planet. Rather than considering dusting a drudgery, light a vigil candle in front of your dust cloth and pray a prayer of awe.

DUSTPAN PHILOSOPHY

A Moslem mystic once wrote, "So long as we are in the dust, we do not see the face of the Beloved." As usual with statements of mystics, the meaning has a variety of turns. Are we to understand that as long as we are in these bodies of dust, we cannot see our Beloved One? Perhaps that is true, but there is another less poetic possibility which is more related to daily life. One war that will never vanish, whether the Kingdom comes or not, is the war on dust. Dusting and sweeping are lifelong chores, unless you are rich enough to have a maid.

As well as being pleasant to live in, having a clean house is seen as virtuous. We often, however, overdo our concern for keeping everything spic-and-span. How easily we can get lost in the dust—in the unwashed dishes, the snowy shoe prints in the hallway, the toys that were not put away or the coat that was not hung in the closet. When we are "in the dust," we do not see the face of the beloved son, daughter, wife or husband, friend or roommate—nor are we able to see the face of the Beloved.

Each time we get lost in the "dust" of the business, programs and projects of life, we also fail to see, to experience, our Beloved God. How much better to tolerate a little clutter if it promotes an environment where people take on more importance than a clean house or a finished report. Finding the balance point, as always, is far from easy. Having a clean and orderly environment can indeed bring us into greater harmony with God and others. But as soon as we cross the fine line where things need to be just so, we lose contact with the Source of harmony.

I expect that one of heaven's surprises will be that God doesn't mind a certain amount of dust and disorder. For we are not to be judged on our skills in housekeeping or in flawless administration, but rather on how we have loved. There is an old Jewish tale about why God stopped the construction of the tower of Babel which makes the point in a different way. It seems that as the tower grew higher, the work grew more and more hazardous and accidents began to happen frequently. It got to the point where if one of the laborers fell from the tower, no one seemed to be very concerned. However, if a brick were dropped, there would be an uproar of anger, for bricks had just been invented and were very expensive. The worker who dropped a brick would be severely punished. God, according to this version of the story, halted the construction because bricks had become more important than people.

In every home, office, community and parish, bricks and dust call loudly for attention, but they should never overshadow our concern for others. Only when we keep that in mind is it possible to see the face of the Beloved in those with whom we live and work. Jesus wrote in the dust to teach and also used it to heal the blind. Perhaps if we learn to ''let it be,'' our blindness to what is truly important will be healed. Perhaps we then will begin to see the Beloved in a world liberated from the harsh demands that make life a struggle instead of a delight.

Invention of the Vacuum Cleaner, 1901. H. Cecil Booth patents this ''dust removing suction cleaner.'' It was the size of a modern refrigerator and required two persons to operate. Dealing with dust and getting rid of dust are age-old problems. As the Moslem poet Rumi said, ''The Beloved has afflicted you from every direction in order to pull you back to the Directionless. When someone beats a rug with a stick, she is not beating the rug, her aim is to get rid of the dust.''

18

Remembrance of Nicolaus Copernicus who was born this week in 1473. This Polish astronomer championed the theory that the sun, not the earth, is the center of the solar system. Martin Luther called Copernicus a ''fool'' for contradicting the Bible. Reality is difficult to embrace when it contradicts our beliefs. Do we call anything ''foolish'' because it doesn't support our present beliefs?

19

A Holiday of Firsts. A day to commemorate the birthday of our first president, George Washington, in 1732 (the actual date is February 22; in recent years it has become a movable feast); have a piece of cherry pie today in his honor. Also on this day in 1962, John Glenn became the first American to orbit the earth. Do something today that you have always wanted to do; make this anniversary date the day of a personal ''first.''

20

THE OLDEST PRAYER

According to a book I recently read, the letter ''O'' is the oldest member of our alphabet. You can almost feel the electric excitement that spread like a Kansas prairie fire when that ancient discovery was made: "Hey, did you hear the news? Mongu just invented the **O**!" Then I'm sure someone must have said, "So? What good is it? What can you do with an O? Pass me some more mammoth."

No history book gives us the name of the actual inventor, so it's possible that the first letter was discovered in the same research lab where the wheel originated. Or maybe the idea was conceived in church. But, of course, in those days there was nothing like church, at least as we know it. People long ago didn't go to church—they lived in it, since all creation was really their temple of worship.

There were no special rituals or prayers separate from everyday living because life was filled with ritual and prayer. "O" was for primal people the holiest expressed response to a divine experience, just as "Amen" is the response to modern prayer. When green shoots broke through the crust of the earth after our ancient ancestors had planted their seeds with a sharp stick, they must have prayed, "Ohhh!" in great wonder and awe. When a rainbow arched across the sky, when a child was born or when the drum was discovered, they again must have prayed, "Ohhh!" That expression of awe is at the heart of the prayer of adoration and praise.

In our modern world, where every day seems to be crammed with new discoveries, the ancient prayer of awe is often absent. The primary priestly caretakers of it now are small children. As the letter "O" no longer creates wonder and is lost in a maze of other letters, so awe and wonder are largely absent from our wonder-less lives. But there is hope, for we potentially say a lot of prayers when we are unaware that we are praying. We also perform numerous sacred rituals like sleepwalkers, unaware that we are worshiping.

The next time you find yourself open-mouthed in o-ness, pause and reflect for a moment on the fact that you are in the midst of a holy and ancient prayer. The next time you see such things of great beauty in creation as a splendid sunrise, a night sky flooded to the rim with stars, or when your small child takes a few first steps, you might consciously pray that great-grandparent of all prayers. As you do, know that like anyone who has created something of great beauty and originality, or like a magician who has performed a deed of unexpected mystery, God loves to hear us respond to the divine creations with the prayer, "Ohhh!"

21 **Feast of the Sun**, the nuclear engine of our solar system. Each yard of the sun's surface produces energy equivalent to 70,000 horsepower. Powered by the sun, our family of planets is at this moment circling around the center of our galaxy, the Milky Way, at a speed of 633,000 miles per hour. This is a festival to remind ourselves that the sun isn't standing still; a day to marvel.

22 **Feast of Moses** encountering God in the burning bush. As the voice in the flames called him to go to Egypt, Moses asked God's name and was told, "I Am Who Am." The Jewish Talmud gives us material for reflection: "Would that they had forgotten my name and done that which I commanded them."

A good day to be awake to God's voice and God's presence all around us.

THE KNEELING PILGRIM

Once, long ago, there was a woman who spent her life traveling across the country crawling on her knees. When people asked her if she was a cripple, she would respond, "Oh, no, I'm only being faithful to the wishes of Pope Innocent III." Then she would merrily continue her journey on her knees. Sometimes, as she passed through a village, people would offer her food or drink. As she consumed their gifts, they would often ask, "Are you a beggar? I don't see your tin cup." And she would answer, "Oh, no, I'm not a beggar, but I appreciate your kindness. For you see, I'm only trying to be obedient to the wishes of Pope Innocent III. Thank you for your kindness." And then, with the smile of a child looking into a toy shop window, she would once again resume her slow journey.

Now since Pope Innocent III had lived a long time prior to this, people had no idea what would have caused a seemingly sane and healthy woman to crawl across the country. Most people thought her to be mildly unbalanced—or perhaps just an eccentric. But one thing was sure: no one who saw her was not touched by her obvious state of happiness, if not bliss.

One night, as a cold rain lashed down on the countryside, making the road a swamp, the woman crawled on her knees past a small village in a remote area. With the weather being so harsh, a couple in the village invited the crawling woman into their home to spend the night. They kindly invited her to share supper with them. But when they all came to the table, the crawling woman did not use a chair; rather she knelt beside the table to eat her meal. The wife asked her, "Why do you crawl all the time and even eat your meals kneeling; are you a cripple?"

With a large smile, the kneeling woman answered, "Oh, no, I'm not disabled. I can stand or sit as well as you or anyone else. But I have to kneel constantly if I am to be obedient to good Pope Innocent III—at least I think it was he who said it, but I may be wrong."

The husband and wife looked at one another in dismay, and, like many before them, they wondered what it was that Pope Innocent had decreed which could cause a person to go about constantly on her knees. Finally the husband asked, "What was it that the Pope decreed that makes you travel as you do?"

The kneeling woman again broke out into an expression of great happiness and answered, "Long ago, in the thirteenth century, Pope Innocent confirmed a custom and made it a tradition. He said that when you come into church, you should genuflect, or go down on one knee. But when you are in the presence of God, you must make a full genuflection, with both knees. That is why if you stay in church for even a short while, or if you ever find yourself in the presence of God, you must kneel down on both knees."

Birthday of George Frederick Handel, composer of *The Messiah*, in 1685. Great music has the power to awaken the soul. If you feel your soul has fallen

23

asleep, listen to some music today that can quicken and awaken your inmost being.

24 **New Calendar Day**. On this day in 1582 Pope Gregory XIII reformed the old Julian calendar, moving New Year's Day from March 25 to January 1. This necessary change returning the calendar to the natural rhythm of the seasons was met with great disapproval and dismay. The beginning of the twenty-first century will call us to embrace far-reaching changes in our lives. Pray today for an openness to the changes that history requires of us.

25 **Day to Take Stock of Your Spiritual Exercises**. Habit can easily make what once was an awakening exercise into one that puts you to sleep. Reflect today on the words of the Buddha, "To insist on a spiritual practice that served you in the past is to carry the raft on your back after you have crossed the river."

TOO FULL TO HUNGER

Once upon a time a spiritual seeker came to a holy woman and said, "I have traveled over the world from one teacher to another. I have studied many spiritual exercises and seen their advantages. Now I wish to become your student to drink from your great store of knowledge and so become more advanced on the spiritual path. May I become your disciple?"

The holy woman did not reply directly to the seeker's request but instead announced that it was dinner time. As the rice and vegetables arrived, the holy woman herself waited on the guest at table. She served him plate after plate of rich food and took great delight in watching the guest eat. The seeker, in turn, was pleased that such a saint should be so concerned about his needs. Then came more fruits, wondrous pastries and desserts. As the guest became full, he started eating slower and slower. He noticed that this seemed to annoy the spiritual guide, and so to avoid her displeasure, the seeker ate and ate until he could eat no more. By now the man was in great physical discomfort because he was so stuffed.

Looking at him, the old holy woman said, "When you came here you were full of undigested teachings just as you are now full of rice and fruit. When you came, you felt discomfort, but it was not a hunger for new insights. Rather you suffered from indigestion of too much previous knowledge. Being a novice in the spiritual life, you mistook the pains of inner indigestion for those of hunger. I will teach you about holiness, but first you must spend a long time digesting what you have already learned. And you can do that by practicing what you have studied. Then when I feel that you are ready, I will teach you." And it is told that this seeker went on to be a truly holy person.

This parable from the East is a good Lenten-time reflection as we decide what our Lenten activities should be. Let us ponder as we look over the list of workshops on prayer and other spiritual exercises, or as we think about reading a new book or listening to some new tapes. Perhaps like the spiritual seeker in the parable, we do not need to go to *another* workshop or read *another* book, but we need to take time to practice what we already know. Wonderful things could happen if people would take time not to learn more and more about prayer but to actually pray!

Each of us must look inward and decide about questions like, "Is my desire to go to a talk on prayer a true seeking, or is it an escape from actually praying?" or "Is my desire to read a new book a true search for knowledge that I will put into practice by living a more virtuous life, or will it just delay a real reform in my life?" Are you truly hungry or merely suffering from indigestion?

Zero Day. In 876 B.C. the first known reference is made to the symbol zero (0) in India. Originally a sacred symbol of the divine emptiness, the zero-quality of the self is essential for holiness. Practice being empty this Lent not just to be vacant but rather so as to be filled with God. The process of "zeroing" is important for any pilgrim who seeks to find the way Home.

26

Dead to Self Day. Bunan, a seventeenth century Zen master, gives us the thought for this day, "When you're both alive and dead, thoroughly dead to yourself, how superb the smallest pleasure."

27

SAVE THE AMERICAN EAGLE

The American Eagle is an endangered species. The government and various wildlife groups are concerned and are working diligently to preserve this noble national bird. We all can identify with the American Eagle, for we feel a similar threat! If you look closely between the lines of the Gospels, you will see that each of us is an endangered species.

"Unless you deny your very self," Jesus says, "you cannot be my disciple" (Mt. 10: 39). Your "very self," in psychology, is called your ego. As an ego, you are in danger each time you read the Gospels, each time you go to Communion or pray! Perhaps that is why we shy away from deep, silent prayer—because we know in those moments of prayer that our little ego is endangered. And certainly in these days at the end of the twentieth century, the American Ego is in grave danger.

The American Ego, not to be confused with the American Eagle, is that image of self as a nation that is described as the biggest, best, richest, most powerful, strongest and most influential country in the world. We feel the right to use up most of the world's resources at the expense of undeveloped little countries simply because we are Number One. That American Ego must die if we are to become a truly Christian nation that shares its wealth with the world, and shares without political strings attached. That ego must die so that we can reduce our lifestyles to a degree of simplicity which will allow others in the world to come closer to the high comfort level of our daily life.

And the American Ego often is a reflection of our own egos, for we frequently seek to be right in every argument, to be the "best," regardless of what such a position might require of others. Our little self or ego seeks constantly to assert itself at the expense of others. We can seek asylum in those special refuges set aside to protect ego wildlife: in outmoded views, in yesterday's glory, in the competitive philosophy of our society and in such un-christian slogans as, "Just take care of old Number One." Indeed, we can exercise enormous care to protect our egos from danger or harm, but if we do, we may miss the Kingdom.

Jesus called for the end to all egos and all the "very selves" we guard so well, because beneath the roles we play, beneath our selfish little selves, is a greater self, the real self. It is this true self who God created us to be: loving, caring, forgiving, non-judgmental, living in constant harmony with God, creation and the rest of the world.

While we should do all in our power to save the American Eagle, let us do all in our power to slay our own egos and thus become true disciples of Jesus.

28 **Car Keys and Small Change Day**. In 1590 the first pockets were placed in men's trousers. Before a cloth pouch became a sewn-in feature, the pocket was first just an opening where a cloth bag could be inserted. Rejoice in this common but relatively new invention in clothing, for it would be hard to function as we do without them!

29 **A Holiday of Calendar Balance**. Usually our calendars are composed of 365 days, but it actually takes our planet 365 days, five hours, forty-eight minutes and forty-six seconds to complete one of its annual pilgrimages around our daystar, the sun. To keep the calendar dates of the seasons balanced year after year requires the regular addition of leap years. A leap year, which has 366 days, occurs in every year which can be evenly divided by four, except those years that mark the turn of a century. For an even-hundred year to be a leap year requires that it can be divided by 400, such as the case with the year 2000. If this present year is a leap year and you are celebrating February 29th, use this holiday as an opportunity to check your own sense of balance in the seasons of your work and worship, prayer and play, solitude and solidarity. If you find your life is out of balance, then "leap" into what is needed to bring about harmony.

March

First U.S. National Park Established at Yellowstone in 1872. May this holiday remind us to make of all the earth a park where wildlife is protected and nature is reverenced and enjoyed.

1

Remembrance of John Wesley, Christian reformer, who died on this day in 1791. Join with your Methodist friends in a day of honoring this saintly and revolutionary founder of Methodism. And do something truly revolutionary today.

2

A CORN FLAKES PARABLE

Jesus knew that the only good revolutions were continual ones, and so he constantly preached, ''Reform your lives, the Kingdom, the Reign of God, is at hand.'' There's a humorous saying that on the morning after every revolution, every revolutionary becomes a conservative. And it is also almost inevitable that every revolutionary becomes a conspirator! A conspirator? Yes, one who works to overthrow or defraud for political or petty personal gain. And a religious conspirator is one who, for personal profit, alters the original purpose of the founder of that religion. But perhaps a parable may assist our understanding of this human condition.

There are different kinds of parables. Some are purely products of the imagination, others are based on real-life stories from history. In such cases, history is pronounced HI-story. Here's a High Story that's called the Corn Flakes Parable.

In 1890 John Harvey Kellogg, a physician and a Seventh-Day Adventist, was the medical superintendent of the Battle Creek Sanitarium, the Western Health Reform Institute. Dr. Kellogg promoted a meatless, low-dairy diet that included his original idea of a dry cereal which we today call granola (he also created the world's best-selling breakfast food, Kellogg's Corn Flakes). Doc Kellogg could well be called the grandfather of today's health-food movement. As a health revolutionary, he tirelessly condemned the evils of alcohol, tobacco and caffeine.

One of his patients, Charles Post, also a Seventh-Day Adventist, saw profit as well as good health and spiritual purity in Kellogg's radical ideas about diet. Charles Post joined the revolution against the nineteenth century American diet of greasy pork, beef and starchy foods. Post set up his own health clinic and created his own health foods: Postum, Grape Nuts and Post Toasties.

The parable of these two health food revolutionaries and the breakfast-food companies which they founded ends as you walk along your grocery store breakfast-food section. Read the names on the boxes of their "natural" breakfast foods, "Super Sugar Crisp, Frosted Flakes and Froot Loops!"

Recently breakfast foods have undergone a kind of Lent, a reformation. Many companies have removed harmful sugars, salts and preservatives from their products. In so doing, they have given us a model for our Lenten work. This season of reform called Lent is a time to purify ourselves of the creeping conspiracy of compromise that creates a junk-food religion. Lent calls us to a diet of "sugar-free" religion, to a religion of discipline as well as healthy prayer and daily dying. If it is anything less, we have abandoned the spiritual revolution of Jesus and have perhaps even become co-conspirators against the Kingdom.

---

3 **Feast of St. Jonah**, the unwilling prophet who was eaten by a whale. After three days, having his fill of a prophet being in his belly, the whale pitched Jonah out and up onto the shore. This is a festival to ponder how disagreeable are our modern day prophets who after three days are too much to stomach.

---

4 **Inside-Out Lesson Day**. Each day we all can learn wisdom in life from the negative behavior of others. As Kahlil Gibran said, "I have learned silence from the talkative, tolerance from the intolerant and kindness from the unkind." Observe carefully today the behavior of others that you do not want to be your own, and do the opposite. A good day to practice saying "No" to what limits life for you and "Yes" to what promotes fuller life.

SPARE THE ROD, AND...

Hanging in the bathroom in my childhood home was my father's leather razor strap. He used it to sharpen his straight razor, but it was also a symbol of the discipline in our home. While I do not have a single memory of my father ever using it on me, it hung there as the ultimate possible discipline for misbehaving. And it was referred to whenever I needed to improve my behavior.

Generations have grown up with the motto, "Spare the rod and spoil the child." Discipline is essential for children in growing toward mature adult behavior. Ideally, as we mature, we learn the art of self-discipline so necessary for wholesome living.

Discipline is essential also for that child spoken about by Jesus: the child within for whom alone the gates of heaven open wide. We need the discipline to stop, look and listen as we hurry through life. We need discipline to keep from being slaves of that dictator—Der Digital, the clock—which keeps us glued to a schedule and keeps us constantly "on the run." Those who run quickly through life soon run out of life.

No is such a beautiful word when it is the doorway to **Yes**. "*No*, I will not run blindly through my day...*Yes*, I see you, delicate green of the budding oak leaf"; "*No*, I'm too busy...*Yes*, mom has lots of time for you—come sit on my lap and tell me what you did in school today." Such important "yeses" require saying "no" to finishing the laundry or having supper on the table at the usual time. To say such a "no" is to use the rod of discipline on yourself so as not to spoil the child within.

But **no** is such a difficult word, if not the hardest word to say to ourselves. The other day I was in a store, and ahead of me was a woman shopping with her small three-year-old. The woman looked tired and preoccupied. She kept repeating again and again to her small child: "No...I said NO!" Shopping with her child, who was eager to examine each item along the way and wanted everything, was a nerve-straining experience for her. But the exchange between this mother and child awakened in me the question: how many memory tapes of my parents saying "no" to me do I have unconsciously stored away? And do all those "no" memories make it difficult for me now, as an adult, to say "no" to myself?

Without personal discipline, I will spoil the inner child. I need that "rod" of discipline if I am to find time to pray, to do a bit of spiritual reading or even to share my financial gifts with the needy. Such personal discipline is essential to any inner life of prayer or compassionate service to others. "No" is also essential to enjoying all the beauties with which God has flooded this world. Unless I can say "no" to my list of things-to-get-done-today, when will I find the time to enjoy the earthen sacraments of the sunset, the full moon or an evening stroll?

Perhaps I should try to find an old leather shaving strap and hang it up in my room as a reminder of discipline, lest I spoil my child and so lose my ticket to the Kingdom.

Festival of Tobacco. Today commemorates the introduction of smoking tobacco into Europe by a Spanish physician, Francisco Fernandes, in 1558. In 1559, Jean Nicot, the French Ambassador to Portugal sent tobacco seeds to Queen Catherine de Medici. She said it cured her of headaches and, in honor of Jean Nicot, named the plant "Nicotina." A good day to decide whether tobacco is a "yes" or a "no" for you during this Lent.

5

Birthday of Michelangelo in 1475. This Renaissance painter, sculptor, architect, poet and genius once said, "The more the marble wastes, the more the statue grows." What do you need to chip away today in order for the hidden beauty within you to be revealed?

6

YOUR OCCUPATION?

In the days of the French King Louis XIV, a celebrated chef named Vatel killed himself because he had created an unsuccessful sauce! This is a culinary case of too much personal identification with one's work. We can shake our heads at Vatel's excessive reaction to a bad job, but we are often guilty of the same basic error. How easily we feel that we *are* what we do! In our industrial society, one of the first questions we ask a stranger is, "What do you do?" And the answer usually greatly affects how we treat that person. If the person says, "I am a doctor," we are likely to make the appropriate respect-edged response, and if the person is a nuclear physicist, we might add a bit of awe. On the other hand, if the answer is, "I am a janitor" or "I'm a trash collector," we tend to view that person in quite another way.

In reality, what people do as a lifework often has little to do with who they are, with their personal worth or giftedness. While it is of some assistance in initiating the flow of a conversation to know what area of work someone is in, it can also make it difficult to *really* know that person. There is another way to begin to know someone that takes much longer but is free of the predisposition we attach to certain roles in our society. That way is to visit with the stranger about life, love, food and drink, pets and politics. Gradually we begin to get a feel for the other's personality and begin to experience his or her uniqueness of spirit. And not knowing the profession or work of the stranger, we can more naturally treat the person with a basic reverence and respect.

Janitors should be given the same respect given to judges, ditch diggers should be shown the same dignity as doctors, and painters reverenced as much as priests. Jesus called us to look beyond occupations, sexual differences and the color of skin to see the awesome mystery of God dwelling within both stranger and friend. This unusual vision must begin by our looking inside ourselves to find the God-seed. Once we perceive the divine mystery within our own hearts, we will have the scope from which to recognize it also within the heart of every person, regardless of age, religion or profession.

Louis XIV's cook, so it seems, took his work in the royal kitchen too seriously. And so do we when we forget what our primary vocation is. The lifework that we do, even if it is "holy" work, is not our fundamental vocation. Our essential life-calling is to become that unique self-expression of divine creativity, that once-in-history person that each of us is. Lent is the time to take that self more seriously—and our professions less seriously.

And Lent is the time to treat each person we encounter in life with great respect. Those who understand their essential identities tip their hats to junk dealers as well as judges. The removal of our biases about others, shaped by the amount of money they possess, the extent or quality of education they have received or the various titles before their names will not be easy. Lent, thank goodness, is not a season for easy tasks. So, if you've been dragging your heels about a Lenten resolution, today should be a good time to choose one. How about a resolution to sit quietly each day and look inside—to take time to see with the eyes of your soul the Divine Guest within.

---

7 **Patent for the Telephone** received by Alexander Graham Bell on this date in 1876. Celebrate today the awareness that the telephone is only a servant, and it can be given brief vacations from its duty by being unplugged at meals, prayer and other times during the day. A day to ponder whether it really must *always* be answered.

Feast of St. John of God, born in 1495 in Portugal. His love for the sick moved him to found a religious community to care for those who are ill. He is the patron saint of the sick and of hospitals. On this feast may John of God bless all who serve society in health care.

8

Lenten Day of Repentance. As we celebrate this annual season of Lenten reform, we can ponder that Arabic proverb, "The best part of repentance is the sinning." This is also a good day to reflect on the passage, "It is mercy I desire, not sacrifice" (Mt. 12: 7).

9

THE GOLDEN GATE BRIDGE

Bridges are marvelous and useful creations. Think about what our lives would be like if we didn't have them! Crossing even small creeks would be a difficult chore, and a river? Well-nigh impossible! Like many conveniences, we easily take bridges for granted and do not reflect on what life would be like without them.

We would consider someone crazy for blowing up a bridge because of resenting another person. For such an act would prevent that person as well as the "enemy"—and everyone else—from using the bridge. And if the bridge spanned a very wide river, the act would be viewed as even more insane.

In the Orient there is an interesting expression: "Those who cannot forgive others break the bridge over which they themselves must pass." And Gandhi added, "To forgive is divine; not to forgive is diabolic." And to his words we could add, "and insane!"

Why is the refusal to forgive another person (or even an institution) the act of an imbalanced person? Recall the words of Jesus in the prayer he himself gave to us: "...and forgive us our sins, as we forgive those who sin against us." Each time we say that prayer, we determine the condition for the forgiveness of our sins. Each act of pardon on our part strengthens the bridge over which we must carry our personal heavy load of failings, sins and mistakes. Each refusal to forgive and forget the injuries that others have done to us explodes a bomb under the bridge that we must cross someday if we are to go to God.

In a couple of weeks, we will celebrate a Feast of Fools. But the real fools are those who find sick pleasure in their negative thoughts about others, who find dark joy in nursing their wounds with the oil of self-pity and resentment. Only fools would destroy a bridge that was their only crossing out of hate and anger toward another.

Lent is the annual season of reform and renewal. It is an excellent time to examine carefully our lives, past or present, to see if we have unknowingly destroyed the most important bridge of our life. And if we find that we have, then this is the time to rebuild what we have destroyed. For the moment we release others who have caused us pain by granting them forgiveness, a bridge more beautiful than the famous Golden Gate Bridge suddenly springs across the vast ocean that separates us from God. Forgiveness is truly the bridge to heaven.

10 **Feast of the Forty Martyrs of Sebaste**, Turkey, in 320. Forty soldiers of the Sebaste garrison refuse to adore idols under Emperor Licinius and are exposed naked on a frozen lake at night. The next morning their limbs are broken and bodies burned. What are we willing to suffer not to adore today's idols?

SAVE YOUR SKIN

A dog flushed a rabbit out from a bush and gave chase. The dog was fleet but still fell behind the scampering rabbit who raced through the fields. A crow watching the chase began to laugh at the dog. "Look at you," said the crow, "you're much bigger and faster, but the rabbit is out-running you!"

The dog replied, "It is one thing, my dear crow, to run because you want to catch something; it is entirely another matter when you run to save your skin!"

This adaptation of one of Aesop's fables is worth some reflection. Saving our skin is a major concern of Americans. We spend billions on complexion oils, creams and soaps. We watch with dismay as liver spots or wrinkles appear and rush to the drug store to purchase the newest skin-saver. We are careful not to expose our skin to an excess of sun, and we treat it with oil when it becomes dry. We "run fast" to save our skin.

But is the purpose of life to save one's skin or to save one's soul? Jesus frequently warned us that we could indeed win the whole world and yet lose our souls. Souls cannot be lost like car keys, but we can cause them to be undeveloped, immature and lazy from neglect. The spirit is a constantly growing reality, having a hunger for "soul" food. And the spirit needs exercise just as much as the body. When we are too busy attempting to win the world, we neglect our spirits. We can find an excellent parallel with our skins.

What would happen in the world if people invested as much care and concern on their souls as they do on their skin? Imagine the result if we spent as much time on the inner spirit as we do on our outer skin. How much time each day do you spend in caring for your skin—all over your body—bathing, shaving, combing hair, washing and creaming your face? Then compare that with the time spent grooming your soul through prayer, silence, reflection and acts of love and generosity. The comparison may surprise you.

Running to catch something—even the world—should not lend swiftness to our feet. But if we know what life is all about, then we will run as fast as the wind, like the rabbit in Aesop's tale, to save our souls!

11 **Invention of Paper Day**. Celebrate today that little-known Chinese inventor, Ts'ai Lun, who was privy counselor to the Emperor Ho Ti. In 105 A.D. he created the first sample of paper made from bamboo, mulberry and other fibers, along with fish nets and rags. He enjoyed a brief period of wealth and fame and then became involved in the wrong side of palace intrigue. The eunuch Ts'ai Lun went to his death as he took a bath and drank poison. Paper would not appear in Europe until 1102. Pause for a moment as you gaze at the paper of this page and be grateful to Ts'ai Lun. And also give some thought to what kind of involvements or attitudes have the power to terminate your prosperity, especially your spiritual "success."

A DRY WELL

From Arabia there comes a story about a well. One dark night a certain holy man was passing a dry well when he heard a voice calling from the depths of the well. "What's the matter?" he shouted down into the well.

"I am a teacher of grammar, and I was on my way to the university when I accidentally fell into this dry well."

"Hold on, friend," replied the holy man, "I'll jest fetch a ladder and git you outta there."

"One moment," replied the teacher, "your grammar and diction are terribly faulty; what you should have said is... ."

But the holy man broke in, saying, "If my grammar is so much more important than what's essential, then you had best stay where you're at until I've learned to speak properly!" And bowing to the well, he continued on his way.

How frequently do we also place our attention on minor details and overlook what is essential. Like the grammar teacher in the Arabian story, all of us are habit prone to such an attitude. And, as in the story, the behavior that flows out of such a habit can be costly.

In recent years, we have seen great changes in many non-essentials of our Faith; a number of practices, attitudes, customs and even certain objects have been removed from our places of worship. But the essentials of our Faith remain the same, as they have during times of change throughout the ages. We need to be reminded of what is essential and to distinguish it from the non-essential. What is more important: the hymn or the instrument upon which the hymn is played? Which is of greater significance: the marvelous gift of the Holy Eucharist or the sex or the ordained status of the person who gives us the Body of Christ?

The same is true in our daily lives. How often do we suffer and cause others to suffer because we have lost sight of what is truly important? And just what is essential? **Life** is essential. The enjoyment of another's presence, love, friendship, health and living in harmony with God's way are essential, not things like how people choose to dress, the manner in which they wear their hair or how they park the car in the garage. Yet it is the little things, the unimportant things, that eat away at us and cause us to create unhappiness. As Jesus said, "Is not life more important than food? Is not the body more valuable than clothes?" (Mt. 6: 25). He was speaking about our tendency to get trapped, as was the grammar teacher, in dry, lifeless wells.

Examine your attitude, especially toward those who are closest to you, and see if you are stuck on the non-essentials. Change now, while there is time to change. Death or loss can come to us as the messenger of Truth, harshly opening our eyes to what is truly important.

An excellent spiritual exercise for us people of the well would be to take time today to carefully overlook the unimportant while establishing a pattern of giving thanks for the essentials in our lives—in our marriages, families, religious expressions and our relationships with God.

Jesus told us that where our treasure is, there also will be our hearts. Let our hearts rest in the treasure of what is essential. For when our hearts delight in that treasure, we will live happy and holy lives.

12 Anti-Commercial Day. Be mindful today of the pollution of life created by the constant flood of advertisements. According to one study, Americans are bombarded by 1600 commercial messages every day. Only eighty of these are consciously noted and less than fifteen evoke some response. Take time today to carefully judge those fifteen to see if you really need what you have been told that you can't live without.

HORSE SENSE

One day an old man heard the sounds of a horse approaching his village at great speed. Like a whirlwind the horse and its rider galloped through the town. The old villager cried out to the rider as he passed, "Where are you going in such a hurry?" The man on the horse turned around and shouted back, "I don't know; ask the horse. I'm only riding it!"

This story from the East fits us like a glove. Most of us feel like we are astride a galloping horse, racing madly to some unknown destination. How often do we hear, "We have to learn how to slow down, to have time for the important things of life." Yet how often do we actually slow down; we usually only cling tighter to the galloping horse of modern life and do our best not to fall off.

Once again we are in the midst of the season of Lent, that sacred season of discipline and prayer. Our various Lenten disciplines should not have a lifespan of only forty days, but should rather be a step forward in our ongoing growth in holiness. Whether we are eight or eighty, we are still growing; our minds and especially our souls know no point where they are "finished" and can no longer learn, change and evolve.

Lent is an ideal time to stop smoking or to change those habits that are harmful or lacking in love. In Lent we are surrounded by the energy of countless millions practicing self-denial. These forty days are rich in grace for conversion, for a change of habit and of heart. And when Easter comes, we should not return to our limiting behaviors but should continue to live free of them. So the choice of our Lenten practices should be easy: what do we want to be different about ourselves and our lives?

The story of the bewildered rider on the galloping horse suggests a discipline for us to embrace if we still haven't been fully grounded in a Lenten practice. For finding a resolution to the problem of constant rushing will surely be a discipline, a penance. The logical answer to the hijacked rider's dilemma would be, "Get off the horse!" But if you have ever been on a galloping horse you know that such a solution is not as easy as it may sound.

The same is true of our fast-paced lives, since our society is geared to an ever-increasing speed. Yet we cannot very easily live in this world without riding the horse. Our challenge is to find a way to be at peace while still in the saddle.

The discipline of daily prayer, in which we stop our activities to sit still and rest in God, teaches us how to find peace in the saddle. To make room in our day for a quiet moment here and there, to chew our food just a bit more slowly and to sip instead of gulp at life's experiences are other Lenten disciplines that hold the power to change our lives. Such practices can bring us a calm heart even though we are caught up in a hectic, galloping society. But you might ask how one finds the time to sit still.

You can start by making a definite space each day for prayer. And before retiring at night, you can envision yourself the next morning quietly at prayer and enjoying the peace it brings to your heart. Envision yourself the next day slowly sipping your coffee or pausing at midmorning to drink in a bit of beauty, a moment of quiet. Such bedtime preparation, you will find, makes any act of the will much easier.

If you are faithful to this discipline of creating quiet pauses in your day, then when Easter comes you will have a permanent gift. While you will still be riding the galloping horse, you will be less anxious, less out-of-control, and your heart will be calmer and closer to God.

Antique Ashtray Show hosted in Houston in 2057. On display are antique cigarette lighters and ashtrays of the early and late twentieth century when the drug, nicotine, was in wide use. A day to reflect on the fact that all our modern artifacts will one day be antiques.

13

Birthday of Albert Einstein in 1879. Einstein, one of the great geniuses of our time, once said, "Since the splitting of the atom everything has changed except our thinking."

14

HOW TO CHANGE THE WORLD

A devout and holy rabbi once said, "In my youth, fired with the love of God, I thought I would convert the whole world. But soon I learned it would be quite enough to convert the people who lived in my village. I tried that for a long time, but I was unsuccessful. Then I realized that my program was still too ambitious, so I concentrated on reforming the members of my own household. But I couldn't convert them either. Finally it dawned on me that I must work only upon myself. But I have stumbled in my attempts to accomplish even that."

This story reminds us of who should be the subject of our reform during this season of Lent. While the world is filled with great injustice, and there are endless lists of causes that we might take up—from "Ban the Bomb" to "Save the Whales"—let us begin to reform the world by a serious attempt to reform ourselves. The world will find itself being changed at the speed of each personal conversion. While we all may sense the truth of this fact, we also do **not** know it.

At times the change of heart that is the central issue of Lent seems to affect only ourselves. But we need faith in what seems too good to be true—that if I myself am different, the world will be different. In our modern age we are able to view the hunger, pain and sufferings of people all over the world by means of electronic media, so we tend to be overwhelmed by the vast, global need for change. As a result of feeling powerless to effect change in the world, we usually do nothing! Lent crashes in upon our apathetic sense of impotence and says, "You *can* do something, *you* can become different!"

As you read this, take time, if you haven't already, to reflect on an attitude present in your life—a habit or addiction, a behavioral pattern that needs to be amended—and make a resolution to change it as your Lenten work. As much as possible, put your resolution into a positive statement and say it aloud to yourself with real conviction. Repeat your resolution each day, perhaps as you stand in front of the mirror in the morning after awakening and in the evening before you retire. Perhaps you could also visualize your actions or responses to important life situations in a new and creative way. If you do this for the rest of Lent (and beyond), you will likely find that a change **has** come into your life. By planting the thought of what you wish to do, by nourishing it and reinforcing it over and over with great conviction, you can create the desired changes much more readily. And as our actions begin to change, we help create a field for a chain reaction so that in time the world will become a better place.

Don't waste the rich graces of the remainder of this Lenten season. Each of its forty days are fertile with divine energy, and it would be tragic not to use them. You can't afford not to respond to those graces; our world cannot afford for you to delay its reform.

---

15 **A New Pope.** Today in 2025, a black African Cardinal is elected as pope. The new black Bishop of Rome announces that he will call a world synod of bishops to bring about radical changes in the Roman Catholic Church to address the needs of the twenty-first century.

---

16 **Feast of St. Sarah**, the barren wife of Abraham. She is the great-grandmother of the three great Western religious traditions: Judaism, Christianity and Islam. In advanced old age she bore a son, teaching us that, indeed, with God nothing is impossible. Reflect today on her great flexibility which allowed her to respond to that great change of life in her latter years.

---

17 **Feast of St. Patrick of Ireland**, patron saint of the Erin Isle. This pre-spring ritual of feasting, parading and wearing the green is a sign of the end of winter. St. Patrick was known to stand in ice water up to his armpits while reciting all one hundred and fifty Psalms by heart. He is also known for introducing the Easter fire into the ritual of Easter.

SHENANIGANS

On Saint Patrick's Day, the wee folk, led by Leprechauns by the thousands, head the parade of rejoicing that is so much a part of this green and glorious feast of Ireland's great saint. The feast is not only an occasion for parades and parties but also for some shenanigans, for mischief and pranks. The word is a shortened form of an Irish blessing or invocation, **Shee nanna gasne**, "the Shee are rattling the dishes." The Shee were invisible fairy folk who were very much in control of Ireland before the coming of Christians. And as the blessing implies, they were very fond of mischief. The purpose of such spirited pranks as making tables tap dance and causing pots and pans to prance was to teach humans some humility.

When any unexplainable events happened in the house, the Irish would pronounce the blessing invocation, **Shee nanna gasne**. It was both a polite greeting to the wee folk and a gentle invitation for them to leave. For although the pranks of the wee folk were reverenced reminders to humans that they were not in total control of their lives, no one wanted the invisible visitors to be permanent house guests.

We are all a bit reluctant to accept the gift of humility. Yet humility is the rich soil out of which grows the rose of holiness. Certainly it was the bedrock of the holiness of Jesus who took upon himself our sins and our shameful shenanigans that cause so much pain in the world. This virtue of humility is often misunderstood. But perhaps the wee folk were agents of true humility when they reminded humans of their lack of control over their lives—or even their pots and pans.

Today's technology can easily give us a sense of false pride. It creates the impression that we are secure in our ability to manage our environments and our daily lives. But, with or without the help of the wee folk, we need to learn the wisdom of insecurity, the value of embracing with humble trust our lack of total control. Our age has a lust for security which expresses itself in countless types of insurance and protection policies. While to a certain extent all these are good and necessary, they can easily produce a false sense of security. And that illusion can blind us to the need to place our dependence not upon modern safety nets, but rather upon the love of an ever-caring and compassionate God.

The Saint Patrick's Day Parade, animated by the spirit of mischievous fairy folk, is an overture to Good Friday's Passion Parade. As Jesus carried his cross up the hill of Calvary, he was painfully aware that every source of security, even the support of good friends and disciples, had been stripped away from him. He who was so much the master of the various events of his life was now totally dependent upon the love and protection of God. In his humility he embraced that reality with as firm a grip as the grip the cross had upon his limbs.

The next time we find ourselves feeling very safe and comfortable, fortified by our various systems of support and security, while we should feel grateful for all of them—from our health insurance to the lock on the front door—perhaps we should also pronounce an invocation. Looking our illusion of security straight in the eye, we could say, "**Shee nanna gasne**," or more simply, "We're not fooled by your shenanigans...in God alone do we trust."

18 **Celebration of Columbus' Almanac.** In 1504, upon landing on the Island of Jamaica, Columbus encountered hostile Indians who refused to provide food and water for his crew. He read in his almanac that there was to be an eclipse of the moon and warned the Jamaicans that God was going to punish them for their lack of hospitality by making the moon go dark. The eclipse occurred, and the terrified natives promised to provide him with all the food he needed if he only would bring back the moon. May this almanac provide you with information to aid you as much in your pilgrimage as Columbus' almanac assisted him.

19 **Feast of St. Joseph**, husband of Mary of Nazareth. St. Joseph is the patron saint of Italians who today celebrate with festive meals. It was an old custom to set a plate at the table for St. Joseph and heap it high with food, which was later given to the poor. A day for all, Italians and non-Italians alike, to do something for the poor and hungry.

20 **Spring Equinox.** This is an earthen feast when our planet begins to lean back toward our star, the sun. One of the most ancient of celebrations when earthlings of ages past rejoiced that the ever-new season of spring had arrived. Celebrate, today, the end of winter with mirth and madness, joy and song.

EASTER POTATOES

A springtime reflection on planting a garden might provide us with some insights into the meaning of Easter. Planting potatoes in some parts of the United States is a ritual that takes place on St. Patrick's Day or Good Friday, but the ritual is ancient. Before planting potatoes, you must first cut out those pieces containing eyes. Then those pieces are ready to be buried in the good soil of the garden. In a play on words we can see a similar relationship between Easter and the destruction of the "I." For without cutting out the "I," without the death of the ego, there can be no personal resurrection experience. Easter is a joyous event which we may express with elaborate alleluias, feasting, new clothes, candy rabbits and brightly decorated eggs. But it is a painful experience as well! Easter is the celebration of the resurrection, but a resurrection implies death. We are eager to celebrate life but reluctant to die first!

The death of Easter is more than the death of the body. It is that deeper death of a superpower—the ego, the "I" and its almost dictatorial position. If we seek holiness and wholeness, we must "cut out" the great "I" and bury it. This is no easy task, for the "I" reacts strongly to any effort to limit its authority. The "I" wants to have its own way and to have it right now, with no compromise and no opposition. We want what we want when we want it!

Part of the task is to find the "I" of the self, just as we locate the eye of the potato. In its daily demands for attention, the "I" wears a thousand and one clever disguises. The ego has mastered countless ingenious maneuvers to make sure that all of its desires will be met. But as long as the "I" remains above ground, refusing to die, it is doomed to death and sterility. Both the potato and the ego must surrender to the knife! But the strength of the "I" should not frighten us, for it is this very potency, which after being cut out and buried, will become the power for fertilizing a new and dynamic personality.

The death of the ego is the hardest of all spiritual sacrifices. The paradox of the Passover, the journey from Good Friday to Easter Sunday, is that we must surrender to death to find Life. When we struggle to say "no" to our needs, dying to the demands of the ego, so that we can say "yes" to the needs of others, then the self is freed from its cramped cocoon. When we can relate to the needs of others—to our family as well as complete strangers—by lives of service, we cut out the "I." No marriage, friendship or community offers an easy, painless escape; it promises only the vital condition of common living. That common life is the rich soil for new life and growth. But unless we have first used a knife on the ego, the soil becomes only a battleground and smells of death and destruction. A wholesome spiritual life encourages self-giving service, that daily learning to say "no" to ourselves in order to say "yes" to the other. In their proper order, both are words of freedom.

The Easter of bonnets and colored eggs is pink and beautiful. The Easter of cut up potatoes and dead egos is one that frightens the hell out of our insulated "I." Hell, the realm of death, is frightened away so that the true condition of life may appear. This hard side of Easter is denied by all the little kings and queens sitting in their tiny but absolute kingdoms. Those, however, who seek a greater life lay themselves bare to the knife. Willingly, they allow themselves to be buried in the rich humus of daily life and love. Such people are aware that only when the potato eye of the ego has been buried, can it come forth as vital new life.

Part of the mystery of this death to the self is found in service to others, and part of it is found in the ability to invest oneself in something greater than the self. We all need a "beyond" to which we can consecrate ourselves, a dedication to something bigger, greater and more transcendent than the self. We need to find something worth the investment of our whole self, an investment that can be made with our whole heart. It is by this sharp twin-tool of service and consecration that we find Life!

Easter eggs have for centuries been a beautiful symbol for the emergence of resurrection life. But perhaps the cut-up Easter potato might be a more **awakening** symbol for this great feast.

First Full Day of Spring. Recent studies show that Americans spend only about 2% of their lives out-of-doors. Today go for a walk and enjoy this new season. And it's more fun if you take your family or a friend with you. 21

---

22 **First Book Printed**, the Gutenberg Bible, in 1457. Celebrate the birthday of this book and the books that have made a difference in your life. Ponder the marvel of the written word and its power to change your life. Do not lament over the lack of a good spiritual director. Find an author who speaks to your heart; let his or her books become your guides as a cosmic pilgrim. There is no good excuse for not finding your way Home.

THE OZARK SIDE-HILL HOOFER

Down in the Ozarks, the old-timers still talk about the Side-hill Hoofer or, as it is also known, the Side-hill Slicker. This strange creature runs around the Ozark Mountains in one direction because the legs on one side of its body are shorter than the other.

This springtime season of Lent offers the best chance of seeing a Side-hill Slicker, and you don't even have to go to the Ozarks to find one. They are not even restricted to the hill country but can be seen in the prairies of the Midwest or in the coast lands; indeed, throughout the whole world! For they are Lenten creatures known for their ability to go down or around—but never **up**—the hill of Calvary, the Mount of Skulls.

Lent is the sacred season of the year when we are invited to take up our crosses and follow Christ up the hill of Calvary. That invitation to share in the suffering of Jesus is not just an offer of a supporting role in some passion play. In fact, there is very little play or pretending in taking up one's cross and so sharing in Christ's redemption of the world.

Side-hill Slickers, having one foot shorter than the other, find numerous ways to go in the "other" direction when they see that the road leads up the hill to a crucifixion! Few disciples of Jesus ever have an opportunity to share in an actual crucifixion, but in some way every disciple is daily offered a chance to surrender to death.

We die a little each time we refuse to react in anger or self-pity when someone offends us. We feel the kiss of death each time we forget about our needs to address the needs of another. We share the mystery of Calvary each time we go out of our way, and so die in a small way, in order to bring comfort or assistance to someone who is in need. And whenever we make room in our hearts for the thousands who are locked in the prison of poverty or who are demoralized because they have lost a job or the family farm, we take on a Good Friday heart. To pray daily for the hungry and the homeless of our world is to share in their sufferings, and it is also to shape our hearts in the pattern of Christ on the cross. His heart on that Good Friday expanded enough to contain all the pain and suffering of this world. To ponder such suffering in a prayerful way isn't easy, but it is redemptive.

Side-hill Slickers find numerous excuses to go in any other direction and so avoid personal sacrifice. By so doing, however, they also miss the opportunity to personally embrace the healing passion and death of the living Christ. Have you seen any Side-hill Hoofers recently around your part of the country—or perhaps in your bathroom mirror?

Birthday of the Spoon, that most common of eating tools, in 19,000 B.C. This is a celebration of that practical implement for eating liquids and foods too soft for forks. But instead of being totally "spoon-fed" today with soft reflections on God, be willing to dig into some substantial theological reading or something that has the capacity to radically change your life. Unfortunately most of us have not advanced beyond grade-school level religious "education" and are not willing to sacrifice comfort for spiritual growth.

23

Feast of St. Gabriel the Archangel. This messenger of God who visited the prophet Daniel and John the Baptist's father Zachary also announced to Mary that she was to be the mother of God. On this feast, we should ask if we are open to divine messengers who bear strange and sometimes unbelievable good news.

24

A NEW VOCATION AND MINISTRY

In the early post-resurrection Church, EVERYONE had some ministry to perform. Just like the parts of the physical body, the Church had a variety of ministries or functions. Each ministry was an integral part of the full expression of the Mystical Body of Christ. Not everyone presently has a formal or identified ministry to perform within a parish congregation or community. But even if you do, would you like to have a ministry closer to the heart of God?

Recall the story of the Annunciation when the angel Gabriel announced to Mary that she was to be the mother of the long-awaited Messiah. For countless generations who had longed for that Messiah, Gabriel's visit and Mary's response were both answers to a prayer.

Being an Answer-to-a-Prayer is a vocation and ministry to which all of us have been called. Daily, you and I have many "divine" opportunities. When we assist a person in need, feed the poor or respond to another's pain, we surely are an answer to a prayer. A stranded motorist may even unconsciously call us by our ministerial title, saying, "You're an Answer-to-a-Prayer!"

When someone comes seeking pardon or to be reconciled to you, it is a royal opportunity to answer that person's prayer and to be part of the removal of the difficulties that divorce the two of you. Or a person's request that we pray for his or her intention can beautifully activate our basic vocation. We assist the other person by sharing in his or her burden as well as by investing the intention with all our prayerful energy. At that moment, we are not just a pray-er but also an answer to another's prayer for assistance. We can enhance that experience by taking time to talk about the issue that is the subject of the request for prayer. We may not be able to bring about a particular resolution, but we can provide a compassionate, listening heart. As we listen with love, we become the ears and loving presence of God. And when we are able to be an answer to prayer by helping someone in need, we become the left and right hands of God!

Mary, the mother of Christ, especially as she appears in the Annunciation, provides a perfect pattern for an open attentiveness to God that also allows God to become enfleshed in the world. If you are looking for a ministry or vocation in life, no more needed or divine calling could be found than being such a pray-er who is also an answer to prayers.

25 **Feast of the Annunciation of Mary**. Before the reform of the calendar by Pope Gregory VII, this was the golden feast that began the new year's celebration which lasted until April 1. This reform was too radical a change for some, who continued to keep April 1 as the beginning of the new year. Such conservatives who refused to embrace the new calendar were called "April Fools." A good day to reflect on how we may be fools today for not embracing the new.

THE JOKE'S ON YOU!

Who doesn't like to tell a funny joke? A good joke is worth a bushel of medicine, and it is the safest drug for stress and depression. An outburst of laughter and a brief island of comic relief in the midst of the serious sea of life is the greatest reward for the joke teller. Bank tellers and joke tellers are both distributors of wealth.

No matter how poorly or expertly we tell a joke, we are enriched by the joy that it brings to others. In short, we feel good; we feel invigorated when we are able to help others laugh and look on the funny side of life.

But how quickly that sense of personal well-being changes if we didn't intend to be funny, if the joke is on us! We slip on one of life's banana peels and fall on our faces—a mispronounced word, a stupid statement or an unguarded moment—and everyone laughs. Yes, everyone roars with laughter; that is, everyone but us! Our usual reaction to such a situation is embarrassment and anger, because to us it isn't funny. But this kind of experience is an unrequested gift from the gods, for it's like having our oil checked. To *be* the joke instead of *telling* a joke, to be the cause of a release of peals of laughter and to fully enjoy it, is THE test for the virtue of humility. I don't know about you, but when I become a laughingstock, I usually find that my humility dipstick comes up bone dry!

While we enjoy telling jokes and being amateur comedians, we don't enjoy being the joke. Yet until we do, can we truly be "fools for Christ," as St. Paul invited us to be? We are usually cautious and calculating disciples of the Lord of Fools, disciples who detest losing our respectability and dropping our guard. Only when we have no self-image to protect can we sincerely join others in uproarious laughter when we accidentally become an April fool. One way to begin to learn such humility is to start seeing the humor of our private mistakes. We can also begin to take ourselves and what we say or do more lightly. We can recall the wisdom of Jesus that the gates of heaven are like those of a playground; they open only to children. Then when one of life's unseen banana peels turns us temporarily into a fool, we may be ready.

If we can sit on the kitchen floor or in the middle of a meeting and enjoy our stupid mistakes or accidental falls as much as others, then we will have come a long way toward developing a true sense of humor and a true sense of the holy. When we are able to allow ourselves to be fools, then we will know that the virtue so highly prized by Jesus has found a home in our hearts.

Pied Piper of Hamelin Anniversary. In 1284 an underpaid rat-removing piper seeks revenge on the city council by leading all the children out of the German town of Hamelin and into a hole in a hill. Has your inner child been kidnaped? If so, go in search of it today by being more playful and childlike.

26

First Zoo in China, the Park of Intelligence, is founded in 2000 B.C. Zoos, like religious rituals, are resources for the healing of anxieties. When you visit a zoo, you see wild animals safely behind bars. A visit to the zoo calms the heart since we have deep-seated fears of things that "go bump in the night," the inhabitants of our inner recesses who play in our nightmares.

27

Respect Your Cat Day. By royal edict in 1384, England's Richard II condemned cat eating. The peasants, out of resentment toward King Richard, whom they called "the royal cat," took it out on cats, killing and eating them by the thousands. But they also cooked cats because of food shortages. Our expression, "There is more than one way to skin a cat," came from this period during which cats were cooked for supper. A 1399 recipe book had an entire chapter on "cat stews." Do we still harbor any of our ancestors' attitudes toward our canine friends—or any other part of our creation family?

28

Feast of St. Barachisius who died for his faith in 327. After being pierced with several spikes, he was put into a press and squeezed to death. An eye witness to Barachisius' death said that "while enduring terrible tortures, he said that he thought he had bought heaven too cheaply." What price today do we, as pilgrims, put on achieving our ultimate destination?

29

LIE YOUR WAY TO HEAVEN

Lying? That's a sin! How can it be a way to heaven? The rabbis of old used to say that there are only two times when telling a lie is not sinful. If people ask you about your sexual life, you can lie because it is none of their business, being a private matter. The only other time is when you are asked about the hospitality of a host—the quality of his or her food and wine. To protect a host from an invasion of unwanted guests, it is permissible to lie and say that the food and drink were terrible.

But there may be a third situation when lying is permissible—or even a way to heaven! Such a situation may come up, for example, when someone asks, "Does anyone care for this last piece of cake?" and we sense that the person who makes the offer really wants it! Untrue answers such as "No, thank you, I don't care for any more cake," are lies of the third kind. So are statements like, "Yes, I'd be glad to do it," when asked the question, "Would anyone here like to volunteer for this task?" It is an especially "true" lie if the task is an unpleasant one and we do not want to take on another job at this time.

Such lies can assist our way to heaven because they go directly against the strong urge within us to think only of our wants, desires and preferences and not consider the needs of others. These heaven-bound lies are made by our hearts, that small part of us that truly cares about serving others, at the expense of what the rest of us wants. But as we begin to make this kind of lying a habit, slowly the personality begins to move naturally toward joyful self-sacrifice. At some point we actually begin to enjoy volunteering, giving others what we would like to have or going where they would like to go. Do not worry, however, if after years of effort to sacrifice with joy, there still remains a trace of insincerity and deceit in your personal responses. Time is required for our hearts to grow into the fullness of the heart of Christ.

Blessed are the lies that are spoken by the heart, for by such lies we slowly climb up the ladder of holiness and into the arms of God.

---

30 **Festival of Maimonides, Moses ben Maimon,** who was born in 1135 A.D. This Spanish born Jewish scholar, physician and philosopher once wrote, "Anticipate charity by preventing poverty; assist the reduced fellowman either by considerable gift...or by teaching him a trade or by putting him in the way of business, so that he may earn an honest livelihood...This is the highest step and the summit of charity's golden ladder."

---

31 **Third Vatican Council Begins** on this date in the year 2062. The first truly "catholic," that is universal, council meets, with two bishops attending from each Earth-orbiting diocese in outer space. The Third Vatican Council also has voting delegates from all the major Christian denominations.

April

Feast of Fools. St. Paul told us to be fools for Christ's sake. Since God's ways and thoughts are not our ways and thoughts, those who think and act like God are likely to appear like fools or clowns. For the origin of this feast see March 25.

1

A DOSE OF FUN

This week of foolishness which begins with our annual celebration of April Fool's Day, the feast of fools, is only a faint relic of its once robust and jovial origins. Yet it can still help us recall the need for a little foolishness and fun. In our busy, busy lives, where we have mortgaged away our time, two important functions of life are the first to be sacrificed. The paradox is that they are the very things we cannot afford to sacrifice when we are truly busy.

The first activity we usually cut out of our over-scheduled day is prayer, and the second is play. While we can understand the necessity for prayer in a busy life (for how else can we remain balanced in the midst of intense activity if we do not take time for a prayer that centers us), we seldom see a real justification for fun. Play, fun and foolishness are the extras in life, the activities of children. Since we are now adults who deal with matters of grave consequence, we find little basis for any frivolity.

And yet, while we have the finest medical treatment in the world, the United States ranks no higher than thirtieth in the overall health of its people. The reasons are as complicated as our country, but I wonder if one cause could be that we relegate fun to a non-essential status. Henry Shaw, who wrote under the pen name of Josh Billings, said, "There ain't much fun in medicine, but there's a good deal of medicine in fun." Perhaps our national health might improve if we had more fun in life, if we did things just for the fun of it. So many of our waking hours are filled with the practical, the functional, the necessary—because life seems to require it. But we need to take time to simply play—to be totally involved in non-productive activity. Such "fun" comes in ten thousand flavors, and it is essential for staying healthy and human. Only machines work constantly, and even machines break down.

Taking the time for fun, and being willing to spend the necessary funds, will help make us both healthy and holy. For the activity of prayer among industrious people like ourselves requires an attitude of non-productivity. Only when we approach it as time to waste, time to throw away on our Beloved, will our prayer become fruitful. May this reflection—and April Fool's day—encourage you to take time in your busy day to do something just for the fun of it.

2

First Movie Theater Opens in Los Angeles, 1902. While realism in motion pictures has its value, movie theaters are the great dream temples where we can be inspired to live lives of heroic greatness. Also a day to celebrate the joy of having your own theater in your home through the miracle of VCR's. Have fun with film today!

3

Close Call Day. In April of 1989, an asteroid a half-mile wide, traveling at 46,000 miles an hour, missed Earth by only half a million miles—in cosmic terms, a very "close call." If this mountain-sized projectile had struck the earth, it would have had the effect of 20,000 1-megaton hydrogen bombs. It would have left a crater five to ten miles wide and a mile deep and would have caused destruction for a hundred miles in every direction. Effects would have been felt thousands of miles away. One scientist predicted its return in April of 1990, and if not then perhaps in years to come. Maybe the next time it will be a *closer* call.

4

April Showers Possible. And when it rains, remember that old Arab proverb: "All sunshine makes the desert." Don't run under an umbrella when showers come, in whatever form, today. Rather, open yourself to the fertile rain. In time you will reflect its liquid light.

JUST A DROP IN THE BUCKET

We realize that a single drop in a bucket of water or one raindrop of a spring shower are very insignificant. But often we ourselves feel even more insignificant—like a drop of rain falling into the ocean! Indeed, the fact that millions upon millions of people inhabit our earth seems to suggest that our individual actions and even our whole lives are of little importance. But we can also look at that reality from another angle. The Saadi of Shiraz, an Islamic saint, once wrote,

> A raindrop, dripping from a cloud,
> Was ashamed when it saw the sea.
> "Who am I where there is the sea?" it said.
> When it saw itself with the eye of humility,
> A shell nurtured it in its embrace.

A tiny drop of water, lovingly embraced by a shell, becomes a pearl. But the process by which it becomes a pearl is a long one. A bit of sand enters the shell with the water; then the oyster slowly surrounds that grain with layer upon layer of the bodily substance that is also the lining of the shell.

As we come to view ourselves with the "eye of humility," as Christ himself embraces us, we begin ever so slowly to reflect the luster of God and become as precious as pearls. If that process is forced or hurried, for whatever reason, we can easily become imitation pearls—imitation saints! We might resemble the real thing from the outside, but the quality of our lives will reveal the difference.

Instant holiness does not exist. It takes time for April showers to produce beautiful blossoms. It also requires humility, patience and an openness to change for us to become a mirror of the sacred shell in which we have made our home. In our hurried society, such a statement may itself seem like an irritating grain of sand rubbing us the wrong way. But the luster of right living only appears when patience and modesty are learned and practiced. When we see ourselves with the "eye of humility," we can assist the process of slow transformation by refusing to make a "big splash" at every opportunity. We seem to love to splash about, attempting to be "number one," to be different and better than all the other billions of droplets. We love to live in special parts of town, to have certain kinds of houses, to wear designer clothes or to acquire degrees, honors and titles. But nothing changes our identity if we are blind in the "eye of humility."

Look for peace, and in your daily efforts at prayer promise to surrender quietly to the Divine Mystery that surrounds and slowly transforms you. Don't rush away from the daily, quiet embrace of prayerfulness. Let the luster of silence, the wordless prayer of meditation, lovingly convert your spirit into a "pearl of great price."

Feast of St. Noah who rode out the Great Flood, patron saint of boat builders and sailors. This is a feast that attests to the fact that oceans build up drop by drop, day by day; and also that one can survive a storm with one's essential nature enhanced. A festival day for raincoats and rainbows.

5

Admiral Peary Discovers the North Pole, 1909. As Peary was making his difficult journey, thousands were reading about the adventures of that arch-pilgrim, Dorothy of Kansas. Lyman Frank Baum's book *The Wonderful Wizard of Oz* which described Dorothy's pilgrimage to the Emerald City was very popular at the time. Like Dorothy and Peary, each of us as prayerful pilgrims must face great trials on the long journey of returning "home."

6

Festival of P.T. Barnum who died on this day in 1881, a genius of showmanship and the circus. His saying, "A sucker is born every minute," is worth pondering in our age of advertising—in one way or another the promise of happiness is hidden in every ad.

Also, on this day in Japan, the **Death of Gautama Buddha**, which took place in about 483 B.C., is commemorated.

7

Feast of the Humming Bird. According to the religious belief of the Aztecs of ancient Mexico, when a warrior died in battle or offered his life in sacrifice

8

to the sun, he went on to live in the sun for four years. At the end of that time, he returned to earth as a humming bird! A day for those who feel the call of the warrior to take on the gentle ways of the humming bird.

I WILL NOT...

Isabella, the daughter of Philip II of Spain, the king who launched the Armada at the end of the seventeenth century, once swore an interesting oath. Isabella vowed not to change her underwear until Ostend, a city in the Spanish Netherlands, was recaptured by the Spanish army. The siege took three years before Ostend was recaptured.

While we may smile at such a silly and smelly vow, we are often guilty of making the same kind of rash oaths. When we have been offended by another person or our heart has been captured by anger in league with injury, we are prone to say, "I will not speak, smile or act in a natural and loving way until she/he apologizes." Or "I will be as cold and distant as the North Pole: polite, mind you, but cool and remote until... ."

Isabella's dirty, yellow underwear was a sign of her Spanish pride. Our chilly silence and refusal to address properly the cause of our private war with another person can also be a sign of pride and fear. We retreat into chilly non-confrontation because we fear the pain of direct confrontation. We are also afraid that we will look silly and petty if we say that we were offended because someone was twenty minutes late—a small matter, but one of those situations that can really set our teeth on edge! Jesus called us to face the music, to go directly to the person who has offended us or whom we have offended and seek reconciliation. Such an act requires humility, courage and, most of all, love. But it is of supreme importance in the ongoing growth of a relationship.

No doubt poor Philip II and the rest of Isabella's family suffered as a result of her vow not to change her underwear until the victory at Ostend. When we respond with silence and withdrawal of love when our hearts have been captured by anger, our families and those who live with us must suffer as Isabella's family did. Even if the vows of withdrawal are only between two people, remember that there are no private wars. Every conflict, even between two people living together, feeds the disease of war, the cancer of our human family.

Our world will not find peace at the great powers' summit conferences or at the meetings of the United Nations. Peace spreads outward in the world at the speed that it spreads in your home, to the degree that it is present between you and the persons who share life with you. The next time you change your underwear, think about these things.

9 **American Civil War Ends** with Lee's surrender to Grant at the Appomattox courthouse on this day on 1865. A day to remember that all wars are civil wars; all wars are family fights. All wars are suicidal, one part of the body killing another part of the body.

Birthday of General William Booth in Nottingham, England in 1829. The founder of the Salvation Army, Booth was often ridiculed and violently opposed because of the organization's uniforms and brass bands. But he remained steadfast in his mission to care for the poor and the homeless. Celebrate, today, with all the members of the Salvation Army, the birthday of its founder. And may the compassion of General Booth spark a real concern within you for the poor and homeless.

10

Feast of Non-Spectatorism. A day to consider the Zen principle of life: "Being a spectator while one is also a participant spoils one's performance." To totally forget yourself, refusing to be a critical observer of your behavior, is the best way to be spontaneous and natural.

11

THE PURSUIT OF HAPPINESS

"If life were a game," said Dennis Wholey, "the happy people would be the players, the unhappy people the spectators." If that's true, in which of those two groups would you place yourself? As Americans, part of our national heritage is the pursuit of happiness. But one wonders how many have caught up with happiness—and if they haven't, why not? A Zen riddle may help us to understand the major cause of most unhappiness.

Once there was a monk who left his temple to make a pilgrimage. He vowed not to take a step backward in his journey until he had reached the shrine to which he was traveling. After days of travel he came to a deep canyon with a river flowing through the bottom of the ravine. A single large rope served as a bridge spanning the canyon. To assist the traveler, there was a hand rope fastened to the swaying rope-bridge.

The monk carefully crossed the swaying bridge, placing one foot slowly ahead of the other as he tried not to look down at the roaring river far below. When he reached the middle of the bridge, he came face to face with another monk who was on a pilgrimage to the very same temple from which the first monk had come. The second monk had also vowed never to take a step backward until his pilgrimage had been completed!

See if you can help these two pilgrims. How can they each continue on their pilgrimages without breaking their vows? Take a few minutes to consider the problem; see if you can resist reading on until you have your own solution.

The Zen answer is that there are no monks, no rope bridge and no deep canyon! No, this is not a weird practical joke. Think about it for a moment: the two monks, their conflicts and even the swaying bridge all exist in your mind. The meaning of this religious riddle is that unhappiness in life is located in the mind.

It is our thoughts that cause our distress and unhappiness. Thoughts such as, "People should be on time" or "She must be angry with me or she would have said 'Good morning'—I must have offended her somehow" or "Parents with crying children should take them out of church." The list of thoughts that cause our conflicts with what is happening around us could fill several pages of this book.

If there are pockets of unhappiness in your life, first examine what your thoughts are about those situations. Then see if you would still be unhappy if you removed those thoughts. Without the thought, like the thought of the problem of the two monk pilgrims, the problem often easily disappears. While it might sound simple, however, it isn't as easy as it seems. We are often hung up, literally, on our ideas. Such thoughts are like hooks upon which we dangle in distress.

Dealing with the ideas that flow through our minds is one of the most important aspects of the spiritual life, as Jesus and spiritual masters of every religious tradition tell us. As it has been said many times, we each, at this very moment, have everything we need to be happy. If we are not happy, then the place for change is not necessarily in those around us or in the external conditions of our lives but rather in the arena inside us. In the game of life, we are all given a choice. We can be players if we wish, or we can simply be spectators.

---

12 **Spaceship Earth Day**. On this day in 1961 Russian Cosmonaut Yuri Gagarin becomes the first earthling to orbit Earth in space. A good day to reflect on the words of Marshall McLuhan: "There are no passengers on Spaceship Earth. We are all crew."

---

13 **Saint Prince Hermenegild Martyred** on this day in 586. The son of the king of the Visigoths, he surrendered his life rather than deny his faith. He chose another type of crown other than the regal one that was his heritage. A day to ask if we would give up what we desire most in life—and our very life—to preserve our faith.

---

14 **Discovery of the Location of Happiness**. On this day in 2301 B.C. the Chinese scholar and saint Hi Ling Su found that happiness lies in the heart and not in a special place or in the circumstances of life. This significant discovery was also made in other centuries by countless other discoverers who had no direct contact with each other's cultures. For large numbers of people the search continues to this very day in spite of many well-documented maps and reports.

---

15 **Sinking of the Titanic**, the "invincible" ocean liner goes down on this day in 1912. Those individuals, groups and institutions that go on as though they were unsinkable should seriously reflect today on the myth of permanence and security in this life.

PARABLE OF THE TWO LITTLE PIGS

Once upon a time there were two little pigs who went into the forest to build homes for themselves. The first little pig labored at great sacrifice and built an immense two-story brick home. It was even necessary to take out a large loan in order to pay for the construction. And when it was completed, he invested in an insurance policy that covered loss by storm, fire or attack by wild beasts. The house was so large and the debt so great that most of his time and energy was spent in upkeep of the house, paying off the loan and making payments on his insurance policies. As a result he had little time to play and less time to enjoy life.

The second little pig built a home out of sticks and straw. It didn't take much time to construct, and he had so little invested that he was free to learn how to play the fiddle. His life was filled with a good deal of enjoyment as he entertained himself and his friends with music. He took walks in the woods, enjoying sunrises and marveling at sunsets.

One day the wolf came to that corner of the forest, and everyone was fearful. Arriving at the house of the first pig, the wolf huffed and puffed, but he couldn't blow down the brick house. Inside, the first little pig smiled to himself and only momentarily paused in his busy work-day when he heard the wolf at the door. Worn out and unsuccessful, the wolf moved on to the straw house of the second little pig. Inside, the second pig was worried sick. He was terrified because there was nothing between the wolf and a pork chop dinner but a thin straw door. The little pig knelt down and began to pray, "O God who watches over the simple and the weak, come and save me from the wolf at my door. I place myself into your hands." As the wolf filled his lungs with air for one more mighty huff and puff at the door, he was struck dead by an acute attack of emphysema. The danger now past, the second little pig made a sign of the cross, picked up his fiddle and began to play a jig.

As a society which has an addiction to security, we might find such a turned-around parable a bit strange if not totally unreal. As disciples of Christ, however, we are called to live lives that are secure—but secure in God's providence. Living as we do in the midst of security-anxious neighbors, we also can become overly concerned about the future; about our retirement, our income, our fire coverage, our safety from robbery. Continuous exposure to advertisements that talk about protection from a host of possible dangers can add to our fears. Indeed, we need some security from the high cost of hospital care or from the possible threat of fire or theft, but where is the limit to such needs?

Jesus calls us to live lives that are providential, lives that leave room for God to act. In the parable, there was little space for the divine activity in the case of the first little pig with his super-secure brick house. If God seems distant in our daily lives, if providence seems to be only a word, perhaps it is because we are overly secure, overly protected. We can wonder if Christ intended the Kingdom to be a spiritual empire equal to any of the world's great organizations in its power and security. Or is the Kingdom of God intended to be small and unprotected so that it might find its shield, its rock, in God instead of some insurance company or large bank account? Today, most of us can look out the door and see the wolf sitting at our front step. The times are becoming increasingly difficult. Yet there may be a gift hidden in the hardship, for it can open us to a real opportunity to invest our trust in God's "Good Hands."

It demands time, effort and energy—not to mention money—to be continuously secure from all potential danger and loss. That time and energy spent on protection from possible threats in the future might be better spent enjoying the blessings of today. Think about it. Instead of buying a new lock for your door, why not open the doors of your heart and mind to the beauties of life that surround you? Or, you might take up learning how to play the fiddle!

16 **Birthday of the Spiritual Security Act.** In 505 B.C. in India Gautama Buddha taught that one's good works and acts of compassion go on ahead of one to the next life. They are there to welcome you like family and old friends when you finally arrive. Give thought today to how you need to live to make sure that when you step across the threshold of the next life a large crowd of good friends will be there to greet you. (See the **Birthday of the Social Security Act,** August 14.)

17 **Sparrow Festival.** The English or House Sparrow was not known in North America before 1847. Thomas Woodcock decided that they should come to the U.S. and first introduced them in that year, but they did not survive. He again brought them over in 1852 and this time was successful. As the poet Alexander Pope wrote, "Who sees with equal eye, as God of all, a hero perish or a sparrow fall." Consider today how God watches over each sparrow—and over you.

18 **Earthquake Day.** At 5:13 a.m. on this day in 1906 a massive earthquake destroyed 497 blocks of the city of San Francisco and killed nearly seven hundred people. Will the next great California earthquake happen in 2006 or even tomorrow? Since we know not the day or the hour, we should live prepared. Use this feast to remind you to live fully today.

A TOAST FOR LIFE

The green paper hats have long been put away, and the parades and parties of St. Patrick's Day are month-old memories. But echoes of the melodies of that green spirit still linger in this Irish spring heart, particularly the tones of a couple of Irish toasts. The first one goes like this: "May you live to be a hundred—with one extra year to repent!" And the other, which is one of my favorites: "Here's to your coffin; may it be made with hundred-year-old oak trees which I will plant tomorrow."

Both of these, like so many good drinking toasts, are about a long and happy life. To toast someone with that wish seems only natural. But how many people really want to live to such an advanced age?

The commanding officer of the Fourth Battalion, Queen's Regiment of the British army in 1811 was badly wounded at the battle of Alburea. As he lay battling old bony Death, he called out to his men as they fought on, "Die hard, men, die hard!" Today we give the name "diehard" to those persons who refuse to give up on an issue even when it is clear that they have lost the fight. Our own George Washington, at his death, is reported to have said,

"I die hard, but I am not afraid to go."

Today it is not fashionable to die hard. We prefer to have those of advanced age slip out of sight and quietly conclude their existence without a fuss. We live in an age of enforced retirement and comfortable senior citizens' homes. Once there was great pride in dying "in the harness," to use a term from the old days, or as we say here in the Midwest, "with your boots on."

The heart of the issue isn't retirement or non-retirement, but rather the strong passion to live life to the fullest—the passionate fight to resist the demon of death in our daily living. Who wants to live to be a hundred if our years are devoid of life and vitality of spirit? The lust of the spirit for life isn't something to be acquired at sixty-five or seventy. The passage of time has the power to intensify a person's life attitudes. As a result, you can take whatever you are at the age of thirty-five and double that attitude in its expression, and you will have a fairly accurate picture of the person you will be as a senior citizen. Woe to those who at thirty-five are always negative, critical of others and prone to self-pity—and woe to those who must live with them thirty-five years from now!

If we wish to "live to be a hundred"—to die hard—then we must learn how to live today with gusto. We must resist the daily tugs of the angel of death and keep the heart of a child. Then whether or not we live until the oak trees grown for our coffin reach the century mark, we will be ready. Jesus promised that he would give his disciples life in great abundance. But it is the depth at which we dare to live rather than the length of our lives that brings about the fullness of that promise.

Long Life Festival. In 1989 over 10,000 Americans were over the age of 100. The prediction at that time was that by the year 2000, there would be over 100,000 Americans over 100 years old. Reflect today on how you want to spend your added years. Each period of your age is a prophet of the next one. If you want a peek at what you will be like twenty years from now, just double your present personality traits. If you are mildly impatient today, be prepared for an irritating retirement. Now is the time to choose to live life fully.

19

MOTHER BUNCH

Even her name speaks of abundance: Mother Bunch. She was a well-known alewife—or barmaid, as we would say today—of late sixteenth century London. It was said that Mother Bunch spent most of her time telling tales. And when she laughed, "she was heard from Aldgate to the monuments of Westminster, and all the Southwarke stood in amazement...She dwelt in Cornhill near the exchange, and sold strong ale...and lived a hundred and seventy and five years, and two days and half a minute!"

It's the "half a minute" that is especially intriguing. What a vital woman Mother Bunch must have been to have her life measured down to the last half minute! Would that more of us could be filled with the same sort of zest and liveliness. Indeed, we are very aware of the promise of Jesus: "I have come that you might have life and have it to the full'' (Jn. 10: 10). But it seems that we usually regard such divine promises as forms of burial insurance! Perhaps we should instead look at them as **life** insurance, intended to yield an abundance of life both now and in the future. Many times it is not so much a lack of faith as it is feelings of fear that hinder our ability to experience the fullness of life that Jesus spoke of so often. We fear a host of things: ''What will people say? What will the neighbors think? What will I look like to others?'' In fact, our fears come in as many flavors as Baskin-Robins ice cream. They stalk us night and day and ride piggyback on our lives. Mother Bunch, whose laughter rocked the buildings of Westminster and made the citizens of Southwarke stand in amazement, was a woman who overcame those fears, a woman who was always fully alive, not just each day, but each minute—each half minute of life.

If we were to look for the most repeated admonition in the Gospels, beginning with the message of the angels who appeared at the birth of Jesus right up to those who were present at the tomb, that admonition would probably be ''Fear not!'' And if, in our day-to-day lives, we are to look for the fullness of life promised by Jesus and sealed by his rising to new life, we will, like Mother Bunch, have to forget our fears and be ourselves.

The power and presence of the feast of Easter live far beyond the feast itself for those who are willing to ''fear not.'' The gift of the Resurrection seals the promise of Christ, but that gift will have little effect in our lives if we are not able to let go, to free ourselves of the numerous shoulds and should-nots of our sometimes drab and dull society.

What better testimony to our life in Christ than to have our tombstones carved not only with the number of years we lived on earth, but also with the hours, minutes and, yes, even the half minutes!

20 **Birthday of the Alarm Clock**. Plato is said to have invented a water clock with an alarm in 381 B.C. Salute, this morning, that ticking servant, your alarm clock, and its great-great grandfather, Plato's clock. And let it awaken you this spring morning to living life more fully—even the part of life that involves death.

THE POOR WIDOW'S PARTY

The feast of Easter is a festival of joy and hope, as we rejoice in the victory of Jesus over death. And each Easter is an overture to a personal joyous party, our final reunion with Christ after our death. But perhaps a story may give us a better insight into what I mean by an ''overture.''

One night, an old Irish woman sat alone in her little cottage. In the cupboard was a jug of good Irish whiskey, saved, she always said, ''Fer a wake or a wedding.'' This night, however, she took down the jug and poured herself a glass of special whiskey, saying to herself, ''Well, tonight's nothin' special. But I feel the need of a wee bit o'warmth.'' As she sipped her whiskey, she remembered the good times and the hard years, the parties, the wakes and the countless blessings of her long life.

She put some more peat on the fire and began to pray, "Ah, if only the men o'heaven could be here tonight in me little cottage havin' a wee drink with me. Oh, 'twould be wonderful indeed! And I wouldn't be so lonely on this chilly night." Suddenly her prayer was answered, for there they stood in her cottage! "Ah, welcome to you, Peter and John, Andrew and Matthew, and all the rest of ye. It's an honor to have ye in my home, tellin' stories and drinkin' my fine Irish whiskey. And Jesus—havin' you here, hearin' you laugh with the men o'heaven. Sure an'now, if we could only have the three holy Marys here too... ."

Her prayer was answered straight-away, for there they were. "Welcome Mary, gentle mother of Jesus, and you, Aunt Mary, mother of James and John; ah, and even Mary Magdalene. Lord, what a party this is! But if I might be askin' a small favor. I know me cottage is small, but could some o'the other good saints come as well?"

That very instant her prayer was answered. Through the door came St. Bridget, St. Patrick and a host of others laughing and talking. She recognized most of them from her old dog-eared holy cards or from statues in the parish church. "Come in, come in, one and all. Ah, 'tis wonderful that you could come to me party. Here, have a glass of my good Irish whiskey." And the songs, stories and laughter overflowed from the little white cottage, as the old woman prayed, "Oh, Lord, what a grand party this is. Even the fine and the mighty in their big houses surely never had such a party as the one I'm havin' tonight. 'Tis the best of me whole life. Oh, I wish I had an ocean o'beer for Jesus and his friends so me party could go on and on... ." And at that, Jesus leaned over and whispered in her ear, "Ah, Mary, my dear, why should it end?"

The next morning, as was her custom, Kate O'Reilly stopped by the widow's cottage to check in on her. As she opened the door with a cheery "Good Mornin'!" she found the old widow in her chair, asleep in the arms of death. Beside her on the table was an empty jug of whiskey. And on her face, now white with the kiss of death, was a smile as wide as the Shannon River.

Remembrance Feast of Saints Basilissa and Anastasia, holy women and martyrs who professed their faith before the Emperor Nero. Their tongues and feet were cut off before they were finally put to the sword. Reflect today on how well and wisely you use your tongue. Does it ever spread gossip or speak unnecessary words that only harm the reputation of others?

21

Zip It Up Day. Zippers were patented in 1913 by a Swedish-American engineer, Gideon Sundback, who improved an 1893 design by Whitcomb Judson called the "clasp-locker." Judson's invention was unpopular since it frequently jammed. First used in World War I by the military, the zipper only appeared on civilian clothing in the 1920's. Consider Sundback's invention today when you are tempted to repeat some gossip or to speak some negative words and zip your mouth shut!

22

PASCAL PUMPERNICKEL

The Easter Jubilee lasts fifty days to allow us to explore all the gifts that are contained in the resurrection of Christ from the tomb. Among those Easter gifts is one which, like an Easter Egg, has become hard-boiled. The victory of Jesus' resurrection was the birth of hope for the world. By our faith in his victory we have hope that the powers of death, darkness and evil have been destroyed. As Easter people, we Christians are also hopeful people. We have hope about the future, and that hope expresses itself in our sense of joyfulness about life.

But like those colored eggs in our Easter baskets, hope today is hard-boiled, devoid of illusions but also of feeling. Hope, that second gift of the Holy Spirit, has been hard-boiled by the perplexing and global problems of our age. As we look at the collapse of so many once-stable social institutions, the increase of divorce, the numerous local but deadly wars across the earth, the continuous threat of terrorism, the poverty and unemployment of millions of people, the sad decline in family farms and countless other tragedies, we find little hope in the future.

Today, if you are overflowing with hope about the future of the Church, the vitality of religion and the faith of our youth, as well as the condition of our world, your friends will likely think of you as odd, at best. You may be considered out of contact with reality or even feeble-minded. Yet, if we believe in the Easter mystery, should we not **live** on hope?

Ben Franklin, in *Poor Richard's Almanac*, gives this bit of wisdom: "Fish and visitors stink after three days." And just below it: "One who lives on hope, dies farting." To which I reply, "Yep, pumpernickel!" That dark rye bread gets its name from the supposed effects of eating it. It is composed of two German words, "pumpen," which means "to fart," and "nicken," which means "the devil." Ole Ben Franklin was right: those who live on hope do pumpernickel. They get rid of those diabolical gases of the heart that make life so unpleasant: despair, cynicism, sadness, gloom and doom.

Such indigestion of the heart is a sign of a lack of faith in the presence within us and our world of the Spirit of God who makes all things new, who is constantly creating life out of death. Indeed, entire ways of life, including beautiful and old religious traditions, are dying. But if we are Easter people, then we live on hope instead of a diet of despair.

So the next time you have contact with a hand-wringing gloom-and-doomer and are feeling worried about tomorrow or sad about today, just pumpernickel.

---

23 **Feast of St. George**, the dragon slayer. This saint became the patron of the Crusaders who on their return from their quest in the Holy Land were responsible for making him the patron saint of England. Are there any dragons lurking in your home or neighborhood that need to be slain?

---

24 **Legalized Drug Day**. In the year 2019 on this date, the United States legalizes marijuana and cocaine. As it did when it removed the prohibition of alcohol, the U.S. seeks another answer to the social problems of drug abuse and crime.

Drugs are now sold by the government and profits go toward drug education and rehabilitation programs. At the same time, heavy penalties are placed on drug abuse.

Candle Clock Day. In England in 870 calibrated candles were used for the first time for the purpose of measuring time. It was the custom in monasteries at that time to awaken the monks an hour before dawn for prayers by having them sleep with lighted candles between their toes. For obvious reasons there were many complaints which led to the early invention of the clock. Today's Easter Candle is a throwback to calibrated candles since it is intended to measure fifty days of joyous celebration.

25

ANOTHER NEW CHANGE!

In the past twenty years Christians of all denominations have made many changes in their religious expression and so have become well-practiced in that difficult art of change. I would like to propose yet another change, one that affects this Easter season.

In 1829, Dr. Joel Roberts Poinsett returned to his home in South Carolina after serving as United States Ambassador to Mexico. Dr. Poinsett brought with him a flower found in great abundance in Mexico to see if it would grow in this country. The immigrant flower flourished in its new home and soon became the traditional flower of the Christmas season—that's right, the poinsettia.

Red and white poinsettias have been used for Christmas for only a little over a hundred years. Similarly, using the Easter lily to decorate our churches on the feast of the Resurrection is also an infant tradition compared to Easter eggs and many other Easter customs. The lily was introduced to America a few years after the poinsettia, in 1882, by the florist W.K. Harris. Like the poinsettia, the American people immediately adopted it; it became **the** flower of Easter.

Since both are relatively new traditions, it would not be a terrible jolt to change them. I would propose that the poinsettia and the Easter lily trade places as the traditional flowers of their celebrations. I am suggesting this switch because Christmas is celebrated for only twelve days, while Easter's season is fifty days. And, as you probably know, the poinsettia continues to bloom for weeks, even months, after Christmas, while the lily lasts only a week or two. If we used white poinsettias at Easter, we could have them in our churches and homes for the entire Easter celebration. Having a flower with holding power might help us sustain the celebration of the feast of Easter. For although the flame of the Easter candle dances for fifty days to remind us to keep this jubilee of Easter joy, we find it difficult to rejoice for so many days. For some strange reason it seems that it is easier for us to enter into purple penance for forty days than to rejoice that long. Often our Easter joy lasts only about as long as the bloom of the Easter lily.

Have we lost our ability to be joyful? Has contemporary life with its many pressures and demands made us into industrious worker bees who have no time to playfully party and celebrate? Or is our failure to maintain joyfulness, to echo Easter until Pentecost, an indication of a lack of faith in what the feast of the Resurrection proclaims? Do we *truly* believe that by his death and resurrection, Jesus has freed us from death and given us life in great abundance?

Realizing how much we all deny and reject death, I conclude with a question. If today someone guaranteed that you would never be destroyed by death—that, like God, you had become immortal—would you dance and sing as long as a bloom lasts on a lily or on a poinsettia?

26 **Birthday of Our Galaxy, the Milky Way**. While she is secretive about her exact age, she's likely to be about 8,000,000,000 years old today. Celebrate this wonderful galaxy that is home to our tiny solar system. She has a diameter of 480 million billion miles from our point in space to one of her spiral arms. Traveling at one hundred miles per hour, it would take a total of two hundred and one billion years to reach the center of our galaxy. A good day to reflect on the Risen Christ as the Alpha and the Omega, the beginning and the end.

UNDOING DEATH

Indeed, we have reason to rejoice! For in the resurrection of Christ, God's eternal springtime has been proclaimed. Death and winter have been conquered by Life. Easter is not only remembering; Easter is happening. It is unfolding in creation which in much of the northern hemisphere has laid aside its drab grays and browns to dress up in a new spring robe of bright green, yellow, white and purple. But Easter is also happening to and within each of us.

In the death and resurrection of Jesus there lies a mystery and meaning for each of us. Jesus came as a kind of anti-hero. He came not to do something but rather to "undo" something. Unlike the traditional hero, his mission was not to find a secret treasure or the fountain of youth, but to destroy, to undo the power of death! Jesus was defeated in a sense in his hand-to-hand struggle with bony Death, was stretched out upon a cross. But his defeat became the very means of his victory.

The mystery and meaning of Easter carries over into our lives in that our mission, like Christ's, is not to do something but to undo the power of death. The dominion of death is present in so many ways in our world—when personal gifts and talents are buried, when people are dead to one another because of fear or prejudice, when the joy of the adventure of life is entombed by the morticians of routine and over-seriousness, when the natural struggles of life are seen as numbing problems rather than challenges to human growth. The life mission of those who have set foot to the spiritual journey is to destroy even the Great Death, to undo its power by living lives which proclaim that love and life will always be victorious over bony Death! Easter is more than eggs, new bonnets and greeting cards. Easter can have real significance in how we live and love, how we view our journeys in this short life.

In our mission to undo the power of death, we gradually strip away our selfishness, perhaps in some interior crisis, perhaps just in the everyday challenge of living. Such stripping away is always painful, and it helps to have the support of a friend or a community. As pilgrims we sometimes have to be carried when we lack strength or when it seems that hope is gone. But God is actually part of the process of undoing, of our seeming helplessness, for it forces us to relinquish any feeling that we can achieve salvation by our own virtue. It also makes us more aware of our interdependence with other Easter pilgrims. The Christian spiritual quest cannot be a solitary journey, even if the process of transformation is part of one's **personal** path. For each of us is involved not only in the process of undoing the power of death for ourselves but also for all of creation.

Natural Law Day. In 1417 on this day in Basel, Switzerland, a chicken lays a brightly colored egg. The townsfolk, horrified at this violation of the ''natural law,'' accuse the chicken of being the devil in disguise. The chicken is put on trial, found guilty and burned at the stake. A good day to reflect on how easily, because of fear or prejudice, we also misjudge what is unnatural and so condemn to the stake those who do not conform to our standards.

27

EASTER EGGS, LILIES AND TURTLES

To the many symbols of Easter, such as brightly colored eggs, lilies, sunrises and flowers, I would like to suggest a new one: the turtle! The turtle can symbolize that the spiritual journey that each of is making is a slow one. And there are no short cuts. At times we can feel like we are making little headway. We often wish that we had more time to pray, to spend with God, if only somehow the circumstances of life would stop interfering and spoiling our good intentions.

We frequently set goals for ourselves—healthy activities to engage in, books to read, spiritual practices to perform—as our humanity longs to be completed, but the grind of daily life seems to prevent us from these goals. However, the everyday challenges of living and loving one another can properly be seen as the quest itself. To be human is to be a pilgrim—and a slow one at that, as slow as a turtle. Many refuse to start the journey, and some turn back because it takes so long. Others settle down halfway or try to decide for themselves the route and the goal, ending up going to the wrong place in search of the wrong things.

The success of our journey to Life, undoing death, depends not so much on courage or goodness of heart as it does on obedience to the divine will as it unfolds in the circumstances of our lives. We can be obedient to the overall design of the search even though we may not at all times understand what is happening. At the same time we are called to use all our resources to keep inching ahead. Easter is a feast that proclaims patience with our gradual growth in becoming perfect as our heavenly Father is perfect. Slowly the resurrection is taking place in our flesh. Slowly, like the coming of spring to the forest, we undo the stranglehold of death in ourselves.

The resurrection of Jesus was not a private Easter victory over a private Good Friday, but a step—a giant one—toward the destruction of the universal Good Friday. By our turtle-like daily undoing of the power of death, we join with Christ in ending the corporate Good Friday that holds humanity in its icy grip.

28 **Festival of Easter Eggs**. Easter Eggs were first brought into use as home sacraments by European Christians in the year 700. May this feast remind us that while Christian holy days are usually observed in church, their real celebration is in the home. Start your own holy day and holiday traditions of special foods, decorations and symbols for your home.

29 **Festival of Tradition**. In an age of enormous and rapid changes, including the very act of moving into a brand new millennium, do not abandon your personal and family traditions. A day to reflect on the sense of stability and the healing effects that come with keeping ageless traditions as well as personal rituals. Be aware also of how such rituals can be vehicles to direct communion with the Divine Mystery.

30 **St. Walpurgis Night**, the eve of May Day. Northern European countries celebrate this old Viking feast of fires with bonfires, masquerades and merrymaking. Ancient feasts should not be forgotten; they should be redesigned for fun and feasting so that we will not become technological robots or lose touch with our spiritual roots.

May

May Day, an ancient spring festival. Originally it was an occasion for maypole fertility dances, picnics and parties. Let us not allow such an ancient holy day to go by without fitting celebration. On the more sober side, usually preferred by an industrial age, today is also **International Workers' Day**.

1

HAPPY EASTER AND EVERYDAY

The traditional Easter greeting of "Happy Easter" still lingers in the spring wind in these days after the great feast of the Resurrection. But it's so faint that it can barely be heard. Perhaps the brief life span of this age-old greeting is due to the fact that happiness itself is, for most of us, so short-lived! It is our custom to wish others the gift and blessing of happiness as a normal part of our holiday, birthday and wedding greetings. But while many people wish us happiness, and do so on countless occasions, it seems to be a gift that eludes us.

When I was in the seminary, there was an uncommon janitor who cleaned the buildings. Every Friday, as he mopped the floors, he would greet each student with a broad grin and say, "Well, Happy Sunday!" While he was a man of limited education and of simple means, he was always happy. Looking back, I realize that he was one of those rare individuals who is truly content with life, who knows the taste of happiness.

Harper's magazine recently announced a national study of persons making less than $15,000 a year. Asked if they thought they had achieved the American Dream and were content, five percent answered "yes." That same question was asked of persons earning more than $50,000, and of that group only six percent responded with a "yes." This survey holds a lesson for us. While most of us believe that we could be happy if we only had more money, this study seems to say that it is not necessarily true. Happiness is the fruit that grows from contentment. Happiness comes when we are content with what has been given to us and with what we have achieved with whatever gifts we have been given. But to possess such a sense of contentment is not easy since our consumer society is based on creating discontent. Daily in the media we are persuaded to buy something bigger and better. We are called to constantly upgrade our appliances and improve our possessions so that the market will remain strong. While breakthroughs in technology mark these times of great advance, we do not need a large TV set or a self-cleaning toilet bowl in order to be happy.

An excellent Eastertide reflection would be to take time to appreciate all the sources of happiness that are ours today. Be grateful for good health, shelter, clothing, good friends, family, the peace of our national life and that most precious of all gifts: life. Easter is the feast of New Life. And if we could truly appreciate what a gift it is to simply be alive, how could we help but be happy?

Taking time each day to experience contentment with what you have and with who you are, especially in the light of the Resurrection, would make it easier to wish others the gift of happiness. When you are content, you can offer others a gift that you already possess. Then every Sunday, if not every day, would be what I believe it was for that joyful janitor I knew long ago: an Easter Sunday!

2

Festival of Leonardo da Vinci who died on this date in 1519. A true genius in many and varied fields. When commissioned to paint a portrait of the wife of Francesco del Giocondo, he found it very difficult to make her smile. Da Vinci even resorted to hiring people to play, sing and jest while he painted her. Today, Mona Lisa's smile is renowned. A good day to let the grace of the Easter season make your smile unforgettable.

3

Primal Teachers Day. A feast to ponder the delightful Spanish proverb, "An ounce of mother is worth a pound of clergy." And in India the same truth is expressed as, "One guru is worth ten paid teachers. One father is worth one hundred gurus. And one mother is worth one hundred fathers." The most important sacred teachers in our lives are our parents.

KITCHEN GURUS

That bit of folk wisdom, "An ounce of mother is worth a pound of clergy," reminds us of what we so easily forget—that our parents, and especially our mothers, are the arch-teachers of our religious values. In our specialized society, where authorities abound in every field, we sometimes expect experts to perform functions for which we are actually better equipped. How easily parents play down their influence as teachers and their God-given gifts to be the priestly patterns for their families because they feel that they are lacking in professional learning!

At its core, the Gospel is a profoundly simple message. When we reach the heart of prayer, it is also simple; the more we pray, the simpler it should become. The day-to-day living out of our religious values is not complicated and does not require a degree in theology. Such life-teaching requires only great love and self-discipline. And parents, if they are willing to live out their faith, can be the most inspiring teachers their children will ever have. An old Islamic adage points the way: "Good students study their text. Truly good students study their teacher." Each of us is a teacher, and we teach our best lessons when we are not attempting to teach and when we are unaware that anyone is studying us. In a society where nearly everyone reads and writes, a great deal of importance is placed upon textbooks. But we forget that *we* are the textbooks from which others learn their most profound lessons.

Abraham Lincoln said, "There is just one way to bring up a child in the way he should go, and that is to travel that way yourself." Don't send your children to school to learn to become something, be that "something" yourself. And when you doubt your ability to be a primal teacher for your family just remember that "an ounce of mother is worth a pound of clergy." Also recall the Indian echo of that Spanish proverb: "One guru is worth ten paid teachers. One father is worth a hundred gurus. And one mother is worth one hundred fathers." The image is truly wondrous: one kitchen guru, a mother, is worth ten thousand holy guides!

Feast of St. Monica who died in 387. The mother of St. Augustine, who in his youth was no saint. Monica prayed day and night for her rebellious, sinful son. Eventually he was converted to a life of holiness and became one of the most influential saints in the Church's history. Today is the patron feast of mothers with difficult sons.

4

"OUR MOTHER..."

Since 1915, when Woodrow Wilson authorized the annual national observance of Mother's Day, we have set aside the second Sunday in May to honor our mothers. As we do this, we bring honor also to women like Julia Howe and Anna Jarvis who campaigned for the national observance. Anna Jarvis appropriately wanted the celebration to focus on peace. For the relationship between peace and motherhood is an ancient one. In our times, when we live on the narrow edge between peace and war, we might once again make Anna Jarvis' idea the theme in remembering Mother's Day. It could also be a day for more than remembering our earthly mothers—we could also celebrate the Motherhood of God!

We know that God has more names than anyone or anything in the universe. Over the long sweep of history a litany of titles has been used to express the mystery of the Godhead. Still, praying to God under the title of "Mother" seems odd to some and highly offensive to others. And it may appear contrary to the holiest prayer in the Christian faith which begins, "Our Father... ." Jesus himself gave us that prayer to a Father-God, and he called God by that title numerous times in the Gospels. That identification of God as Father was most shocking to his listeners because it suggested an intimacy that seemed too close for creatures. We know that Jesus' favorite title, the Aramaic "Abba," was extremely intimate.

But Jesus could just as easily have called his God "Mother," for he frequently emphasized the maternal divine qualities of nurturing care, unconditional love and compassionate wisdom. And we can address God with that child's call for "Mother" if we wish. But if we do, we should be prepared for the same reaction that Jesus experienced in referring to God as "Abba." To call the Lord God, the Supreme Creator and Judge, the One Who Always Was and Always Shall Be by the familiar title of "Mom" would certainly raise an eyebrow or two. And with two thousand years of tradition behind us, with all the scriptural support for the use of the term "Father" for God, and considering the strong social bias against making God feminine, anyone who desires to worship God as "Mother" must be prepared for considerable "static," if not outright attack. But these are times of change, when we are redesigning and reforming many of our outdated, narrow and restricting religious concepts. Perhaps it's time to open the door for an either/or Lord's Prayer. Depending on personal choice we could begin that prayer with "Our Father" or "Our Mother" and interchange the personal pronouns "his" and "her" when speaking of God.

At this point, Catholics might reply, "Yes, several mystics and saints of the Church have addressed God as 'Mother' and a freedom of choice does sound more democratic, but, really, what would the Pope say?" In answer to such a question, in 1978 a recent chief teacher of the Catholic tradition, Pope John Paul I, said, "...(God) is Father; even more, God is Mother."

5

Tango No Sekku, Japanese Feast of Kites. The Chinese in 1200 B.C. first used kites to communicate coded messages between army camps. They built lightweight kites as one-person aircraft, and the first airborne attack was the invasion of an island by kite troops. Today kites survive only as toys—would that all weapons of war were turned into toys! Kite flying allows both young and old to enjoy the outdoors, the wind and fresh air and the spirit of free flight. It is heresy to think that only children should fly kites.

6

Senior Citizens Sunlight Day. Sunlight travels at the speed of light and so takes only eight minutes to reach you from the sun. But the sunlight that touches you today was created in the heart of the sun over 20,000 years ago! It has constantly been detoured on its journey to the surface of the sun by colliding against solar particles. Today, even if you aren't elderly, let your smiles be senior citizen sunshine in the lives of those around you.

7

Feast of St. Stanislaus, Archbishop of Cracow and patron saint of Poland. He was murdered at the order of Boleslaus II while celebrating Mass in 1079. A day to be in solidarity with the Polish people both in prayer and in celebration. Also an occasion to consider: if you could choose a place and time for your death, what would it be?

NO POLISH JOKE

The Poles invented the boomerang; no joke, I'm serious. Before the invention of the bow and arrow, somewhere around 20,000 B.C., the people of what is now Poland made boomerangs from the tusks of the great mammoths that roamed their land. It would take 13,000 years before that creative hunting weapon would reach Australia, the country with which we associate it today.

The purpose of this bit of trivia is not to present the Polish people as ingenious and creative—which they are, if you take into account all their gifts to culture in the areas of music, literature and science—rather, it is to awaken us. The boomerang traveled at a turtle's pace across Eastern Europe and Asia before it arrived in Australia. Consider that American blue jeans which became popular here in the 1960's took only twenty years before they made the Most Wanted List in the Soviet Union and China, cultures apart from ours.

In July we will celebrate our Declaration of Independence and our struggle for democracy. Today, in spite of heavy oppression, peoples across the earth are yearning for this American invention of independence. What once took hundreds or even thousands of years to migrate across the world now takes only a few years or even days. To be alive today requires a virtue that we all find difficult: the capacity to change. We no longer have the luxury of a slow, evolutionary embracing of new inventions or ideas.

Those who resist change in their daily lives will experience a good deal of suffering and stress as we move into the beginning of the twenty-first century. If we wish to taste peace and happiness, we will have to learn the virtue of elasticity. A brief 2000 years ago, Jesus proposed that virtue with his image of new wine skins. Be rigid, like old leather wine skins, and you will be burst open by the new wine of change.

If you find ideas like married clergy or women in the priesthood too novel, if you can't adjust to changes in education, employment or things as simple as how young people dress or act today, here's a prayer that might help you acquire one of the most needed virtues for these turbulent times.

A PRAYER OF NEW WINE SKINS

Come and awaken me, Spirit of the New,
    O God who makes all things supple and life-giving,
    and grace me with the gift of elasticity.
For high are the walls that guard the old,
    the tired and secure ways of yesterday
    that protect me from the dreaded plague,
    the feared heresy of change.

Yet how can an everlastingly new covenant
    retain its freshness and vitality
    without injections of the new,
    the daring and the untried?
Come, O you who are ever-new,
    wrap my heart in new skin,
    ever flexible to be reformed by your Spirit.

Come, O God of endless creativity,
    and teach me to dance with delight
    whenever you send a new melody my way.

8 **First Use of the Boomerang** in Poland in 20,202 B.C. Consider today the boomerang principle: what goes out, comes back. Think evil thoughts today, and tomorrow evil will come arching back to strike you. On the other hand, be grateful for the gifts of your life, and an abundance of blessings will return to you.

THE BOOMERANG PRAYER

The vocabulary of the Old Testament people did not have a word for "thank you." That does not mean that they were a people who were devoid of gratitude. For when they felt a need to express thanksgiving, they pronounced a blessing: "Blessed be God, who... ." Part of the prayer life of Jesus' heritage was an almost endless list of such short blessings that praised God for everything from rainbows to a good bowel movement. As a devout Jew, the life of Jesus was saturated with short prayers of gratitude. This spirit of gratitude carried on to the prayer and worship of early Christian communities whose central expression was the "Eucharist," a Greek word for thanksgiving.

The prayer of Jesus was simply a response to life. As such, thanksgiving arose organically from the events of life, hour by hour, day by day. We usually think of prayer as something that is done at special times, such as upon rising or going to bed or before eating a meal. But prayer for Jesus was a river that flowed out of life and back into it again. Prayer was a natural, at times spontaneous, response to a hundred different aspects of being alive.

Our prayer life also holds the power to awaken within us a need to live lives of continual gratitude. If we could acquire a habit of making short expressions of gratitude to God for the countless daily gifts of our lives, we would find that such a prayer is a Boomerang Prayer. When we pray "Thank you for such a beautiful day," we sail our prayer of gratitude off to God, only to have it come whirling back to us as we taste the beauty of the day. Each time we say "thank you" for the gift of a hot shower or for the faithfulness of a friend, we open ourselves to the giftedness of hot water or a friend's fidelity, and all that can so easily be taken for granted.

The person who prays "thank you" tastes life twice. Those who make their lives a litany of thanks need never fear that they will be counted among life's zombies. Their very prayer opens the floodgates to even more gifts as well as enhancing their enjoyment and awareness of existing ones.

I have found it of value to pray a thanksgiving rosary. With each bead I pray "Deo Gratias...," or "Thank you, God...," and then add the gift for which I am grateful. I move from bead to bead, listing the fifty things, in sets of ten, for which I am grateful that day. For example: "Thank you, God, for a clean bed in which to sleep tonight. Thank you, God, for my parents. For the gift of sight, thank you, O God... ." Whatever form of prayer you use, such a litany can awaken you to countless gifts which we so easily take for granted. And such a prayer is habit-forming and self-generating. You will soon find yourself making spontaneous responses—on-the-spot short prayers of gratitude—to life's perpetual parade of gifts.

Such thanksgiving prayers, I promise you, are blessed boomerangs which will whirl back to hit you on the head, awakening you to an amazing fact: "At this very moment, I am as rich as a millionaire."

Hurray for Buttons Day. With the invention of the button hole in 1247, buttons—which until that time had been used only for decoration—became functional as a means to hold clothing together. Before this date clothes fasteners were either garment pins or belts. The first button factory didn't appear in America until 1800! As you hurry to dress today, give thanks for the unknown genius who invented the button hole. Even the most common of blessings are worthy of our gratitude.

9

Festival of a Royal Privilege, the Mailbox. The delivery of letters to a private home was for centuries a privilege reserved for royalty. The postal system began in Egypt in about 2000 B.C. with a courier service for the royal government. China had an imperial postal system by the year 1000 B.C. But it wasn't until the mid-1800's that common people had the opportunity to mail and receive correspondence with a dependable postal service. Mail a letter today to a friend and enjoy an imperial feeling. A good day to be grateful for those paper sacraments that carry love and news across the miles to and from those we love.

10

Feast of St. Mamertus who died on this day in 480. He was Bishop of Vienne in France during the time when Goths, Huns, earthquakes, fires and crop failures were all sweeping the land. He initiated *rogation* or "asking" processions which became central to the worship and prayer of agrarian Christians. Today, go for a walk and make a mini-pilgrimage of prayer for today's evils.

11

SAINTLY VICES

One of the functions of organized religion has been to confirm and support the moral codes of society. We are aware that in past ages when slavery was an integral part of society, the religious establishment was able to find appropriate scriptural quotations to confirm the slave holder's right to possess another human being as property. It also taught slaves to live obediently confined in their chains.

Pope Urban II, while proclaiming the first Crusade in 1095, said, "Christian warriors...go and fight for the deliverance of holy places...if you must have blood, bathe your hands in the blood of the infidel! Soldiers of hell, become soldiers of the Living God. God wills it." Such papal statements did not even raise an eyebrow at the end of the eleventh century, since making war and washing one's hands in the blood of another son or daughter of God were socially appropriate behaviors.

Ralph Waldo Emerson, American poet and philosopher, reminded us that "the virtues of society are vices of the saint." It would be interesting to list a litany of social virtues we tend to accept without question and then place next to them the virtues that Jesus invited us to seek. The comparison might prove disturbing.

Here are a few of the social virtues a saint might view as vices: "You can tell a book by its cover," which implies that outward appearances can tell you the inward state of a person. Jesus, on the other hand, warned us that those who are poor, in prison or who are social outcasts are like books whose shabby covers hide the reality that they are tabernacles of the Divine Presence. Likewise, the social virtue, "Cleanliness is next to Godliness," has placed great emphasis on being externally clean, without giving much attention to being pure of heart. Here again, Jesus warned us not to be as concerned about having clean hands as clean hearts. And the social virtue, "Mind your own business," is often really an excuse not to become involved, as the Good Samaritan did, in the troubles of a neighbor or stranger. Such a list of social virtue-vices could go on for pages, but I think the point is clear from a few examples.

To be a saint, which is the primal vocation of everyone who is a disciple of Christ, requires the cultivation of some social vices! The religious code that Jesus proposed ran counter to his culture, and continues to run counter to every culture since then, including our own Christian culture today. And Jesus' crucifixion was the product of an alliance between State and Religion, since Jesus was a threat to both.

For several centuries after his death, the small communities of Christ were outsiders to society and often its victims. A happy compromise was reached in the middle of the fourth century which allowed Christianity to become the official religion of the State. It is an agreement that has enabled a real flourishing of both Christianity and culture, but it also has cost Christian life dearly. Each of us fears social rejection, and so we understandably make compromises, the continuous necessary adjustments that allow us to be canonized by our culture as good, loyal and law-abiding. But in the process we can easily lose sight of our primal vocation of becoming saints of God.

12 **Birthday of Florence Nightingale**, founder of the nursing profession, on this date in 1820. She made it her lifework to bring acceptance and dignity to women as nurses. She and her followers served in the Crimean War; before her time, the prospect of women nursing the sick on the battlefield was considered unthinkable. Compassion for those who suffer should inflame each of us to battle against great odds and social customs, as did Florence. Is there a call of compassion that you ignore or reject today because it goes against social norms?

13 **Feast of Florence Nightingale's Pet Owl**. Florence never traveled without her pet owl which she kept in her pocket. Perhaps the care of cats, dogs, fish, birds or even owls has the capacity to make one compassionate toward all living beings!

AN EMBARRASSING QUESTION

I recently enjoyed reading a small book entitled *The Book of Questions*. It poses the following situation. Suppose someone offered you a complete four-week vacation for two anywhere in the world, with all expenses paid. The only condition placed upon this gift is that you must first systematically tear off the wings of a butterfly, causing its death. Would you accept the free vacation on those terms? Take a few moments now to ask yourself this question.

I've asked that question to many people, and over 90% of them have responded, "No." Then I ask them a second question from that book: "Would you accept the same free vacation if the only condition were that you step on a cockroach?" After an embarrassing pause, 80% of those I asked answered, "Yes." And some even added that they would crush a cockroach even if they were not given an all-expense-paid vacation.

How readily do we discriminate in our respect for life. Since a cockroach is a dirty, germ-carrying insect, we easily feel free to kill it without a thought. But a beautiful butterfly? This attitude, however, doesn't stop with insect life. Jesus, aware of our tendency to make such distinctions, said to us, "Whatever you do to the least of my disciples, you do to me!" (Mt. 25: 45). Whatever we do to the law-breaking "cockroaches" of society, we do to Christ. Whatever we do to the disowned parts of ourselves, we do to Christ.

Lewis and Clark Expedition. On this date in 1804 these explorers set out from St. Louis on their great adventure with the firing of a shot to mark the occasion. It was a long and arduous trek through the Rockies and all the way to the Pacific. Both Lewis and Clark kept journals of the journey. A good day to consider that the best adventures are those that are shared.

14

Remembrance of St. Isidore the Farmer whose feast is this week. A day of thanksgiving for all those who grow and tend the foods and fruits that we eat. Also a good day for those who garden to consider that work to be saintly.

15

KNIFE AND FORK PRAYER

Recent surveys of George Gallup show that only 28% of Americans pray daily. In 1952, by contrast, 42% of Americans said that they prayed at least twice a day or more. Prayer is slowly slipping out of our daily routines. Yet 80% of Catholics and Protestants said that prayer is an important part of their lives! Gallup's poll also revealed that over 90% of our prayer takes the form of asking God for something! Our daily routines provide numerous opportunities for us to change those dismal statistics and to revitalize our relationship with God.

One prayer that formerly was part of every "good" Christian home was grace before meals. Rather than asking God for something, grace before a meal was an expression of gratitude for the gifts of food and for those who made the meal possible. Very religious families also said grace after meals.

Many who were raised in traditional religious homes still pray before they eat to thank the Divine Source of all gifts. But after-dinner prayer has invariably been replaced by clearing the table or, if eating out, by paying the bill. Since every meal can be a sacrament, a grace-filled reminder of the Great Meal of the Eucharist, we would do well to maintain a sense of prayer whenever we come to or leave the table. Such a prayer can be verbal, or it can be a silent ritual as simple as a sign of the cross. Another simple ritual of gratitude which could be reintroduced after eating is an old European custom about positioning the knife and fork at the end of a meal.

Surprisingly, forks did not become part of standard table equipment until after the American Revolution. Before that time, forks were considered a symbol of luxury and status. As a result, only the wealthy or the noble class ate with them. But today almost everyone uses a fork, knife and spoon at meals.

In Italy, after silverware became commonplace, there arose a custom of placing the knife vertically across the empty plate and the fork horizontally across the top of the knife. This became a sign to the hostess or waiter that the person was finished eating. And more to the point, because it formed the cross, it also was an expression of "grace" after the meal. It was a prayerful ritual of thanksgiving for the gifts of the bounty of God which had been received through Christ.

To make such an after-dinner ritual part of the daily flow of life would not be at all difficult. It would only have to be practiced a short while before becoming a natural way to conclude every meal. At home or away, it could be a hidden, yet holy, silent prayer of thanksgiving.

16

Feast of the Common Table Knife. Today we honor the French Cardinal Richelieu who created the table knife in 1639. Richelieu was distressed by the uncouth custom practiced by the courtiers of his day who used their sharp daggers to carve their meat and pick their teeth. He ordered that all knives at his table have the points rounded off. Consider, today, how your knife can be an instrument of prayer rather than a tool to attack your food.

17

Pie Plate Day. In 1873 a New England baker, William Russell Frisbie begins to sell his pies made in circular plates with the name "Frisbie" embossed on them (Richard Knerr trademarked the name "Frisbee" for the present day plastic toy). The bakery is located in Bridgeport, Connecticut, near Yale University, and when the students begin tossing around the empty pie tins in the 1940's, it becomes a case of—as Sherlock Holmes would have said—"Ah, Watson, the game's afoot!" A good day to remember that instruments to prepare food as well as instruments of prayer can also be fun!

18

Feast of St. Eric, patron saint of Sweden, king and martyr. Like his namesakes, Eric the Red and Leif Ericson, who sailed off in unknown oceans and discovered new lands, St. Eric was an adventurer for the faith. Set off, today, on uncharted courses and search out new spiritual ground.

19

Feast of the Birthday of St. Abraham in Ur of Babylon in 2001 B.C. St. Abraham is the great-grandfather of the three great religions of the West. He is famous for his faith response to God's call. For even though he wandered long without a homeland, he trusted that God would be with Sarah and him. On this feast, reflect on this saying of Alcoholics Anonymous: "Faith is not a possession, it's a decision." Make a decision today.

Relief for Sore Feet Day. In 1310, for the first time since the fall of the Roman Empire, shoes were made for both the right and left feet. Until then, even royalty did not have shoes shaped for their individual feet. Right and left shoes were not made in America until about 1750. Reflect today, as you enjoy the comfort of your footwear, how you might pray with your feet, and take a mini-pilgrimage.

20

ADIOS INSURANCE

The pre-revolutionary Russians had a proverb about leaving home that is worthy of some reflection: "With God, go over the sea; without God, not over the threshold." This idea that the abiding company of God was an assurance which could give one the courage even to cross the ocean is more ancient and universal than even the roots of Russian culture. Yet today some might smile at the childlike dependence that would prevent one from even going out the front door if God weren't coming along. As modern people we tend to pride ourselves on being strong and resourceful. Technology has cleansed the world of so many dangers that previous generations found truly frightening. We have "taken control" of so much of our daily lives and have no need, we feel, for God to shield us from harm on our way to work or to inspire us as we begin a meeting or seek a solution to a problem. Prayers before and after meetings are more like pious bookends than genuine pleas for help. We cross our thresholds, begin our meetings and eat our food as capable and competent people. Who needs God?

The fact is that we are more inclined to seek the company of God if we are crossing the sea, our lives in possible danger from terrorist's hijackings, than when we "run down to the store." The modern religious believer has neatly put prayer, religion and even God into compartments here and there in daily life. Indeed, we bring God out in times of crisis, death or fear; but we seem to have little need for the divine presence in the business of daily life. Instead, business-like, we have placed our fears and concerns under another protective umbrella—the insurance company!

Our lives, homes, property and cars are all covered by insurance policies which provide us with all the sense of security we feel we need. While insurance is a necessity in our modern life, it can never provide the kind of **assurance** that the Russian proverb implied. To feel that kind of security, perhaps we could use a prayerful ritual to remind us of our need to "go with God," the meaning of the French word "Adieu" and the Spanish "Adios." The function of such a prayer-ritual would be to frame our entire lives within the mystery of God. We do not have to ask God to join us in our travels and trials, for God is always at our side and constantly within us. Rather, it is *we* who must be awakened to this loving, protective presence, and prayer is the alarm clock.

This reflection began with a reference to the threshold, and it is fitting for such an "Adios" prayer-ritual to take place at our doorways. As we leave home, even to "run to the store," we could trace a small sign of the cross on the door with our thumbs. We could even add a short prayer, like, "Bless this house, O God, in the name of the Father, Son and Holy Spirit. Keep it and we who live here safe, and bless our comings and goings.'' And upon returning after a safe journey to find our home secure, we could again trace a small sign of the cross on the door and simply say, ''Thanks be to God.'' Such short but mindful rituals at the intersections of our lives can awaken us to live fully aware of the Mystery of Love that always envelops our comings and goings.

21 **Travel with God Day**. On this date in 1927 Charles Lindbergh took off from New York on his historic transatlantic flight to Paris. Pause today to consider that old Russian proverb, ''With God, go over the sea; without God, not over the threshold.'' May we never leave home without inviting God to be our co-pilot and companion on the journey, even if it is only trans-street or trans-city.

22 **Remembrance of St. Basiliscus**. During the persecutions by Maximian, Basiliscus refused to sacrifice to the gods. His body was cruelly cut to shreds, his feet wrapped in oil-soaked cloths, and then he was set on fire. After these tortures he was cast into the sea. Pray to St. Basiliscus for the gift of holy endurance, for the patience to embrace the discomforts encountered in prayerful silence as an act of love for God.

LA-Z-BOY PRAYER

A psychologist at a Midwest university has released studies showing that those who meditate do not have any less tension than those who recline in a La-Z-Boy chair. The research of this psychologist was in response to claims made by some meditation teachers that their techniques greatly reduce tension, curb alcoholism, relieve asthma and generally ease daily stress.

Those who see meditation as an alien from the East may not realize all the implications of this report. It is important to be aware that this ancient spiritual practice is also deeply rooted in the silent prayer of the Jewish-Christian tradition. And while members of the scientific community have recently recommended this form of prayer as a means of finding freedom from stress, that aim alone greatly reduces its real intent. Those who pray the prayer of meditation do not do so for the reduction of muscle tension or to relieve asthma, even though those benefits may follow. Meditation is practiced as part of one's spiritual life, as a means of opening to and listening to God. In meditation we quiet not only the lips but also the ever-talkative mind, at the same time opening our heart so that we can be fully present to the quiet voice of the Spirit within.

Prayer, for the great saints and mystics of the past, was hardly La-Z-Boy comfort. Prayer is that awe-full place, that desert where one goes with fear and dread as well as with love and joy. For in the quiet of prayer, God reveals to us our failures to be kind and forgiving. And the silent wind of meditation carries the voice that calls us beyond the comfort of our society, beyond the easy solutions to our problems, beyond concern for self to sacrifice and service.

If you are looking for relaxation and freedom from tension, then lean back in your La-Z-Boy chair for fifteen minutes, close your eyes and take it easy. If you are seeking to become **more** than you are now, if you are seeking to know the will of God, then pray the prayer of stillness. But realize that in the process you may not always feel at peace. If you have carried anger toward another within your heart, you will be challenged always to bring it to a resolution, called to forgiveness. If you are able to release or resolve that anger, then you may indeed be less stressful and full of peace. But the peace of body and soul that you will taste will be the result of an infusion of grace rather than merely lowering the blood levels of the hormone linked to human stress.

The prescription for good health, both body and soul, isn't difficult if we can discipline our lives to practice it. Try fifteen minutes a day in silent prayer, and *then* relax for fifteen minutes in your La-Z-Boy chair!

Feast of Fire, marking the first productive use of fire by early humans, 1.4 million years ago. Such a major step in technological evolution is easily forgotten in our age of daily technological miracles. Celebrate, today, by lighting a fire, a candle or even a match, and appreciate all the efforts of days past that allow us to enjoy the comforts and advances of our day. **23**

Feast of St. Sarah. Gypsies made a pilgrimage to France for a two-day festival of dancing and feasting in St. Sarah's honor. A new name for the Church is really a very old name: "The People of God." We are God's gypsies whose home is a mobile one; we are only passing through this place on our way back home again. **24**

Feast of the Cook Stove. Today celebrate that most essential piece of equipment in your home. A cook stove was installed in the White House for the first time in 1850. The cooks who until that time had prepared food in a fireplace took one look at the new contraption and quit! A day to wonder at the marvel of having such a convenient, efficient and clean instrument for preparing your food. Celebrate your stove today by placing a lighted vigil candle on or by it as you cook your meals. A stove can be an altar where meals are made sacred because they are prepared with love and prayer. And reflect today on the food you give your soul and on the "instruments," the spiritual practices, that assist you in providing that nourishment. And as you appreciate your stove today, renew your appreciation of your spiritual exercises. **25**

EXERCISE AND INNERCISE

As spring prepares to turn into summer, it's not uncommon to see large numbers of people on the streets and roads running, jogging, walking or cycling. America's recent renewal of personal fitness is encouraged not only by the medical profession but also by business leaders who understand that a healthy person makes a better employee. And entire industries have arisen to support the fitness movement, by supplying technologically advanced athletic shoes and bikes, all-weather sweat togs and a host of other accessories for the well-equipped-and-dressed exerciser.

Furthermore, it makes no difference whether it is spring or winter, for health spas and exercise clubs now make it possible to give your body a workout regardless of weather conditions. Other companies sell home exercise equipment that allows you to perform your daily disciplines within the privacy of your own home. And in short, there are so many benefits from regular exercise that we would hope that the fitness trend continues.

Many of us care about the condition of our bodies, but are we also concerned about the condition of our inner persons, of our souls? The soul, like the body, needs regular exercise. A truly healthy person is not only engaged in frequent physical exercise but also in daily spiritual exercise. The latter, however, does not require any special clothing, shoes or equipment. Like physical exercise it can be performed in the privacy of your own home. And it does not require a membership in any spiritual spa. But while you need spend no money on these inner-exercises, they are not free or even cheap!

For one thing, "innercises" demand time, and because of our busy schedules we often find it too costly. But they really only require ten or fifteen minutes in the morning and evening—no more than a quick jog. They **do** require facing into some uncomfortable facts about ourselves—whether we are resentful, manipulating, overbearing, greedy, jealous or petty. Yet this is not so different from seeing the flab in the various parts of our body.

But what are some of these innercises (or spiritual exercises as they were once called), and how can we go about starting to innercise? We might first set aside some time each morning for silent sitting, for quiet prayer of the heart. We can dedicate our day to God, using a brief reading of Scripture and simple prayers of adoration and petition. In the evening before supper (since we're usually too tired by bedtime) we could again take some quiet time to read a few lines from a good spiritual book or say a prayer of gratitude for the day and its many gifts. A brief review of our words and actions during the day that is ending and a prayer of surrender to the divine will could conclude our daily innercise.

Such a practice develops our devotion and also our will power. It strengthens our commitment to a life of communion and opens our eyes to see the events of life within the framework of faith. And being faithful to such spiritual exercise establishes us in the gift of peace.

Daily physical exercise is truly beneficial. But if we seek to be really healthy, we also need some daily exercises for the soul, our inner person. For, as Jesus might say, "What have you gained if you have a strong, lean and healthy body, but your soul is weak and flabby?"

26 **Feast of David Meeting Goliath**. The young David was delivering cheese to King Saul's camp on that fateful day. Cheese had been invented in 4000 B.C. by the Sumerians and was a common food by 2000 B.C. in Egypt. It was the favorite "health food" of Greek athletes who believed that it provided increased endurance. Have a cheese sandwich today and take on the neighborhood giant. Or better yet, use that extra energy to renew your disciplines as a spiritual athlete.

Remembrance of St. Bernard of Montjoux, after whom the famous Alp mountain passes are named, on the eve of his feast. He labored to aid and care for travelers in the Alps and thus has become the patron saint of mountain climbers. All pilgrims are mountain climbers who are scaling the Seven Story Mountain of God. The best way to travel up that Mountain or any mountain is to be roped to other climbers. Good pilgrims find others to whom they can be linked, assisting one another when the climbing becomes difficult and supporting a pilgrim who slips and falls.

27

FOR HEAVEN'S SAKE

As we continue to celebrate these days of rejoicing after the feast of Easter, a parable may help us understand how complex real resurrection is.

Once upon a time, long ago, a great king set out for the mountain of heaven. He traveled with his wife and three children and a group of loyal friends. In addition, the king brought along his faithful dog.

It was a hard trip and the way was long, and one by one each of the king's friends and family died as they journeyed toward heaven. Only his faithful dog remained as he neared the end of the way. One day, as they were climbing the great mountain, God appeared to the two and announced that it was time for the king to enter heaven. However, God said that his dog could not accompany him, for dogs were not allowed in heaven!

As anxious as he was to be admitted, the king refused, saying, "If there is no room in heaven for my dog, then I choose not to go!" At that very instant, in a flash of crystal blue lightning, the dog changed into Christ! For his faithfulness, the king was ceremoniously ushered into the great hall of heaven.

As he walked about the great hall, he saw many familiar faces, both of his followers and also his enemies. He saw those who had spoken unkind words about him and even some who had plotted his downfall. But though he looked everywhere, he did not see his family or friends. So the king went to God and asked, "Where are my wife and children and my dearest friends?"

God replied, "I do not know where they are, but you are welcome to search for them not only throughout heaven but even in hell if you wish."

So the king was taken by the Spirit of God down to the regions of hell, to the place of torment and great pain. And there he found his family and his friends. But before he could speak to them, the Spirit said to him, "Come, it is time to return to heaven; we are allowed only a brief time in this place."

But the king refused to return with the Spirit, saying, "I must stay here, for I desire to be with my wife, children and friends more than I long for heaven."

Again, a crystal blue flash of lightning split the sky asunder, hell vanished and God appeared to the king, saying, "Because of your great love and fidelity, you, your family and friends have all earned eternal life in Paradise."

Festival of Gratitude for Pets. Celebrate that day in 50,000 B.C. when dogs were domesticated and became such good friends of us uprights. And

28

be patient with your "untrainable" cat: its ancestors haven't been domesticated for more than five thousand years. Cats were sacred in Egypt where the cat-god Bast was a symbol of the kindly powers of the sun. Cats were also worshiped in Babylonia, Burma, Japan and China. Egyptians embalmed cats by the thousands and even mummified mice to be entombed with the cats as food for the day of their resurrection. A day to enjoy the sacredness of your pet.

29

Pop-Up Day. Charles Strite of Stillwater, Minnesota on this day in 1919 filed for a patent for the pop-up toaster. Strite had decided to do something about the burnt toast served in the company cafeteria and so invented a convenience that required no human attention to produce perfect toast. But Strite didn't invent toast. The ancient Egyptians toasted bread not to change its taste but to remove moisture. It was a form of preservation, giving bread a longer shelf life. This morning as you have your toast at breakfast, salute Charles Strite. And when at work, keep your eyes open for ways to make life easier for others.

THE MARTYRDOM OF ST. CHICKEN

Although Easter has already passed, perhaps some of you still have an Easter Egg or two around the house. Gathering those brightly colored eggs which come in all shades of the rainbow is one of the most delightful Christian folk-customs. But "colored" eggs have not always been a sign of the Resurrection.

As was mentioned in the April 27 entry, in 1471 a chicken in Basel, Switzerland laid colored eggs as beautiful as any we dye at Easter time. But the people of Basel were horrified that this chicken in their midst was transgressing the "natural law." The strange chicken became the subject of an ever growing tide of tattle-talk and accusations. Since chickens are only supposed to lay white or brown eggs, this chicken was thought to be "the devil in disguise!" "Yes, the chicken is possessed of the devil," was the readily accepted answer to its unique conduct.

So the citizens of Basel had the chicken put on trial, the evidence of its diabolical possession presented before the religious judges. The chicken was found guilty and condemned to be burned at the stake. As the fire burned down, leaving only a pile of ashes, the townsfolk returned home, secure in the knowledge that Satan had been purged from their midst.

We shake our heads today at such fearful logic, and may even find the story humorous. But how often in history have we treated persons as possessed by the devil simply because they were different? Joan of Arc was burned at the stake in Rouen, France in 1431 as a heretic, as one possessed of the devil—like the chicken in Basel. Yet we have canonized her as a saint.

St. Joan, like the colored-egg-laying chicken, was also found guilty of behavior contrary to the "natural law." It wasn't "natural" for a woman to wear a soldier's armor or lead an army into battle—or to have extraordinary results. It wasn't "natural" that she heard voices in her garden when she prayed. She was considered possessed when she said that they were "heavenly voices" telling her to lead the French army to victory over the English forces. In 1456, twenty-five years after her death, the proceedings of her trial were annulled by the pope, and she was finally canonized a saint in 1920.

What is the purpose of this reflection on a chicken and a young French girl, both burned at the stake for being possessed by the devil? St. Joan's martyrdom at the stake was in 1431, and this is the end of the twentieth century; we don't burn heretics or chickens at the stake any longer. But like the citizens of Basel and Rouen, do we not also pass judgment on those who are different or whose behavior we consider to be a violation of the natural law? And our harmful actions and words which follow such judgments—will they be viewed in the year 2600 as we view the deeds of the people in 1431 or 1471?

Feast of St. Joan of Arc. At age nineteen in 1431, she was burned at the stake as a heretic. The Sufis, Islamic mystics, say, "Until you have been called a heretic a thousand times, you cannot say that you are a disciple of truth."

30

Feast of the Visitation of Mary to Elizabeth. Is it possible that what we call interruptions in our well-planned day are really divine visitations? Whenever you are interrupted today by a visitor, a person requesting something of you or even an unexpected difficulty, pause and remember St. Elizabeth's response when she answered the door.

31

RENT-A-WOLF

Folk wisdom teaches that only a fool goes looking for trouble, so who would want to rent a wolf? Most of us yearn for a life free of problems and troubles; but a life without difficulties **creates** troubles!

There's a saying that if there is no wolf at your front door, you should hire one to come and howl at your doorstep. The imagination draws a picture of a huge wolf standing with its paws up against the door and howling, as, inside, the family is huddled together in fear. This image holds the secret as to why you should rent a wolf if none is presently on your doorstep.

Troubles hold the magic to bring us together or destroy us. In his poem "How Did You Die?" Edmund Cook wrote:

> Oh, a trouble's a ton, or a trouble's an ounce,
> Or a trouble is what you make it.

Life is trouble; how we deal with that ever-present and annoying fact shapes us and our homes. Trouble can call forth greatness from us, heroism as well as creativity, or it can breed self-pity, bitterness and a host of other evils.

Trouble, if nothing else does, tests our faith and our love of God. When our work and life in general is going smoothly, how easily we tend to forget about God and about others who are in need. We can easily live in our comfortable but cramped little world, unwilling to go outside of it. But have you noticed what happens to people's normal isolation from others when some trouble occurs while traveling on a bus or plane? The ice suddenly melts, and complete strangers begin to talk to one another about the difficulty they are sharing—and to actually help one another when needed. The wolf named "Trouble" could also be called "Glue." Natural disasters like floods, fires and tornadoes are able to bring together entire communities of people who respond to the trouble with assistance and friendship. Those who share a misfortune often find themselves in a holy communion that enriches their lives.

Jesus taught us to respond with love and compassion to others who are in trouble. He called those who wish to be his disciples to come to the aid of both family and stranger, friend and enemy. Jesus, it seems, was aware of the wolf-at-the-door theory. He knew that if we become compassionate and hospitable toward a stranger, we discover that the person is not really a stranger. By sharing in the holy communion of trouble, we become bonded more tightly together as members of the great family of God.

The next time trouble comes howling at your door—or you see it howling at another's door—think twice before you look upon it as evil. Trouble—by ton or by ounce—can be good or evil: it all depends on you.

June

First Negro Slaves arrive in Virginia on this day in 1619. The "New World," full of promise and freedom, adopts one of history's oldest and ugliest traditions. A day to mourn the evil seeds of slavery in America and to ask a question: "Am I, today, a slave to anything?"

1

Dinosaur Day. The age of dinosaurs began 225 million years ago. They disappeared from the face of the earth around 67 million years ago. They had a long and varied life and left their mark on the land, but we can still learn a valuable lesson from our friends the dinosaurs: those who are unable to adapt and change must pay the price of becoming extinct.

2

ARE THERE FLOWERS IN YOUR WILL?

For many, many years, the origin of flowers has been a great mystery to scientists. Where did they come from? When and how did they first appear? A few years ago Robert Bakker, a research scientist, suggested that flowers may have emerged as a result of the browsing habits of dinosaurs. It seems that flowers are part of the last will and testament of dinosaurs.

Angiosperms, as flowers are called by scientists, may have been part of the inheritance left to us by dinosaurs who lived about one hundred-million years ago, at the time in which shorter dinosaurs replaced their taller ancestors. As a result of this size change, the diet of dinosaurs shifted from tall trees to low-lying shrubs and tall grasses. The change in diet may in turn have hastened the evolution of new plants capable of rapid growth to replace the bare space left by the dinosaurs' large dinners. The plants that eventually appeared were flowers. How fortunate we are that the dinosaurs altered their eating patterns and so willed to us such beautiful gifts as flowers.

Regardless of the validity of Bakker's theory, it can be an occasion for us to look at what we are leaving to the world in our personal wills. Will the earth be a more beautiful place because of our behavior? It is within our power to plant seeds to make the world more just, tolerant and loving. Each deed we perform today that breaks down the walls of discrimination which separate people of different religious beliefs, skin color or sex will create a more beautiful world in ages to come. Each effort to replace war with understanding, greed with generosity and despair with hope creates the sacred space from which flowers will bloom for all ages to come.

The great, lumbering dinosaurs who munched away at their lunch of tall grasses and low shrubs never saw a flower. But their behavior helped create the flowers we so enjoy today. Those who strive to remove poverty, discrimination, religious separation and sectarianism will not likely live to see those goals realized. But the Christ-flowers of harmony, justice, peace and love will bloom for the earth in the future if we plant the seeds today. Not by our diet but by our deeds of compassion and our decision to live lives of holy communion will we create flowers for centuries to come.

3

Flower-Smelling Feast. Only children (at heart) and bees know the smell of the intoxicating perfume of flowers. The rest of us usually only approach them with our organs of sight. Awaken your sense of smell today to the world of aromas in which we live.

4

First Woman in Space. In 1784 Marie Thible of Lyons, France, together with a male companion, ascended to 8,500 feet above the French countryside. According to her companion, Marie was so filled with joy that she was "singing like a bird." On this June day do something that can make you "high," like being kind to a stranger, and then sing like a bird as did Madame Thible.

5

Feast of St. Boniface. This English Benedictine monk who was a missionary to Germany took the name Boniface after being made a bishop. He was put to death in 754 in the process of proclaiming his faith. Whether we are aware of it or not, each of us is a missionary of some "god." On this feast of St. Boniface take time to reflect on whether your life preaches the true God or some lesser god. It is not usually by words that missionaries proclaim their beliefs but by the deeds and attitudes of their daily lives.

6

New Religious Identity Day. The 2010 census shows that there are more Moslems in the United States than Jews. America's religious tradition is reworded to fit its new identity as a "Jewish-Islamic-Christian nation."

WANTED: A PROPHET

His personality, and especially his voice, was like the desert wind. When he spoke, there was a fiery force which gave his voice a power unlike any other that had been heard in the fierce desert wastelands of Arabia. Mohammed the prophet did what six hundred years of Christian missionaries had been unable to do, what thousands of years of association with Jewish believers had failed to achieve. He led the warlike tribes of the desert away from the holding up of many gods to the worship of the one God. The religion he founded is called Islam, which means surrender, and his followers who are called Moslems worship Allah, the one God. Recent events in world affairs have made these terms commonplace on our television news broadcasts, but often, like the name "Mohammed," they are without much meaning to many of us.

The prophet Mohammed did more than bring a large portion of the world to a living belief in one God; he also instituted social reforms against the injustice of the wealthy, limited the practice of polygamy, restricted divorce and helped the poor. He banned war and any form of violence, permitting it only in the case of self-defense or for the cause of Islam.

Mohammed's words, which he believed came from God through the Archangel Gabriel, called people to change their lives. And if that forceful desert prophet were to appear today in the center of an urban shopping mall, such words as these would be as fitting for us as they were 1300 years ago for the people of the desert: "Riches are not from the abundance of worldly goods, but from a contented mind."

The virtue of contentment is one that each of us should seek, for we live in a land that also worships many gods. We worship wealth and power; we are easily caught up in the rituals of consumerism and rapidly changing fashions. And along with these, advertising fosters our feeling continually discontented, wanting more and more.

Jesus also called the world to embrace the fullness of life that flows from simplicity, from a contented heart. His words teach us to seek real treasures, the only wealth that cannot be stolen or devalued by inflation. And 400 years before Jesus, the Greek philosopher Socrates taught that "those who want the fewest things are the nearest to the gods." Christ, Mohammed and a long line of great philosophers all teach the same lesson. Why is it that we, as well as so much of the rest of the world, seem unable to see and embrace this obvious truth? Who among us ever really expects to find lasting happiness in embracing our checkbooks or our many possessions? Why do we allow ourselves to be fed a continuous diet of addictive advertisements that make us constantly itchy to go out and buy something?

Perhaps, like the unbelievers of the desert in Arabia 1300 years ago who had rejected the words of Moses and Jesus, we need a new prophet whose voice is strong enough to call us to where real happiness and true wealth can be found. Or perhaps, if enough disciples of Jesus really believed in what he taught and lived contented and simple lives, *they* would be the prophets needed by our modern world.

Death of the Prophet Mohammed in 632. Mohammed founded the Islamic religion based on the teaching that there is only one God, Allah, and that everyone should surrender (the meaning of the word *Islam*) to the one God. This feast is an occasion for us to be awakened by the Prophet of Islam's words, "Riches are not from abundance of worldly goods but from a contented mind."

7

The Laki Volcano Erupts on this day in 1783 in southern Iceland. One of the most violent volcanic eruptions in recent history, it caused the death of ten thousand, and its acid rain after-effects brought about climatic changes worldwide. Every violent eruption of anger follows the same basic principles

8

of the volcano and has the same effects. Check today to see if deep inside your heart there is a bubbling fear that churns into a roaring anger ready to erupt, later to rain down more fear into the environment.

ACID RAIN OF THE HEART

The acid rain that falls on the forests of North America and Europe, destroying the trees and harming wildlife, is usually a result of the spread of poisonous industrial waste. Polluted rivers, even in the "clean" Midwest, contain fish which cannot be eaten because of the high ratio of deadly chemicals they contain. And Denver, in the midst of the fresh air of the Rockies, is one of the most polluted cities in America, the air filled with the various toxins given off by automobiles and factories. These are only a few of our environmental problems of pollution.

National and local monitoring agencies keep careful watch to insure our good health in the midst of these invisible but deadly by-products of our society. But maybe we also need a federal or local agency to monitor another poisonous pollution: fear! And in addition to smoke alarms, perhaps our homes should have fear alarms which would trigger loud signals at the approach of anxiety and fear.

As deadly as any poison is fear. In these last years of the twentieth century waves of collective fear and panic have swept over the atmosphere of our lives. The fears of global war, terrorism, the spread of crime, drugs and violence are like acid rain to the heart. Even milk cartons with pictures of kidnaped children speak an unconscious message of fear to small children, reinforced by the anxieties of parents who constantly preach vigilance against a variety of evils that lurk about the home. Fear feeds fear, and fear always cripples both freedom and life.

Largely because of our mass media, the presence of the dark side of humanity seems out of proportion compared to the good side. Some respond to the barrage of evil events in the news with aggressive behavior, while others flee into isolation, hiding behind triple-locked doors and iron-barred windows. To be cautious in such a troubled world is to live wisely, but to be a prisoner of fear is not to really live. It is certainly not to be a disciple of Jesus.

"Fear not" was one of Jesus' most frequent expressions. Only when we free ourselves from the overwhelming flood of collective panic about drugs, crime and violence are we truly able to do something about them. And so the paradox is that only when we cleanse ourselves of constantly feeding our minds with the acid rain of fearful thoughts do we become free enough to most effectively better our "environment."

Our thoughts are forms of electric energy that obey the laws of attraction. Energies of like nature magnetically draw one another. Think negative, fearful thoughts and you will attract dark, negative energies to yourself. Today's world presents each of us with a challenging opportunity to follow the teachings of Jesus to "fear not." We do this by placing our trust in God—but also by monitoring carefully the kind of thoughts that dwell in our minds. We call the Kingdom into existence not only by good deeds but also by constantly creating good, peaceful, trusting and loving thoughts within our hearts and minds. For by so doing, we are creating an environment free of spiritual acid rain; we are helping to create the Kingdom of Peace.

Birthday of Donald Duck on this day in 1934. According to United Press International, in the 1985 Swedish Parliamentary elections, Donald Duck received 291 votes! A good day to take elected officials a little less seriously—it will be good for their humility. Whom among the folks of "Loony Toon Town" would you give your vote to in a Senate race?

9

Alcoholics Anonymous Founded on this date in 1935 by William Wilson and Dr. Robert Smith. The great success of this movement is founded on the un-American principle, "You can't do it alone."

10

Feast of the Living Sun. Recent studies show that our daystar, the sun, pulses every two hours and forty minutes, moving in and out six feet per second. It is a theory that these vibrations originate deep within the sun and make it possible for vast amounts of energy to travel rapidly from the interior of the sun to the surface. Pause today to view the sun and take its pulse. And realize that the magnetic pulse of Love is present everywhere in the universe.

11

GONE FISHIN'

Among the most pleasant summer leisure activities is one that Jesus gave to his followers as a special sacred vocation. He sent his disciples into the sea of humanity to be fishers for God. We usually think of that vocation as one restricted to ordained ministers, but it's actually a vocation of everyone who is a disciple of Christ.

Actually, it's God who is the Fisher, and we who are the game. Love is the fishhook; but there's a problem. Anyone who has handled fishhooks knows that they are very sharp and dangerous. And just as we stay clear of fishhooks, we tend to stay clear of God's love. We know all too well from the stories of saints and from Scripture what happens to those who get hooked on God. We who do not want our well-ordered lives upset avoid getting "hooked" on the radical love of such a demanding Lover who wants not just part of us, but **all** of us! Obviously, the fisher can't catch a fish unless it takes the hook. So the hook must be hidden with some tempting bait like a big, fat, juicy worm.

Jesus was the alluring bait that hid the hook of God's love. His humanity was the incarnation of God's love in the flesh, and, oh, how attractive it was. Sinners, those who had been excommunicated from their religion and social outcasts all wanted to be near him. Why were these persons who normally would have felt uncomfortable or out-of-place in a religious environment so lured to a person who was so prayerful and religious? Hidden in the answer to that question is the pattern for how you and I are to evangelize (to use a religious term) the world, to go fishing in the sea of humanity.

From all the Gospel stories it is clear that Jesus respected others, loved them for who they were at that moment. He didn't preach at them, didn't demand their conversion as a requirement of his companionship with them. He was just among them as one of them, loving them as God loves: unconditionally. Being hungry for such love, they swallowed him, hook, line and sinker. The paradox is that the more they were caught, the more they were liberated.

If we wish to go into the world as Christ sent us, as fishers, we need to make ourselves into the same kind of bait that Jesus was. Rather than attempting to convert anyone to anything, let us simply love everyone, the good and the bad, with unconditional love. If our love has strings attached to it, hidden motives other than to love as God loves, the "big" fish (who always get away), are clever enough to see the hidden motives and will swim away.

Of course, the best way to go fishing in this Christlike way is to be first caught by the big, sharp hook of God's love and to wiggle with joy and delight. When we little fish are caught by unconditional love, we will become alluring bait for other fish. Fear not the hook, for to be caught by God is to be truly free.

12

Falling in Love Feast. In Portugal an annual festival is celebrated on the eve of the feast of St. Anthony, the patron saint of young lovers. The best way to stay young is to perpetually keep falling in love—and each time to fall deeper into the Beloved.

13

Beyond the Solar System Day. The U.S. spacecraft Pioneer 10, launched on March 2, 1971 on a mission to go beyond Mars, on this day in 1983 passes the orbit of the furthest planet and leaves our solar system. If it continues to travel onward and does so at its present speed, it will reach our nearest neighboring star in the year 851,989. A day to pray the prayer of wonder.

Also, in 1966 on this day, the **Miranda Decision** is handed down by the Supreme Court, requiring police to read prisoners their rights before beginning to question them. Take time today to reflect not only on your rights but also on your duties as a citizen.

THE NEXT "ANTI" CAMPAIGN

The war against cigarette smoking in public is almost won. With a passion, laws have been passed which ban smoking or limit it to very restricted areas. Such enthusiasm from non-smokers to free their environment of the cancer-causing effects of another's habit is understandable. And the passion with which the war has been waged might be explained by the fact that we feel so out of control today. We feel impotent to alter such great global issues as nuclear war, terrorism, acid rain, economic disaster and unemployment. And being able to do something about the problem of smoking has revived a sense of personal power in our lives. The driving force in this anti-smoking war is the basic American concept of not violating personal rights: "I have a right not to have to sit next to someone who is fouling the air with cigarette smoke."

But the drive shaft of the Ban Smoking campaign—the protection of "my right"—is also being installed in other vehicles of society. Many restaurants in the eastern part of our country have No Children sections as well as No Smoking sections. "I have my rights: when I go out to dinner, I don't want to sit next to a crying baby or some toddler playing with food."

If this concept of the American freedom to protect personal rights, the freedom not to be bothered by the behavior of others, spreads with the speed of non-smoking laws, it could have a dramatic effect in our lives. It is not impossible that we might have airplanes, theaters and other public places posting white signs with a circle and a large red slash across the picture of a child! There are some people who already would like to see such signs on the walls of their parish churches! Indeed, how can a person pray when some baby is bawling away or some little children are constantly asking questions of their parents? How can anyone hear the sermon, or worship in a church filled with children acting like children?

With Flag Day upon us, and in a couple of weeks the annual celebration of our nation's independence and the commemoration of our Bill of Rights, we should reflect on our duties as well as our rights. We have a duty to be involved in our government, to vote—to take an active part in the direction of our country. But duty implies sacrifice, a word that we do not like to hear.

Christian worship is more than prayer, good sermons and a quiet place to pray. Christian worship is sacrificial. Both at church and at home, it implies a spirit willing to sacrifice our personal needs for another's good. It even calls us to die to self in a love for the other. And if we can make such sacrifice without feeling diminished, we have truly found a royal road to holiness. We can live out our baptismal priesthood in such seemingly unholy and un-American ways as letting families worship together as families, even if little Harriet is cutting a new tooth or little Herman has brought his toy truck to church. Or we might tolerate, without complaint, being a bit chilly in an air-conditioned church that is "just right" for the guy in the pew three rows behind us. We might even give up our rights and allow a smoker who really needs a cigarette to cloud up our environment for a time.

Flag Day, U.S.A. While we celebrate this festival that honors the flag of America, we can also reflect about how the ideal flag for the United Countries of the World would be a white flag. For the white truce flag was originally used not for surrender but as a sign of God's peace, employed to bring fighting to a halt in order that dialogue might take place. We should also reflect, today, on how burning a flag is not the only way it is abused and dishonored.

14

THE LORD THUNDER

It's nearly summer, the time when the thunder rumbles across the prairies. Thunder is a welcome sound to farmers in need of rain and a sour note for people on a picnic. Previous ages have regarded thunder as a god and at other times as the voice of God. From East to West, Greek to Native American, each culture has its legends about thunder.

The Chinese tell about a deity named *My Lord Thunder, Lei-Kung*, who is represented as a being of repulsive ugliness, complete with wings and claws. My Lord Thunder wore only a simple loin cloth and had drums hanging at his side; in his hands were a chisel and a mallet. By divine ordinance, Lei-Kung had the authority and the duty to exact punishment on all the guilty whom the law courts on earth had let go free. He also punished with lightning those who had escaped justice by never going to trial. For the Chinese, then, to be struck by a bolt of lightning was an act of being punished for some hidden crime. Lei-Kung had no temple, for no one came to pray to him except when seeking to strike down an enemy who had gone unpunished. All this background information leads us into a story about the Lord of Thunder.

Once upon a time a hunter went into a forest and was caught in a great storm. Lightning and thunder filled the sky. The hunter saw that under a large tree, a short distance away, there was a child with a flag. As the thunder drew close, the child waved the flag fiercely and the thunder retreated. At that moment, as if in a flash of inspiration, the hunter remembered that the Lord Lei-Kung was repelled by the blood of black dogs, and it occurred to the hunter that the flag may have been saturated with such a repellent. So he took up his bow, aimed at the flag and let fly an arrow. When it struck the flag, thunder and lightning crashed down on the tree which fell, crushing the child. One great limb of the tree fell on the hunter, throwing him to the earth unconscious.

When the hunter awoke, he saw at the foot of the tree the corpse of a huge black lizard, the true form of the child. In the hunter's hand was a piece of paper on which was written, "Life prolonged for twelve more years for helping onward the work of heaven."

The next time you help rid the world of some evil, speak or act against the dangers of nuclear war, perform an act of kindness to a stranger or another task that brings the Kingdom closer, remember the story of the Lord of Thunder, Lei-Kung. You may find that you have been rewarded with twelve more years of life—or, better yet, that the life you have is twelve times more zestful and vital.

15

Signing of the Magna Carta, the English "Bill of Rights," by King John on this day in 1215. This landmark historical document of political and personal freedom stated, among other things, "To none will we sell, to none deny or delay, right or justice." An excellent day to ponder if we extend such rights to others in our daily lives.

16

Soweto Day, the international day of solidarity with the struggling peoples of South Africa who are denied their basic human rights. Reflect, today, on these words of Lenin: "I am not free until everyone is free," and lend your voice and your hand to the international movement for justice and equality.

SAINT UNCUMBER

Sir Thomas More wrote fondly of the virtues of St. Uncumber but not of the dangers of following her example! Tradition and legend say that she was a very beautiful woman who wanted to live a single life but was surrounded by suitors. So she prayed with great devotion to God that she might grow a beard—and her prayer was answered! (Which might entitle St. Uncumber to be named the patron saint of bearded ladies of the circus.)

But her answered prayer didn't solve her problem of being pursued. One of her suitors was a Sicilian who didn't take lightly to the beard on the face of his beloved Uncumber. He was so enraged that he killed her. One moral of St. Uncumber's story might be that we should choose carefully what we ask of God in prayer, lest the answered prayer have tragic consequences.

When it came to prayers of petition, Jesus admonished his followers to pray for the right things: "Look at the lilies of the field...Your heavenly Father knows all that you need" (Mt. 7. 32). If we are not to be concerned about tomorrow's material needs, for what should we pray?

At the Last Supper Jesus said, "It was I who chose you to go forth and bear fruit. Your fruit must endure, so that all you ask my Father in my name will be given to you" (Jn. 15: 16). It seems then that we are to pray not for material necessities but for what is needed to be fruitful.

In our consumer society which is constantly intoxicated by a thirst for more possessions, it is easy to pray for those material things that we think will make us happy. Such petitions might include a promotion, a scholarship, a new home or an "easy out" from some difficult situation. But might not, as was true for St. Uncumber, the granting of your fondest desire lead to something very undesirable?

Together with daily prayers for what we truly need, such as an increase in faith or love, we could also include prayers for those in our world who are afflicted by poverty, the lack of shelter or not having a decent job. Yet how seldom do we pray for such gifts from God. How easily are the dire needs of the poor overshadowed by our immediate concerns and personal, material needs.

This reflection on St. Uncumber's hairy prayer gives each of us an opportunity to examine the content of our daily prayers of petition. Let us not ask God for an easy way out of our difficulties but rather for the strength of grace to resolve them according to God's will.

And in our prayers for those who are crushed by oppression or discrimination, who are easily forgotten by the well-fed and well-dressed of the world, let us do more than pray words. As the poor and hungry find a daily place in our heart-chapel, their needs become a more vital part of our lives. Such prayer changes us and enables us to speak and act in a different way to those who are broken. Then our voice will be added to theirs in a great chorus calling for justice.

Right prayer, then, is the womb of social change, since thoughts lead to words and words lead to action. Prayer can indeed be transforming when our daily devotions include petitions for the poor, since such prayers cannot help but find concrete expression in our lives! Daily social prayer leads to deeds of justice as our prayers take flesh in such ways as voting or writing letters to our representatives in Congress on behalf of the poor and helpless. It can also lead to generosity with financial gifts as well as gifts of time and energy in such work as helping out in soup kitchens. And it can surely make us more responsive to those right around us in their times of need.

Surrounded by so much suffering in our society, so clearly seen on television and in newspapers, we can often feel helpless to do anything. We don't even know where to begin to change the situation when we consider the complex structures and rigid systems that create the injustices of our society. But one place, if not the best place, to begin is in our prayer.

17 **The Law of Karma is Discovered** in India in 980 B.C. An unknown Hindu saint recognized the truth that every thought, word and action has its consequences. Besides its short term effect, each emotion or deed is a seed that gives shape to events in the future. As we act and walk in the path of life, so we become. Evil seeds produce evil plants, good seeds produce good plants. This law of life, which is reflected in Jewish scriptures as well as in the parables of Jesus, is revealed again and again before our eyes. Yet some people are so careless with something as seemingly harmless as a thought that it would seem that they do not take the existence of such a cosmic law seriously. (See again the entry on February 9.)

18 **Blind Pilgrim Day** *or* **No Headline Day**. Today 40,000 people died from starvation! Yet no headline or news broadcast announced that fact. The same number will die tomorrow, and by the end of the year the body count from starvation in the world will be 15,000,000!

19 **June Wedding Days**. For those who are about to be married and for those who already are, a day to reflect on the words of Friedrich Nietzsche, ''It is not the lack of love but the lack of friendship that makes unhappy marriages.'' A dash of kindness and courtesy toward each other also helps!

R.S.V.P.—B.U.S.Y.

We've all received invitations with the initials R.S.V.P. printed at the bottom. They stand for the French, ''respondez s'il vous plait'' or ''please respond.'' These initials are more than a formality, for only by responding to them can the host or hostess make the necessary preparations for food and drink. Weddings, parties and celebrations require the knowledge of how many guests will be present so that they can be properly entertained.

According to social reports, there is a growing number of persons who do not respond to written invitations. The question that arises is how to consider this lack of response. Is it only an unfortunate symptom of a general disregard for courtesy in our age? Good manners, kindness and polite behavior seem to be out of style, discarded as old-fashioned and out-of-place in a modern age. But what or who is the villain? Do people not respond to an R.S.V.P. because they are B.U.S.Y.?

Indeed, polite behavior requires more time than does rudeness, but how much more? How long does it take to pen a brief response that you will or won't be able to attend a future function—one minute? Three minutes? True, we are all busy and often over-committed, but I do not believe that B.U.S.Y. is the arch-villain.

In the lives of most people there is too much going on. We suffer from an excess of commitments, invitations and activities to which we "should" go. As we battle to keep our heads above the rising tide of obligations, we face a new invitation with anything but glee. Yet we often feel that this or that gathering is something that we "should" attend. It's our old enemy **should** that paralyzes us, that prevents us from taking pen in hand and responding at once to an invitation. So we set it aside with its haunting R.S.V.P. silently calling us to respond, and we wait. We wait for the gods of fate to intervene, for something legitimate to prevent us from having to attend. Who knows what may happen before the appointed date—a sick child, the visit of a mother-in-law or an emergency of any number of sizes or shapes? And if no such angel of mercy appears at our front door to save us, good old **should** will usually push us with half a heart to the event.

The parable of Jesus about the king who had a feast to which the invited guests didn't show up makes one wonder if perhaps Jesus may have experienced such a lack of courtesy in his life. What is courtesy but a form of charity, a loving concern for others? As our society moves away from courtesy and gentle behavior, we do not have to move with it. Using expressions like "thank you" or "excuse me" are simple but graceful ways of living out the charity of Christ in daily life. "S'il vous plait—if you please" is a request for the kindness of a reply, expressed with the kindness of a "please."

Instead of waiting for the fates to decide our choices in life, let us call upon charity and prudence to help us take charge of our lives and decide what we are able, or unable, to do—and what we *really* want to do!

Midsummer's Eve, ancient celebration of feasting, fire, song and dance on the eve of the Summer Solstice. This is a pilgrim feast to reflect with wonder on the fact that since the beginning of this year you have traveled almost 243 million miles in our planet's annual pilgrimage around the sun.

20

Summer Solstice. This is one of the great sun feast days, marking the year's longest hours of daylight. Plan a picnic today, or take time for a celebration of watching our daystar disappear over the western horizon as our planet slowly turns eastward on its twenty-four hour pilgrim's revolving journey in space. Today begins the new season of Summer; celebrate its arrival as an opportunity to begin something new in your life. Examine your life patterns, and if you find that you are stuck in old ruts that keep you from being fully alive, today's the day to jump out of them and start afresh.

21

Feast of St. Basil the Great, Bishop of Caesarea who lived from 330 to 379. Founder of monastic institutions and friend of the poor, Basil said, "The bread in your cupboard belongs to the hungry; the coat hanging unused in your closet belongs to the one who needs it; the shoes rotting in your closet belong to one without shoes; the money you put in the bank belongs to the poor. You do wrong to everyone you could help, but fail to help."

22

SUMMER CLEANING

Simplicity is a magnetic word that holds great charm. Most of us would like to live more simply, especially when we look at our closets and basements. How easy it is to collect all kinds of things that we never use. They can fill our closet and garage space to overflowing. J.K. Jerome said, ''Let your boat of life be light, packed only with what you need—a homey home and simple pleasures, one or two friends worth the name, someone to love and someone to love you.'' When we lack such a simple list of good things, how prone we are to begin to collect stuff and fill our attics and basements with unused possessions.

To come to the point of possessing ''only what you need'' is never an easy task; we need changes of clothing for each season, a place to live, food and the other necessities of life. But besides these material requirements we need good friends and someone to love and someone to love us. When we lack these latter essentials, our lives often cease to be simple, causing us to fill our attics instead of our hearts. Empty spirits usually lead to full closets.

If our ''boat of life'' is to ride high in the water, we must make sure that it is buoyed by the ''essentials'' of life. When we have good friends to love and to love us, how much easier it is to find delight in poverty of spirit, in the simplicity of Jesus. In fact, once we attend to the true blessings of life, getting rid of non-essentials can enhance our happiness. We are familiar with spring cleaning, but maybe a good summer cleaning might be an occasion to enrich the soul. Open your closets and go down into the basement. As you do, keep in mind the words of Gandhi that if people possess something they do not use, they become thieves. For the poor have need of such possessions and keeping them ''in storage'' robs the poor of their rightful possession of goods.

Your ''boat of life'' will ride higher in the water and so catch the breeze of the blessed when you live with only what you need. And dresses, coats, shirts, shoes, pots and pans which find their happiness only in being used will sing a special song of joy as you open the closet-prison of their captivity and let them find new homes.

But remember that if you attempt to find simplicity this summer and do not have a homey home with simple pleasures and the opportunity to love and be loved, by spring your empty closets may once again be full.

23 **Cosmic Patience Day**. Are you waiting for a reply from a letter you wrote or a telephone call you left on an answering machine? If so, consider this fact today: in 1974 the first extraterrestrial message was sent into space in the hope of reaching an advanced galactic civilization. If someone out there responds to our message at the speed of light (the fastest speed we know of at this time), we'll get their reply in the year 51,974!

24 **Feast of St. John the Baptist**. A Christian celebration of the Summer Solstice; in former ages a day for fireworks, bonfires and festivals. This summer Christmas, six months before Christmas eve, is traditionally a day for giving gifts and dancing on hill tops. Old traditions can become new celebrations that restore us in body and spirit. This is a holy day for communion with the earth, sunlight and the beauty of all creation.

NO MOUNTAINS IN THE WAY

Several years ago a book of photographs appeared entitled *No Mountains in the Way*. It is a book of such Kansas scenes as a sunset on the prairie, old store fronts and stately old homes. The clever title speaks of the beauties of the flat lands where one can see for miles and miles with no mountains to block the view. Kansas and its surrounding states are not usually known for their natural attractions, but the Midwest is rich in beauty for those who look. The same is true of our daily lives—that is, if we can keep the view free.

Whenever we make mountains out of molehills, we block the view of all the beautiful things in our lives and homes. Molehill mountains have that magical power to blind us as they stand in the way. Take any one of your average molehills: the neighbor's dog, a visit by your wife's Aunt Bess, the kids tracking dirt on the floor, your husband's cigar smoke, your son's extra-loud stereo or the fact that your friend didn't remember that it was your birthday. Molehills come in ten thousand shapes and colors, and with a little attention and nurturing one can become a Pike's Peak in no time at all.

Whenever that happens to us, we lose our view of what is wonderful in life. Because it bothers us that the person next to us in church sings flat, we lose an opportunity for communion with the Beloved. Distress at mud on the rug or an overlooked hug can drain the day of happiness and paint our world a dishwater gray.

Molehills are unnatural mountains since they are filled with the hot air of irritability. As soon as we see one "on the rise," we should puncture it with a laugh, a prayer or just plain good common sense. While mutual consideration for needs and preferences is important in living together, a son who plays his stereo loudly in the house is better than no son in the house at all. A house with stale cigar smoke is better than living alone, and a forgotten hug shouldn't bug us, since the most important things in life are invisible. The title of that book of photographs could make a really good tombstone inscription: "Here lies a person who lived with no mountains in the way."

Custer's Last Stand. On this date in 1876 Lt. Col. George Custer and about two hundred of his men were defeated in battle by a group of Sioux and Cheyenne Indians led by chiefs Sitting Bull and Crazy Horse near the Little Big Horn River in Montana. Since most Western movies show the Native American Indians as losing, this is a day to remember their "victories" in art, culture and living in harmony with the earth.

25

Summer Snake Season. When walking in the woods or fields this summer, watch out for snakes. And remember the words of W.C. Fields, "Always carry a flagon of whiskey in case of snakebite, and furthermore, always carry a small snake."

26

---

27 **Birthday of Helen Keller**, 1880. This courageous and gifted woman overcame the loss of sight, hearing and speech to become an example and inspiration to all disabled persons. She learned to read and write in Braille and became an author and lecturer. Though blind, she said, "Literature is my Utopia. Here I am not disenfranchised. No barrier of the senses shuts me out from the sweet, gracious discourse of my book friends. They talk to me without embarrassment or awkwardness." Reflect today on these words of Helen Keller and ask yourself if you make the disabled feel awkward by the way you look at them or treat them. A day to remember that we all, in one way or another, are disabled.

SPACE FOR THE HANDICAPPED

You have probably had the experience of driving into a parking lot and seeing an empty parking space close to the door of the store you intended to visit. But when you reached it you saw a symbol for handicapped persons painted on the pavement; so you drove on, seeking another parking place. If this has happened to you, then you can relate to a strange dream I recently had. I dreamed that I was driving into the parking lot of a giant shopping mall. The parking lot was almost totally deserted, so I thought I would be able to park wherever I wanted to. But as I looked around, I saw that there was a yellow symbol for the handicapped on every one of the hundreds of spaces! No matter which side of the shopping mall I tried, every place was painted with that symbolic person in a wheelchair!

Are we not, each of us, handicapped in one way or another—psychologically, physically, emotionally, spiritually or intellectually? Rather than viewing those who are physically handicapped as a minority, shouldn't their presence—or even those specially reserved parking places—call us to acknowledge that we are all handicapped?

Over the years the word "handicapped" has undergone several changes in meaning. Originally it meant a real cloth cap in which bets or forfeits were kept during a game. Then it came to mean an advantage given in a race to provide all who entered an even chance to win regardless of physical ability. And now it refers to a person who has a disadvantage which makes achievement unusually difficult.

As each of us possesses some kind of disadvantage, shouldn't we be alert to our own shortcomings? And if we have a strength that others lack, shouldn't we make special allowances for those less fortunate rather than using our advantage to "lord it over" others? Rather than being creatures of competition, we would become people of compassion and loving care. The spiritual quest is not a race which only one can win, but a strange sort of event in which the aim is for everyone to win. The virtue of compassion, so essential for those on the quest, is simply a conscious sharing in the ten thousand possible disadvantages—handicaps—of others. Compassion translates into making constant allowances for others, always remembering that the majority of handicaps are not immediately visible to the eye.

In his stories about the end of the world, Jesus presents a true hand-in-cap theme. The winners are those who receive the reward at the end of the contest not because of personal spiritual skills at prayer or other religious exercises, but because of their compassion toward the poor, the sick, the naked, the imprisoned and those with any other disadvantage. And, as Jesus said, what awaits us, the prize that God will hand us from the Divine Cap, is far beyond the wildest dreams of all the handicapped sons and daughters of heaven!

Feast of St. Papius, martyred in 305 during the persecutions begun by Diocletian. Papius was scourged with knotted cords, cast into a cauldron of seething oil and finally was beheaded. A day that puts into perspective having to endure the summer heat while having to wait in line. Can we bear such difficulties because of our love for God? **28**

Feast of Saints Peter and Paul, founding saints of the Christian Church. Germanic lore holds them as patrons of good weather. And because of their Christlike healing capacity, they have also traditionally been invoked for protection against the bite of poisonous snakes. There was an old belief that if on this day you prayed to Peter and Paul, no snake would bite you throughout the year. **29**

THE SERPENT SAVIOR

Summertime in the Midwest brings the snakes out. Rattlesnakes and copperheads, who are residents of this area of the country, are a source of fear to many people—and properly so, since they are capable of inflicting mortal wounds. But our fear of them is often out of proportion to their actual danger. Part of our fear may be deeply rooted in our unconscious, reflected in the story of Adam and Eve in the garden. And because we tend to project our darkest instincts onto them, we often treat them with less than respect and reverence.

Snakes have always been dangerous creatures, but the peoples of the past not only feared them, they also worshiped them! Even in the Old Testament, the snake was more than a sign of evil, it was also a symbol of life and healing. In the Book of Numbers, for example, the fiery serpent was a means to cure and restore the people. This concept of serpents was common throughout the Near East. In Egypt and Greece, the snake was a sign of wisdom as well as healing. The Greeks believed that they had been evolved not from apes but from serpents! And in Rome snakes were kept as sacred signs and sacraments in the temple of the god of healing. In the Far East, in India, the cobra was the symbol of the god Siva.

Even in our modern society the serpent has retained that positive symbolic value. For example, the symbol of the medical profession has two snakes intertwined on a staff. This is the ancient Greek sign of the Caduceus, the staff of the god of healing. We are accustomed in our liturgy and religious art to such numerous images of Jesus as bread, water, a lamb and a vine, but I do not recall Jesus ever explicitly symbolized as a serpent. Yet, Jesus told us, "Just as Moses lifted up the serpent in the desert, so must the son of man be lifted up" (Jn. 3: 14). Such an image of Jesus as a snake upon a staff feels contrary to our Christian tradition where the serpent is **the** sign of evil. In religious art, the Mother of God is shown crushing the serpent. Yet, if we look at it in the context of Jesus' statement, where the serpent was lifted up to heal the people, Christ hanging on the cross is **the** sacred healing serpent. He was and is powerful healing medicine to restore the world to life. Since we do not draw back in horror at the sign of a snake on the door of our doctor's office, we should not draw back if the next time we see a cross in church, it has a great snake wrapped around it. In fact, such a sacred sign might do much to help us to view Christ and the cross as healing.

But we fear the cross in our lives almost as much as we fear the bite of a rattlesnake. We jump back in fright when the shadow of the cross comes into our lives just as we would leap back in fear at the sight of a snake in the grass beneath our feet. But the cross with its pain and suffering can also be a creative and healing gift. The cross, like the serpent, can also be an occasion of wisdom and knowledge.

Snakes are part of creation, and so is the cross. If you and I could learn not to fear the unique and personal cross that has been given to us, we might be more open to its powers to heal us and to teach us. If we could move beyond our fears, the cross, like the serpent, might truly be a sign of God's love. All that is created has a purpose, even if that purpose is not clear to us. We should reverence those aspects of creation which seem death-producing as well as those that are life-giving. We tend to strike out at what we do not understand. People kill snakes because they fear them, even snakes that would not harm them. We often attempt to destroy or evade our crosses with the same attitude of fear.

While it has a good theological and biblical base, I seriously doubt that the snake will ever become a popular religious symbol for Christ as the Serpent Savior! But at least we might be more open to consider the crosses that God has given to each of us as sacred sources of our own and the world's healing.

30 **Meteorite Day**. On this date in 1908, what is said to be the most powerful explosion in history occurs as a giant fireball crashes to the earth in central Siberia, leveling two thousand square kilometers of forest. Scientists believe it to be a meteorite; it produces a seismic shock that circles the circumference of our planet twice! Reread the entry on April 3 and remember that we know not the day nor the hour of our death. Enjoy the fullness of life today.

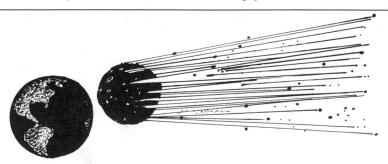

July

Invention of Sunglasses in China in 1200. The original purpose was not to reduce sun glare. Chinese judges wore smoke-colored quartz lenses to conceal their eyes in court, lest their eyes give away their opinion of the evidence presented. Shaded glasses were not used to block the sun's glare until the 1930's when the U.S. Army Air Corps commissioned Bausch and Lomb to create eyeglasses that would reduce the blinding high-altitude glare experienced by pilots. By the 1960's they had become a sign of fashion—and for some, a return to their original use by Chinese judges! If your heart is pure, have you a need to hide your eyes?

1

Birthday of Thomas Cranmer in 1489. The first Archbishop of Canterbury in the Church of England, he was one of the principal authors of the *English Book of Common Prayer*. Shortly after Queen Mary took the throne, he was tried for treason and burned at the stake in Oxford. An ideal day to rededicate yourself to both common and uncommon prayer.

2

A DIME A DOZEN

Our common phrase, "they're a dime a dozen," is a pun that was carried home to the United States by American sailors who accompanied Commodore Perry to Japan on his famous voyage. While in Japan the sailors were introduced to some of the spiritual practices of Buddhist meditation, among them the Daimdu Zen.

The Japanese "Daimdu" literally means "bent nail." It was the name for the meditation practice of focusing one's total attention for long periods of time on a bent nail or some other insignificant object. This religious practice was created by a sixteenth century Zen monk, Subaru Toyota (no relation to the present day automobiles). The monk's intention was to reveal how even the small and insignificant objects and situations of daily life are capable of opening one to holiness. But to the American sailors, this sacred practice signified only a strange obsession with worthless and trivial objects.

In the late 1860's, Daimdu Zen was punned into "dime a dozen" as a form of ridicule of Oriental religions and non-Christian forms of prayer. Today, some serious seekers of holiness are examining Eastern and Near Eastern prayer forms for hidden insights. The doors to this new interest were opened by the Second Vatican Council to promote and reverence all that is good and worthwhile in non-Christian practices.

Like the Zen monk Subaru Toyota, Jesus frequently proposed that his disciples meditate on the "dime a dozen" objects of his day. "Learn a lesson from the fig tree...consider well the fragile beauty of the wild flowers and the lack of anxiety of the sparrows...you are worth more than a hundred sparrows..." are only a few of Jesus' "bent nail" Gospel meditations. Jesus calls you and me to seek holiness—and the Reign of God—not so much in life's great and exceptional things, in miracles and wonders, as in the simple and daily objects and events of our lives.

On this summer day, take time to stop and reflect on whatever seems so common in your life as to escape attention, using it to awaken you to the mystery of God. The possibilities of such "bent nail" meditations are indeed limitless. An example—intended to spark your own creation of them—could be this Bent Nail Closet Meditation: go to your closet and remove some article of clothing that is now out-of-date. Quietly recall how once, not that long ago, it was the "in" style. Sit, holding it in your hands, allowing yourself to be absorbed with the garment and its fate.

Perhaps this outdated garment may teach you to be less obsessed with trends and passing fads. Perhaps, while very insignificant, this meditation will allow you to see the false promise of happiness in those things that are here today and gone tomorrow. So awakened, you will be free to seek with all your heart that which is lasting in life.

---

3 **Feast of St. Thomas the Brave**. While the Apostle Thomas is usually known as "doubting Thomas," he was the only disciple who proposed going up to Jerusalem to die with Jesus! It is also believed that after Pentecost Thomas carried the Gospel through the Near East and into India. A day to resist the discrimination implied in such titles as "peeping Tom" and "doubting Thomas."

---

4 **Declaration of Independence**, 1776, the national holiday of American freedom. Celebrate your independence from all forms of slavery and oppression by checking to make sure that nothing holds you in bondage, especially the chains of discrimination, hatred, greed and indifference. Sigmund Freud once said, "America is a mistake; a gigantic mistake, it's true, but none the less a mistake." Are we doing anything today that lends credence to Freud's evaluation of America?

THE BIRTHDAY OF OUR COUNTRY

For those who follow the way of Jesus, which he promised would lead to God and would set us free, common daily events are of special importance.

Disciples of Jesus pursue the holy, both in ho-hum, daily life and also on the special days marked as holidays.

The Fourth of July offers us an opportunity for more than a civil celebration. Along with the fireworks, watermelon and fried chicken, we can enjoy the Fourth as a feast day. The prayer below is one way to remind us of the hidden treasures of growth and grace contained within this wonderful summer celebration of our nation's independence.

A FOURTH OF JULY PRAYER

We lift up our hearts, O God, on this day of celebration
    in gratitude for the gift of being Americans.
We rejoice with all those who share
    in the great dream of freedom and dignity for all.

With flags and feasting, with family and friends,
    we salute those who have sacrificed
    that we might have the opportunity
    to bring to fulfillment our many God-given gifts.
As we deny all prejudice a place in our hearts,
    may we also clearly declare our intention
    to work for the time when all people,
    regardless of race, religion or sex,
    will be granted equal dignity and worth.

Come, O gracious God, who led your children Israel from slavery,
    keep us free from all that might hold us in bondage.
Bless our country and join our simple celebration
    that we may praise you, our Source of freedom,
    the One in whom we place our trust.

Feast of Interdependence. Reflect today on how true freedom requires a balance of independence and an interdependence with others, the earth and with all living beings.

5

Birthday of Beatrix Potter in 1866, creator of *Peter Rabbit* and other stories for children. A day to be grateful for authors and creators of stories for children and the youthful of heart.

6

Chocolate Day. In 1550 chocolate was introduced into Europe from the New World where Columbus discovered the native's use of cocoa beans. Soon after the beginning of its use in Europe, the clergy of the day, viewing it as an aphrodisiac, denounced cocoa as "the beverage of Satan...a provocative to immorality." Rather than simply laughing off the way the seventeenth century clergy responded to the introduction of chocolate—which is a delight to the child's palate—take time today to ask yourself what custom, trend or activity you find "provocative to immorality."

7

Birthday of John D. Rockefeller in 1839, industrialist, founder of Standard Oil, one of the world's richest men. He summed up the prevalent model

8

of the Free Enterprise System when he said, "God gave me my money." A very different idea is presented in an early Christian document, the *Didache*, "Share everything with your brother/sister. Do not say, 'it is private property.' " And St. Basil added, "The rich take what belongs to everyone and claim they have a right to own it, to monopolize it." A day to reflect on whom you agree with, Rockefeller or Basil and the *Didache*.

STEWART'S $TYLE

The late socialite, William Rhinelander Stewart, one of New York's "400," hated rumpled paper money. Each night before he went out, he had his valet iron his money!

Indeed, a crisp, smooth bill has a good "feel." Fresh, uncrumpled currency has about it a sense of power. I'm not sure about you, but however nice having unwrinkled money might be, I would find it difficult to carry out W.R. Stewart's custom. I can't keep my money around long enough to iron it! But rumpled or neatly ironed, what we think about money tells us a great deal about our spiritual journey.

Echoing Jesus, P.T. Barnum, the American circus genius, once said, "Money is a terrible master but an excellent servant." These words provide a spiritual attitude about wealth that puts it into proper proportion. Money is intended to be a servant, but whenever we allow it to become our master, we are in need of salvation, in need of liberation. Jesus did not so much want us to be poor as to be free. The Kingdom only opens to those seeking freedom. Money has the seductive power that easily allows it to become a dictator. And we all know how easily it becomes a cause of marriage disagreements.

Money is a legitimate need in our families and our society. Yet we really need less money than we usually think we need. In our culture, the main "business" of business is discontent. We are led to be constantly discontented by advertising so that we will go out and buy something we've been told we need. We rarely ever wear an article of clothing until it falls apart. The function of "fashion" is to induce a perpetual discontent—and a perpetual purchase of new clothing that is "in style." An industrial, capitalistic society rolls forward on the wheels of artificial needs.

William Rhinelander Stewart had a need for non-rumpled folding money, and we smile at his quirk, his artificial need. But the next time you find yourself measuring the width of the lapels of your suit coat or the length of your dress, remember the real-life parable of W.R. Stewart, and words that we could easily hear from the mouth of Jesus, "Blessed are the content, for the Kingdom of Heaven is theirs. Blessed are the content, for they are truly the millionaires of life."

9 **Religious Tolerance Day**. On this day in 1850 in Tabriz, Iran, a firing squad killed Mirza Ali Muhammad, the prophet of the Baha'i faith. All the world's great religions teach love and compassion. Why is it that this most important commandment of religions is so often violated when it comes to members of other religions? A fitting day to explore whether you harbor any violence in your heart toward those who hear the voice of God in a different language.

Birthday of John Calvin, one of the foremost leaders of the Protestant Reformation, in 1509. He initiated the first great division in the early Protestant movement by separating from the Lutherans in 1561. His teachings are embodied in the Presbyterian and other Reform Protestant Churches. On this day, have a reformation of your spiritual life as you renew your prayers by investing them with greater love for God.

10

Also on this day in 1962, the **Launching of the First Privately Owned Satellite** (AT&T). It enabled live TV pictures to be transmitted across the Atlantic. Consider, today, the miracle of television which has shrunk our world to the size of a backyard; and as the world shrinks, our hearts must equally expand to meet the challenge of being faced with global concerns.

Detroit Antique Auto Parade of gasoline-powered combustion-engine automobiles of the late twentieth century on this date in the year 2079. Crowds complain of fumes but delight in the old fossil-fuel driven vehicles. People are also amazed at learning how much their ancestors relied upon these small wheeled-boxes.

11

A PRAYER FOR THE ROAD

Summer is vacation time, the season when many of us take to the open road with a different attitude. We usually use our automobiles as machines to transport us to work and to help us meet other obligations. But in these months of summer our cars become escape vehicles from the routines of our work-a-day lives.

Those seeking an integrated holiness do not restrict prayer to Sundays, to church or even to daily times of formal prayer. Instead, every activity of their lives is engaged as prayer. As Americans, we all spend a significant amount of time inside an automobile, and we should not exclude that travel time from our life of prayer.

St. Paul told us, "Whatever you eat, whatever you drink, whatever you do at all, do it for the glory of God" (1 Cor. 10: 31). As twentieth century Christians, it is easy to exclude our use of machines from our prayer lives and so lose frequent opportunities to give glory to God. We usually think that God is given glory by stunning stained-glass windows or deeds of heroic charity. Indeed, how many of us believe that our use of our washing machine or car can be an act of worship? Yet St. Paul was clear in saying, "**Whatever** you do, do it for the glory of God."

Good prayer is like an alarm clock. Its purpose is to wake us up to the reality that all life is intended to be prayer, is meant to give glory to God. So, as you begin to drive with a fresh summertime attitude, why not begin to see your time in your car as prayer time. An excellent way to do this is to make a brief formal prayer before you step on the gas. The options for such a prayer are numerous. You could say a prayer we all know by heart,

"Bless us, O Lord, and these thy gifts which we are about to receive from thy bounty." While we usually restrict that prayer to meal times, it would be a wonderful eye opener to all the gifts of sight, travel and adventure that are available in a car—even in a short drive to the store.

Such a prayer could also be an expression of our need for God to bless us with protection as we take responsibility for operating a machine that is potentially very dangerous to our health and safety and that of others. With the passage of safety belt laws, we have a daily ritual that is hungry to be made holy. As you wrap yourself in your safety belt, you could make it a sacred ritual by praying, "Wrap me in your love, O God, and bless my journey." A small sign of the cross could also be traced upon your safety belt where it crosses your heart.

And as humorous as it might sound, praying our traditional meal blessing would be a double blessing for about 25% of us. According to a recent survey, at least 25% of American commuters eat breakfast in their cars!

12 **Birthday of Henry David Thoreau** in Concord, Massachusetts in 1817. Thoreau once said, "It is a great art to saunter." Sauntering is a good summer prayer. This beautiful word was born in the Middle Ages when idle people roved about the countryside and asked for charity under the pretense of going "a la Sainte Terre" to the Holy Land. Upon seeing one such pilgrim, children would cry out, "Look, there goes a Saint-terrer."

13 **Birthday of Birds**, 150 million years ago. Birds evolved from reptiles and have continued to evolve in diversity. Pigeons and blackbirds came about 60 million years ago and chickens and ducks shortly after that. If you are not afraid of birds, why be fearful of their great ancestors, reptiles?

PRIMAL MAGIC

July 14 is Bastille Day, a good time to recall what the Duke of Wellington once said about that most famous Frenchman, Napoleon: "The presence of Napoleon on the battlefield made the difference of 40,000 men!" While short in physical stature, Napoleon was a towering charismatic leader. He inspired people by his very presence, calling them to courage and strength beyond their normal limits. What was his secret?

Napoleon was fearless! Unlike the common person, the French general was bold and oblivious to danger. That ability is called "primal magic." All leaders, from the great and famous to the kid who leads the neighborhood gang, possess some of this primal magic. We all admired and were willing to follow the kid who first dared to do the things we wanted to do but were afraid.

Jesus was such a charismatic leader. His freedom to speak out against the injustices of his day, to confront those religious leaders who were only skin deep in their religious observances, made him a hero of the people. Jesus acted without fear, and he constantly urged his disciples not to be afraid. Likewise, he calls us to be unafraid of tomorrow, to stop fretting about our daily needs and to be unafraid of death or of those who can kill the body but not the soul. And Jesus' presence was a source of strength to his followers.

One can imagine, then, the fear that must have seized the hearts of the little band of disciples when Jesus told them that he was leaving. But he said to them, "I will leave you a farewell gift—my peace" (Jn. 14: 27). This gift of peace expressed in the Hebrew word "Shalom" means more than the absence of conflict; it implies the very presence of God. That presence within Jesus was the source of his boundless courage. We need to ask if we have tucked away his gift of peace, causing us to face life fearfully.

Most of our sins are the result of fear. Don't we lie because we are afraid of being embarrassed? And don't some people boast and talk only of themselves because they fear that if they do not continuously parade their achievements or knowledge they will be unlovable? Reflect for a moment on your more recent sins and failings. You may be surprised at how many of them have their seeds in fear. "Be not afraid," Christ tells us, "and remember the gift of peace that I have given to each of you."

Also think about what it is that you, at this moment, fear most of all. Then remember that God dwells within you, a God who loves you more than any human can, a God who loves you unconditionally. How different our daily lives would be if we could really remember and enjoy the gift of peace that is ours.

Bastille Day. On this date in 1798 the French Revolution began as a Paris mob attacked the famous Bastille prison. While we may have a mental image of torturous conditions at the Bastille, according to one inmate a typical menu at that time read like this: green pea soup garnished with lettuce and a joint of fowl, sliced roast beef, meat pie garnished with mushrooms and truffles, sheep's tongue, biscuit, fruit and Burgundy wine. Take time today to reflect on whether you are living in a comfortable prison. 14

THE FATAL FORTRESS

Once upon a time, a king who was also an astrologer read in a remote pattern of the scattered stars that a great calamity would overtake him on a certain day, at a particular hour. He therefore ordered a stronghold to be constructed of solid rock, and when it was completed he had numerous heavily armed guards posted outside. On the day that the stars said he would meet his fate, he entered his fortress. But when he got inside, he found that he could still see daylight. He located the gap in the wall and filled it immediately to prevent misfortune from entering. He enclosed himself completely, but by blocking out the last opening against disaster, he also imprisoned himself without light or air. Needless to say, without air the king soon died. The stars had not lied.

We also can become prisoners of fear by our own hands. We bring about the situations we dread in our lives because we fall prey to the power of our thoughts. They are like a magnetic blueprint, possessing the power to attract the things that we imagine. There are countless building blocks that our minds use to construct our personal prisons: anger, resentment, hate, discrimination, feelings of inferiority, shame, guilt, impatience, regret of past mistakes, anticipation of calamities, our fear of our comfortable lives being changed or challenged and a host of other fears. And our spirits can be suffocated by the fortresses of fear that we build around ourselves.

One of our most important spiritual duties is to keep reducing the height and thickness of these walls by patience, trust, vigilance, prayer and perseverance. And the words of Jesus hold the key that opens the doors of our self-made prisons: "Knock and the doors will be opened unto you" (Mt. 7: 7). If we knock each day with passion and prayer, those prison doors will begin to open. As a Lord of Liberation, Jesus also proclaims the wish and will of the God of the great Exodus from Egypt, the Passover, expressing the divine desire that all the children of God live in freedom: "If you live according to my teaching, you are truly my disciples: then you will know the truth, and the truth will set you free" (Jn. 8: 31-32).

We are like the Israelites who in the midst of the hardships of crossing the desert often wished for the comforts they knew in their slavery in Egypt. Because of the hardships of the work of liberation, we often reinforce our prison walls to preserve our comfortable lives. But as we come to taste the fresh air of freedom from our fears, we realize that we cannot settle for less than full life. And as we learn to use truth and prayer as doorways, we will find our hearts becoming gates through which love can freely flow outward and return again.

15

St. Swithin's Day, commemorating this English saint who died in 862. According to an old legend, "St. Swithin's Day, if thou doest rain, for forty days it will remain; St. Swithin's Day, if thou be faire, for forty days 'twill rain nae nair." Rain or shine, be of good cheer. A day to ask St. Swithin to help you make your heart, and not external conditions, the source of your happiness.

Also celebrated today is the 1871 **Invention of the Merry-Go-Round**, a classic symbol for how to live. We should be merry as we find ourselves constantly "going around in circles!"

16

Celebration of the Hejira, the night flight of the Prophet Mohammed to Medina in 622, initiating the Mohammedan era. Today marks the beginning of the Islamic New Year.

Also on this day at 5:30 a.m. in 1945, the **First Atomic Bomb Explosion** occurred on the Trinity site, Alamagordo Air Base, south of Albuquerque, New Mexico. It marked the birth of the Atomic Age.

A PIECE OF MY MIND

That we live in an age of great tension is hardly news to us. We all live close to the boiling point when it comes to anger and frustration. The causes are many—the hectic speed of daily life, over-commitments and financial burdens—but they are all part of the invisible fires that burn beneath us.

As a result, on occasion we "boil over" and give someone a "piece of our mind." The receiver of that "piece" might be a clerk in a store or the next-door neighbor who decides to mow his lawn at 6 o'clock on a Saturday morning. And the "piece" that we give to such people is a red-hot serving of anger!

"What possible harm can come from letting off a little steam?" you might ask. "So what if I respond in justifiable anger to my neighbor or wife: who is harmed by that small explosion?" Dominique Henri Pires, the winner of the 1958 Nobel Peace Prize, once said, "If an atomic bomb falls on the world tomorrow, it is because I argued with my neighbor today."

When we give someone a "piece" of our mind, it usually leads to an argument and to holding negative feelings toward the other. The statement of Pires makes little sense to us unless we also realize that our world is a single web in which each one of us, and all of life, is intimately connected. Everything we say, do or think has consequences for all our "global village." All selfish behavior has painful results—if not immediately, then sometime in the future, the "tomorrow" to which Pires referred.

By our efforts at persevering in personal silent prayer and by constantly watching over our thoughts—undergirded by the grace of God—all of "Spaceship Earth" will come to live in peace. If we are sincere about these efforts, then we need not be afraid to give others a "piece of our mind," for we will give them the **peace** of our mind! And to the degree that each one of us daily gives such "peaces" of our mind to strangers as well as to those with whom we live, we *prevent* nuclear war.

Compass Day. "Wrong Way" Corrigan leaves New York's Bennett Field on this day in 1938 as he attempts to fly non-stop to Los Angeles. Corrigan reads the wrong end of his compass needle and, without a radio or navigational equipment, lands twenty-eight hours and 3150 miles later in Dublin, Ireland! Have you checked your compass today to see if you're headed in the right direction?

17

Feast of St. Symphorosa who because of her great love for Christ endured the wrath of the Emperor Hadrian. She was first beaten for a long time, then suspended by her hair, and lastly she was thrown into the river with a stone tied to her body. A good day to consider what cost you are willing to pay because of God's love for you.

18

THE BLINDMEN'S DINNER

Eulenspiegel was a fourteenth century villager of the German Duchy of Brunswick who was known for his crude jests and mischievous pranks. A storehouse of legends grew around him, one of which is this story of the Blindmen's Dinner.

It seems that one night twelve blind men came to Eulenspiegel's home asking for alms. He opened his door to them with a gracious welcome and heard their sad tale of hunger. "Go to the inn in the square," he told them, "and eat, drink and be merry, my good men. Here are twelve florins with which to pay the innkeeper." The twelve thanked him in a chorus of joyful gratitude and hurried off to the inn.

After they had finished a truly marvelous meal, the innkeeper presented them with a large bill, whereupon they all said, "Let him who received the money pay for the dinner." But no one actually had a single florin! Each had supposed that another had received the money, but all their pockets were empty.

Each time we attend a Holy Eucharist, we sit at a feasting table. But at the end of the dinner, which of us is going to pay the bill? Like the blind men in the tale, we "pass the buck" (or, rather, the bill) to another. No one wants any personal responsibility for the cost of such a dinner, for indeed the cost of the Eucharist is high!

Although we have eyes, we do not see the presence of a bill at the end of the meal of the Eucharist. While we easily "bad-mouth" the poor on welfare for wanting a free lunch in life, that is how many regard this sacred meal. Often it seems that the Eucharist is a handout for which we expect to pay nothing; nor do we like to do the chores afterward in payment for that bountiful feast, although that might be the only way to respond in justice.

At the feast of the meal where God is the innkeeper, there are only separate checks, and no credit cards are accepted. But we can leave an I.O.U. That I.O.U. would state that we owe something and intend to pay our debt by the way we respond to the various requests made of us that day.

Perhaps we should all leave church with an I.O.U. on the altar that reads, "I owe you a sacrifice, a gift of love that involves **my** body and blood," with our signatures below. I would find it fortunate indeed to meet a person who had left such an I.O.U. on the altar if I had a flat tire or needed a favor.

Faith is required to believe that we have attended a banquet when we go to the feast of the Eucharist. If you believe that you have indeed been richly gifted, then justice demands that you pick up *your* tab instead of sneaking out without paying!

19
First Woman's Rights Convention, 1848, in Seneca Falls, New York. Celebrate this historic date by promoting full and equal rights for women in every area of our religious, political, economic and social life.

20
First Moon Landing on this day in 1969. U.S. Astronauts Neil Armstrong and Edwin Aldrin, Jr. land their lunar module on the surface of Earth's moon. According to Pan Am Airlines, there are 92,000 Americans presently holding reservations for a trip to the moon. May the fact that there are human footprints already on the moon, and the fact that potentially 92,000 more will soon join them, not be reason to forget her magical powers.

21
First Homicide by a Robot. In Jackson, Mississippi in 1984, a thirty-four-year-old worker is crushed as a robot turns and pins the man to a safety bar. Consider how the machines that are intended to serve you may be trapping you and crushing the life out of you—and the fun out of your life.

Also on this day in 1873 in Adair, Iowa, **Jesse James Plans the First Train**

Robbery in history. Again, ask yourself today if your machine servants, while saving you time, are also robbing you of something precious.

AN AGING CURE

The other day, while reading the *Farmer's Almanac*, I discovered an interesting quote: "Middle age is the time of life when work begins to be a lot less fun and fun begins to be a lot more work." Those who are at or near "middle age" tend to shy away from that term. No one, even an eighty-nine-year-old, wishes to be called or thought of as old. And perhaps the term "middle age" is avoided because it is seen as the beginning of old age. Yet if the quote from the *Farmer's Almanac* is true, middle age comes early in the lives of many people. Some of us are middle-aged in our early twenties!

When are we middle-aged? When our work becomes a lot less enjoyable. I remember once hearing about a research director of a large corporation. Every day he would walk around the laboratory and ask his researchers a single question, "Are you having fun?" His theory was that if they were having fun, enjoying their work, they would be more creative and would eventually discover a new product of great value to the company.

The same is true for you and me. For when our work ceases to be fun in the fullest sense, it also ceases to be creative and redemptive. The disappearance of enjoyment in our work is usually accompanied by the absence of fun in our free and leisure time as well. As the saying from the *Farmer's Almanac* said, "and fun begins to be a lot more work." When our work ceases to be creative and rejuvenating, we inevitably experience more exhaustion. When we come home from work, we are too tired to spend the necessary energy for enjoyment, and so fun becomes more remote an experience.

One reason why we are worn out is that we are weighed down by the burden of respectability. To always have to be proper and acceptable is too heavy a responsibility for any sane person to bear. Tiring thoughts like, "What will the neighbors say?" or "What will people think?" not only rob us of freedom but also drain us of the energy necessary for enjoyment. Fear of being judged by others makes fun increasingly more difficult and can block any spontaneous fun. Playfulness is as necessary in our work as when we are not working. Titles and playing roles, even the role of being a parent, can also weigh us down.

In these changing times, a sense of respect for persons is frequently absent. The comedian Rodney Dangerfield speaks for all of us when he bemoans, "I just don't get no respect." Indeed, to be holy and wholesome, we do have a need for the respect of our community and of those with whom we live and work. But our need for respect can be an obstacle preventing us from enjoying life. And enjoying life—having fun in living—is one of the major reasons why we were created. God made us to know, love, serve and enjoy—to enjoy the divine presence here and for all eternity. If we cannot enjoy God here in this life, how can we enjoy God in eternity? Gratitude is always a prayer. But the expression of gratitude that most delights the giver is when the receiver of the gift really **enjoys** the gift. The enjoyment of life, having fun with it and in it, is a prayer that God truly enjoys.

Whatever the lifework each of us has to perform, let us look at it and ask ourselves that question, "Are you having fun?" When we look at our family life, our religious vocations, our present activities and the answer to that question is "No," then we should take time to examine what we are doing and how we are doing it. And we should ask another question, "Why?" The time to ask such questions and the time to search for answers is during our prayer. The time we take at work or at home to add a dash of fun to our lives is also prayerful time. Furthermore, we can sprinkle our schedules with space for some spontaneous enjoyment. Then we will find that whether we are twenty-five or seventy-five, we will still be young because our work will be fun, and fun will not be work.

22 **Summer Leisure Day**. Mindful of the fact that since 1975 Americans have lost 37% of their leisure time, steal some time today for leisure. As you do, reflect on the words of the Roman philosopher Marcus Aurelius (121-180), "The greatest part of what we say and do is really unnecessary. If you take this to heart, you will have more leisure and less uneasiness." Reflect, today, on what you may be doing that isn't necessary for your happiness.

THE BLESSINGS OF UNEMPLOYMENT

One of the great tragedies of our time is the large number of those who are out of work. Yet the other side of that sad social reality provides us with a paradoxical truth. For a great number of people, the tragedy of our age is being over-employed! Our lives are so busy, so constantly occupied, that we have no time left to visit our friends, write letters or simply enjoy life.

Having a lifework is an essential ingredient for happiness and for a healthy self-image. We all need meaningful employment, and a truly Christian society strives to make this possible for every person. But since World War II people in our society have become over-employed in increasing numbers.

The word *employ* originally meant to enfold or involve. It seems today that we all tend to be too involved! We are enfolded in so many activities and commitments that we lack time—not only for leisure but also for prayer, that essential element in our spiritual lives. We have precious little time for play and prayer, feasting and friendship or for all the other gracious necessities of living in a truly human way.

While it is normal for workers to have one employer, what do we say of a culture where large numbers of people have several employers? Who are these extra employers? While they are many, they all have the same family name: **Should**. We should: mow the lawn, keep the house spotless, attend every meeting, be present for this or that... . We need the courage to retire from as many as possible of the Mr. or Ms. Shoulds for whom we work. Examine your life and see which of these various taskmasters you can do without so that you can enjoy some of the blessings of **un**employment. Only when our lives have a proper balance of meaningful employment and meaningful unemployment can our basic lifework nourish us and become part of the redemptive work of Jesus.

Be pre-warned, however, that attempting to retire from the employment of the *Shoulds* will not be an easy task. You will be given a long list of reasons why you must continue to work for them. But any effort to quit, no matter how small, brings some of the blessings of being meaningfully unemployed. Set your heart on the old-fashioned joys of being temporarily unemployed for an hour or two each day, and perhaps you will find a greater natural rhythm overflowing into every area of your life, and a greater harmony with the rhythm of God.

Birthday of the Computer in China in 3000 B.C. Called the abacus, it was the first mechanical calculator. The first efficient modern computer, ENIAC (Electronic Numerical Integrator and Computer), appeared in 1946. It was one hundred feet long, ten feet high, had 70,000 resistors, 18,000 vacuum tubes and 6,000 switches. A new age had begun, even though ENIAC was monstrous in size. Look around your home today and see what large inventions may someday be as small as the newest computers. And while you're at it, see what areas of your life you can reduce so that you can enjoy more **life**.

23

Birthday of Amelia Earhart in Atchison, Kansas in 1898. This daring early pilot disappeared mysteriously on a flight from New Guinea to Howland Island in the Pacific on July 3, 1937. Today, as we toast this heroine of aviation, let her be a heroine who calls forth courageous deeds from you. We need more models of inspiration and daring like Amelia Earhart.

24

Birthday of the Birthday Cake in 55 B.C. When the Greeks adopted the Egyptian commemoration of birthdays, they added to it a custom borrowed from the Persians, that of baking a sweet cake. The worshipers of the moon goddess, Artemis, celebrated her birthday with a giant candle-covered cake, since candles were a symbol of moonlight. In the thirteenth century Germans began the tradition of Kinderfest in which a birthday cake and candles were used to greet a child upon awakening. The custom of blowing out the candles and making a wish also originated with this German Kinderfest.

25

Birthday of George Bernard Shaw, famous English playwright, in 1856. His birthday is an occasion to go out and start making "circumstances." Shaw said, "People are always blaming their circumstances for what they are. I don't believe in circumstances. The people who get on in this world are the people who get up and look for circumstances they want, and, if they can't find them, make them!"

26

The Birthday of the Birthday, 3001 B.C. Originally, only the birth dates of Egyptian pharaohs were celebrated, then of male nobility, but never of women, except for queens. The Romans in 44 B.C. made the birth dates of important statesmen into national holidays. Early Christianity did away with the celebration of birthdays and commemorated only the death days of

27

saints. The celebration of the birth of Christ, when proposed in 245, was denounced as a ''pagan'' and sacrilegious idea. But by the fourth century, its presence as a holiday restored the custom of remembering birthdays. By the twelfth century the birthdays of men, women and children were all being recorded and celebrated.

BIRTHDAYS: A BLESSING OR A BLIGHT?

Birthdays are greeted with a mixture of emotions, ranging from joy and anticipation to denial and dread. When we were children, we thought of them as exciting celebrations in which we were the center of attention. But as we grow older, enthusiasm can easily turn into embarrassment when the top of the birthday cake begins to look like a forest fire! Some see birthdays as dark reminders that they have lost another year of their precious youth and are a year closer to death.

But blessed birthdays are birth-days, occasions of re-birth. At a blessed birthday celebration, it is the guest of honor who must do the work. At birthday parties of those who are pilgrims of the Way, the guest of honor must ''labor,'' as does a woman in childbirth. Each Birth-Day becomes a Labor Day, a festival of re-birthing the sleeping child within.

Christmas and birthdays are most enjoyed by children. But regardless of our age, if we can make our birthdays into true birth-days, then they can become occasions of great joy. They also become opportunities to awaken a ''beginner's mind,'' the mind of a child, eager to learn new things. A beginner's mind is full of questions like, ''What if? What would happen if I tried it this way?''

A birthday party is like a New Year's Eve party. It's an occasion to throw off our old ways, our ''graduate's minds,'' so that we can again become students of life. A birthday celebration is not just a commemoration of a past event or another notch on the staff of life; it is a challenge to be created anew.

Even the custom of the birthday cake decorated with candles can hold new symbolism for us. If birthdays were actually signs of losing another year of life, then it would make sense for the cake at our first birthday party to have seventy or eighty candles blazing away on it. Then with each passing year it would have one less candle. But if birthdays are understood not as a blight but as a blessing, then we can again see birthday celebrations as life celebrations which proclaim that we have grown another year's worth in wisdom and holiness. Each candle would then be a sign that we had become more luminous, more a reflection of the Light of Lights.

And for those who fear growing old, who fear the ultimate knock of death on the door, there's another tradition at our annual birth-day party which holds a secret of good news. At every birthday celebration, the party doesn't really begin until all the candles are blown out!

28 **Birthday of the Singing Telegram**, 1933. The singing telegram is almost extinct today—as is singing itself! Regardless of what kind of voice you have or if you can carry a tune, sing to yourself today. Do your part not to let this very human activity disappear simply because you fear that people might think you're crazy if you walk down the street singing. Nor should you let modern media do all your singing for you!

Birthday of "Happy Birthday to You," a song that almost everyone knows by heart. Composed by Mildred Hill, the music first appeared in an 1893 book, *Song Stories of Kindergarten*, under the title, "Good Morning to All." The original lyrics were written by Mildred's sister Patty who was a school teacher. The words of the song were intended to be the teacher's morning greeting to the students. Robert Coleman changed the words to the present birthday theme, without first receiving permission, for his song book which was published nearly thirty years after the original, on March 4, 1924.

29

Birthday of Henry Ford in Dearborn, Michigan on this date in 1863. Known for his development of the assembly line in the production of automobiles, Ford once said, "History is bunk!" Considering the fact that history is only written by the victors, there may be truth to Ford's sentiment.

30

First U.S. Patent Issued on this day in 1790 by George Washington and Thomas Jefferson to Samuel Hopkins. By the mid-1880's a bill was proposed in the Congress to close the Patent Office; it was believed to be a waste of the taxpayers money, since everything that could be a reality had already been invented! Does part of us share that sentiment? If so, that part of us will be amazed at the marvelous surprises that await us as we move into the twenty-first century.

31

August

1 **Ancient Druid Festival of the Motherhood of the Earth**. Have a picnic feast today, sitting on her fertile lap, or go for a walk across her lovely body. Appreciate, today, your communion with all the children of the earth—and all of creation.

THE WEB OF LIFE

Chief Seattle of the Duwamish tribe of the Oregon Territory very beautifully spoke of the mystery of life and of communion: "All things are connected. Whatever befalls the earth befalls the children of the earth. We did not weave the web of life, we are merely strands in it. Whatever we do to the web, we do to ourselves."

All of creation—women, men, plants, animals and all the earth—is intertwined and interdependent as are the numerous strands of a spider's web. Not only is all of creation connected, it is in communion. Since God created it and shares the divine life with it, that web is holy. To live in an awareness of that communion is to believe in these words of St. Paul: "As the human body which has many parts is a unity, and those parts, despite their multiplicity, constitute one single body, so it is with Christ. God has harmonized the whole body...that the body should work together as a whole with all the members in a sympathetic relationship with one another" (1 Cor. 12: 24-26).

Holy Communion is not simply a religious ritual, it is a way of life that expresses a belief in the holiness of the body, the entire body of Christ. The ancient ritual of going to Holy Communion not only places us at the very heart of the web, it is meant to lead to a life lived in communion with all the various strands of the web of life.

Jesus also spoke of this central mystery of our interdependence with one another and with him, of the mystery of our intercommunion: "I am the vine and you are the branches. Abide in me, as I do in you. As the branch cannot bear fruit of itself unless it remains on the vine, so neither can you unless you abide in me" (Jn. 15: 4-5). The branches of the vine, the strands of the spider's web and the interconnection of the various parts of the human body all speak of the same divine truth.

As followers of Christ we are to "love our enemies" (Mt. 5: 44), for even our enemies are part of the web. If we hate anyone, then we ultimately hate ourselves and even God. Holy Communion is not simply oneness with the good and the beautiful, it is also harmony between the rich and the poor, friends and enemies, sick and healthy, old and young—for all peoples are part of the web of life.

Our communion with God must also extend to all of life. Sky and earth, oceans and flowers, birds and animals, the planets and stars are all parts of the holy web. As we struggle with the problems of our pollution of the earth, of its water and air, we begin to see more clearly the mystery of which Chief Seattle, Paul and Jesus spoke: that whatever we do to the web of life, we do to ourselves.

St. Paul was concerned about the proper preparation of those who were about to receive Holy Communion. "One must test oneself before eating one's share of the bread and drinking from the cup. For they who eat and drink, eat and drink judgment on themselves if they do not discern the Body" (1 Cor. 12: 28-29). To discern the Body is to recognize Christ throughout the web of life. A reverence for the Body of Christ in Holy Communion must include a reverence for the various strands of the web of life, a reverence for earth, rivers, trees and the air that we and all the rest of creation breathe. That communion may be as simple as sitting by a potted plant on a window sill, reverencing the earth we walk on, the clouds that float overhead or the trees we pass on our walk. We prepare for Holy Communion each time we are in communion with the rain or snow as well as with the poor or imprisoned.

We also prepare to go to Holy Communion by taking time to be in communion within ourselves. As we take time to pray, being alone to listen to our needs and inner struggles, our awareness expands to embrace the struggles of all the members of Christ's body.

We test our state of preparation by our ability to see God in the children and the aged, in people who are like us and those who are very different. When we reverence the presence of the holy in the suffering, the sick and dying as well as in the members of our own families, then we live in Christ and experience the fullness of life itself. For Jesus said that all who abide in him would bear much fruit, and that fruit is indeed life!

Feast of Cosmic Communion. According to one of the tenets of Zen, "The self and the rest of the universe are not separate entities but one functioning whole." A day to celebrate the web-unity of all that exists, and yourself as part of that wondrous web.

2

New Worlds Day. On this day in 1492, thirty minutes before sunrise, Columbus sets sail from Palos, Spain with three ships. An ideal day to start off on an adventure, prepared not merely to find what you are looking for, but something better. Open yourself to the possibility of fresh new worlds.

3

---

4 **United Americas Day**. Today in 2076 the countries of Canada, the United States, Mexico and Central America form a new nation, the "United Americas." The capital city of the new multi-national union is centrally located, half on the U.S.A. side of the old border and half on the Mexican side. Likewise the new nation is trilingual, Spanish and English and French. Back in 1989, over 60% of Americans were already in favor of Canada and the United States becoming a single nation!

5 **Federal Income Tax Birthday**. On this day in 1861, Abraham Lincoln signed into law a temporary emergency war-time measure, imposing a 3% tax on all incomes over $800. The law was rescinded in 1872 only to resurrect soon thereafter. Spend a little time today reflecting on our responsibility to support our republic with money. And as you ride down the freeway, for example, take pride that your financial resources helped build that road.

SUNDAY POCKETS

August 5 is the birthday of the Federal Income Tax, when Abraham Lincoln signed into law an emergency Civil War measure. While it is doubtful that anyone will hold a party to celebrate the paying of taxes, it is an opportunity to reflect on what we take to church each Sunday.

As a child, I put two things in my pocket when I went to church every Sunday. One was my rosary, and the other was my Sunday collection envelope. The rosary was said before Mass began or sometimes during Mass, and my children's donation envelope was placed in the basket. As I grew a bit older, I also took my English Missal, since the Mass in those olden days was still said in Latin. Today, of those traditional church companions, we usually carry only the collection envelope. It's a religious version of the 1861 Federal Income Tax; it's our Church Tax. For some of us that "tax" is the prescribed 10%, a tithe of our income.

But we need to take along more of the secular world than a token gift of money. Before we leave home for church we should stuff our pockets with everything of the past week that we can get into them. This may sound like an unusual idea for those of us who think that when we enter the sacred space of worship we should leave behind the secular world. Instead of bringing our whole world to the altar, we usually try to separate ourselves from our business affairs and daily concerns.

Most religion tends to cause a division of the world, and time, into two zones: sacred and secular. But the Christian Eucharistic Liturgy is intended to awaken us to the sacredness of the world. The celebration of the death and resurrection of Jesus Christ should heal the divorce in that unity of all life which God originally designed. If we are to see our world as we proclaim it each time we begin the Great Prayer of Thanksgiving, "Holy, Holy, Holy are you, our God...Heaven and earth are filled with your glory," we need to bring our world, all of it, into our Eucharistic worship.

Then at the offertory of the Liturgy you can empty out your pockets and lift up to God **everything** that you have done, said and thought about over the past week. As you lift them up, see these seemingly secular activities, from paying your taxes to taking out the trash, as invested with the glory of God.

This Sunday as you prepare to leave for church, hear the voice of your pastor saying, "Don't forget to put your collection envelope in your pocket." Hear too the voice of Christ, "And also don't forget to fill your pockets with your world!"

Feast of the Transfiguration of Christ, a day of the glory to come. This is also a day of mourning and remembrance. For the first atomic bomb was dropped by an American B-29 on this day in 1945. The Japanese city of Hiroshima was destroyed, killing over 105,000 people immediately. Another 100,000 died later from severe radiation and other injuries. Pause today for a moment of silent prayer for those casualties.

6

First Photograph of Planet Earth taken from space on this day in 1959 by U.S. Explorer VI. The recent photo of Earth taken by NASA is a sacred icon filled with beauty and mystic meanings. Take time today to ponder its lack of division lines that separate nations as you pray for the unity of all the peoples of our planet. And take some definite steps today to establish a base for the kind of communication that makes for true communion.

7

THE DOG DAYS

August settles in upon us, and the hot winds of summer sweep across much of the northern hemisphere, leaving us to search for a cool spot. Here, for your refreshment and reflection, is a cool parable.

There was a business man who had a serious problem. Even though he had received good reports from his plant manager, showing the lowest manufacturing price in the history of his product, the firm was showing no profit. And so he decided to spend a good deal of money to hire a top-rated business consultant. The consultant arrived and did a careful study of the firm. His report to the president of the company was stated very simply: "Your salesmen are unable to sell your product because it has too small a market!"

"What? That's impossible!" replied the president. "This is August in the Midwest, and I am the largest manufacturer of air conditioners in this part of the country. How can it be that in the midst of the dog days of summer no one is interested in buying air conditioners?"

The consultant looked surprised and said, "Why are you talking about air conditioners? Your factory is making electric powered Japanese fans!"

The president thereupon summoned the plant manager and angrily demanded, "Why are you making electric powered Japanese fans? We have *always* manufactured air conditioners, with freon cooling units and all the little buttons on the front!"

And the plant manager answered, "Sir, I would be happy to make freon cooling units, but, when I took this job, you said that our business was to make elegant cooling units. You also said that I was to do that the best way I know how. I know of no more elegant and beautiful cooling unit than a Japanese fan. If they are not selling well, I cannot be held responsible. You specifically said that manufacturing is my job and leadership is yours. If you wish me to make freon cooling units, you will have to say so."

This parable is about a general manager who generaled too much and managed too little. And in it is a lesson for each of us. How often problems arise in our lives because we presuppose too much from one another! We leave unsaid many expectations, and when they are not met, we often explode in anger like the president of the company in the parable. And like the president, we all need to take more time to make sure that those with whom we live or work understand our expectations of them. Husbands and wives, parents and children, friends with friends, all easily commit the same mistake.

Managing more and generaling less, our homes and lives will be more peaceful, and the stress and distress of daily life will be greatly reduced. And each time that happens, we move one step closer to peace in the world.

---

8 **Commemoration of St. Marinus** who was an old man when scourged, racked and lacerated under the Emperor Diocletian in 301. After undergoing many torments, he was finally thrown to the wild beasts and became a martyr for Christ. Regardless of your age, pray to St. Marinus for the holy endurance you need to come to an understanding with others that produces peace, especially when you are on the edge of exploding with anger.

---

9 **Second Atomic Bomb Dropped** in 1945 on the Japanese city of Nagasaki. Half of the city was destroyed and over 70,000 were killed. A day to send forth prayerful energy around the world that nuclear weapons will **never** be used again for any reason.

VATICAN CITY DESTROYED BY A NUCLEAR BOMB

AP News release: Today at noon, a small nuclear device exploded, completely destroying Vatican City. The entire 108 acres of historic buildings were leveled by a nuclear blast felt throughout most of Italy. Destruction of a lesser degree extended to a five mile radius around the Holy City. The Catholic world is in shock, and the entire world mourns the loss of the largest church in Christianity, St. Peter's. Lost forever are the priceless art treasures of Michelangelo, Raphael, da Vinci and other great artists. The entire population of Vatican City, including the pope and other high officials of the Church, together with thousands of tourists and pilgrims who were present at the time are counted among the dead. So far, no terrorist group has claimed responsibility for the bombing.

This fictional news account gives us a feel for how many Christians would respond to the destruction of the ancient center of our faith. It would be a devastating loss. To consider such an event also gives us a partial insight into the effect of the loss of the great temple in Jerusalem and the leveling to the ground of that city by the Roman army in 70 A.D. It must have been a crushing blow to all Jews and to the young Jesus-sect of Judaism, for the temple was at the heart of their faith and worship.

We find the reaction of those early Christian communities to the destruction of the temple in letters written after 70 A.D. With the physical structure gone, they began to understand the words of Jesus about his body being the temple. And being one with him, they recognized that they were part of his body. In the epistle to the Ephesians we find the passage: "You form a building which rises on the foundation of the apostles and prophets, with Christ as the capstone. Through Christ the whole structure is fitted together and takes shape as the holy temple in God; in Christ you are being built into this temple, to become a dwelling place for God" (Eph. 2: 20-21). And in the second letter of St. Peter: "You too are living stones, built as an edifice of the Spirit, into a holy priesthood" (1 Pt. 2: 5).

The destruction of the temple created a crossroads crisis. Without the temple, the Jewish priesthood lacked a place for sacrifice and so disappeared. Now there was a need for a different kind of priesthood among the early Jewish-Christians. Today's historical crisis of an ever expanding number of Christians along with an even more rapidly decreasing number of ordained clergy among some denominations calls for a similarly creative response from lay people. Today, as never before, everyone must take on the vocation of being "living stones" in the Church. We all must begin to exercise our baptismal priesthood.

Those early disciples of Jesus made their homes into what the great temple had been—a place of prayer and sacrifice. We must do the same. It is time for us also to acknowledge our priesthood in Christ, shared by all who are one in Christ. Today's crisis, like the destruction of the temple over 1900 years ago, should call forth from us a new sense of personal responsibility within the Church.

And if we are to be more than "dead stones," we will have to grow in prayer and holiness. This challenge is at the very heart of lay ministry; it must be embraced by all who wish to be a vital part of the Church and to serve in any of her variety of ministries. Yet consider what would happen if only 10% of those who form the Church were to strive to become "living stones," alive in Christ. Such a hunger for holiness would result in historians recording this as an age of saints unlike any the Church has seen in all her twenty centuries.

Feast Day of Deacons. Today is the Feast of St. Lawrence, a Roman martyr in 258. According to legend, the archdeacon Lawrence refused to surrender money that had been entrusted to him to distribute among the poor. As a consequence he was broiled alive on a grill. May St. Lawrence, call you to share some of your goods with those who are in need.

10

Annual Medical Check-Up Day. Visit your doctor today for your annual medical examination. Good prevention is good medicine. But as you do this, be mindful that there is one doctor for every 520 Americans. In Guatemala, however, the ratio is one doctor for every 8,600 and in the African country

11

of Chad, one doctor for every 47,530! Reflect prayerfully today and do not hesitate to do something, however small, to correct this imbalance between Western nations and the Third World.

THE PEARLY GATE MORGUES

In heaven, each morning at sunrise is an Easter. The bodies of those who die on earth arrive in the night and are placed in giant morgues outside the Pearly Gates to await the sunrise. Accompanied by Archangel Michael who carries files and personal data on each of the dead, God visits the morgues one by one.

Opening the door to the first large morgue one early morning, Michael said, "These are the bodies of those who died as small infants. The number stays steady at about 40,000 a day—fifteen million a year."

"And the cause of death?" asked God.

"For 96% of them it's a lack of food and medical care," answered Michael.

God picked up a dead child and rocked it like a sorrowful mother. "I don't understand," wept God.

"Oh, there's an abundance of both food and medicine on earth, but there's a problem of distribution," said Michael.

God gently placed the child back on the slab. Heaving a great sigh, God moved the divine hands over the dead infants. "Let there be Light!" God exclaimed. And suddenly the large building exploded with laughter and vitality.

God and Michael then moved to the next large morgue. It was filled with thousands upon thousands of skinny, deformed, diseased bodies. "And these?" asked God.

"These, Divine One, are victims of starvation, contaminated water and lack of medical care."

"How is that possible?" asked God. "I gave the people of earth all they need to provide food and care for all my children."

"Again, the problem is one of distribution," answered Michael, flipping open his file. "These dead are from Burundi in Africa where they have only one doctor for every 45,000 people. And these are from Somalia, Guinea and Angola, where the life expectancy is only about 38 to 40 years."

"And what is it in America?" asked God.

"The life expectancy is...let's see...about 76 years. But, of course, America has one doctor for every 520 persons. It's the same problem—distribution!"

Like a father viewing the dead body of his only son, God sobbed in agony. Then, drying the tears, God made a sign over the dead, saying, "Let there be Light!" And the morgue instantly transformed into a great festival hall of joy and dancing.

As they walked to the next large morgue, Michael pointed down to earth. "Look, O God, your children are praising you!" God and Michael looked down upon a group of thousands with upraised hands, singing the praises of God. They were led by a preacher wearing a three-piece suit and a gold Rolex watch who had just completed a hell-fire sermon condemning X-rated films, dancing and the sins of the flesh. In another place they saw a white frame church in which people were clutching their bibles and singing of how pure and prayerful are the friends of Jesus. And then there was an ornate cathedral with giant golden candlesticks, silk vestments and clouds of incense rising above gem-encrusted vessels and a massive organ thundering out the music of Bach. God watched for a moment and then said, "It's a mirage, Michael, only a mirage. Pay no attention to it—I don't."

They then entered the final large morguc. It was filled with bodies of the well-dressed and well-fed dead. They hardly looked dead, but only seemed to be asleep. "And these?" asked God.

"These, O God, are the dead who arrived last night from America and Western Europe." God stood stone still, expressionless; then turned and went to the door. Michael asked, "Divine One, your blessing?" But God only turned and stared into the sunrise and then began to walk away. "But God, you are Love without end. You are Mercy itself!"

"Yes, I know," said God. "While my love is endless, I have a problem— what did you call it? Ah, yes, I have a 'problem of distribution!' No, Michael, leave them dead. Store them away in the warehouse with the others."

Feast of St. Clare who died in 1253. She was the first person to practice the total poverty of St. Francis of Assisi. She found her treasure in the simplicity of nature. May we, on this her feast day, follow her example and find our delight in the simple things of life and in our love for God.

12

Festival of Eyeglasses. Celebrate, on this feast, that wonderful day in 1287 when eyeglasses were first introduced. As age weakens the muscles of our eyes, what a fuzzy world we would live in without spectacles. Also salute A.E. Fick, a Swiss doctor who in 1877 made the first contact lenses. A good day as well to pray for improved vision of the beauties of creation and for a compassionate beholding of the suffering in the world.

13

Birthday of the Social Security Act. On this date in 1935 an act of Congress insured a minimum financial security for retired persons. As well as economic stability in your older years, take care of your senior tomorrows by throwing a brick through your TV set (figuratively, of course) and spending half an hour a day doing some kind of creative activity. This is the best security for a happy and wholesome retirement. (See the **Birth of the Spiritual Security Act**, April 16.)

14

Feast of the Assumption of Mary, the Mother of God. A harvest festival in many parts of the world. An occasion to celebrate the harvest of fruits and vegetables by eating them with prayerful delight and gratitude—as we celebrate the "harvest" of Mary into heaven.

15

COMMUNION ON THE RUN

In the middle of August each year we celebrate a feast in honor of Mary, the Mother of God, and her Assumption into heaven. The feast of the Assumption is a harvest feast, a summertime Thanksgiving. It gives us an opportunity to reflect on how we can express our gratitude for the gifts of life in this season by how truly we savor them.

There is a story about Rabbi Bunam of Pzhzha, a saintly man of prayer, who was once attending a formal dinner. The guests at the table were involved in a lively discussion of politics. After a time the old rabbi spoke up, "As it is written in Psalm 33, 'Taste and see that God is good.' What are you tasting in your bread at this dinner? Only the devout who have purified their taste buds by prayer are able to taste bread as God created it. They taste and see that God is good." The dinner guests all became very silent, aware that they had overlooked the essence of the meal.

We can reflect at this season of the harvest of the fruits of the earth about how easily we neglect to truly taste our food, all of which is an opportunity for communion with God. Instead, we often let interesting table conversation or words of disagreement distract us from the gift of what we are eating. At other times we taste TV programs or the evening newspaper and just swallow our bread without savoring it. Would that each of us could be fully aware when we eat our food. If we were, we might come to know the full meaning of that sentence from Psalm 33: "Taste and see that God is good."

Would, also, that our time of communion at the Eucharistic Liturgy allowed for a true tasting of Christ! It sometimes seems that those who come to the Table move through as quickly as people in a ticket line. Would that time could be created for a reverential reception of Holy Communion. Then those who come forward to receive the Bread of Life might be able to taste and see that, indeed, God is sweet. In both liturgy and life, we need to take time to truly taste our bread.

16 **Fast Food** *or* **Bistro Festival**. In 1815 France was occupied by the armies of England, Austria and Russia. The name for wine shops and small restaurants in French, "Bistro," comes from the frequently used word of Russian soldiers when ordering service, "Bystra!" meaning "quickly!" With our shortage of time, we are fast becoming a Bistro people. Take time today to eat your meals slowly and with delight. Also preserve occasions for breaking bread with family and friends. For if we stop eating together and creating time for that action to be a fully human and shared ritual, our sacred times of dining will soon become extinct.

17 **U.S. Woman Suffrage**. This is the eve of the effective date in 1920 of the 19th Amendment to the U.S. Constitution. It is a day to remember the many struggles in the long process of securing equal rights for women. It is also a day to be aware that we are still on the "eve" of women standing on truly equal ground economically and politically.

18 **Birthday of Virginia Dare**. On this date in 1587, Ananias and Ellinor Dare gave birth to the first child born of English parents in America. Reflect, today, that every birth, including yours, is special and historical. The birth of each person marks the appearance of a unique Word of God made flesh. There is no such thing as a "common" person.

THE NAZARETH SYNDROME

The Gospels tell us that Jesus did not work miracles in his own home town. The reason was that his relatives and neighbors did not believe in him. Jesus himself said that a prophet is not without honor except in his native place. It's a situation which we might call the Nazareth Syndrome.

It's strange that the citizens of Nazareth failed to see in their carpenter anything divine. We could ask, "Didn't they see his halo? Didn't they experience his gentle yet transforming care, his great love, his profound wisdom or the force of his prayerfulness? The townsfolk of Nazareth come under constant attack because of their blindness. How could they have missed someone so extraordinary, so divine?" The reason is easy to understand if we see how the Nazareth Syndrome operates.

For Jesus' neighbors, the extraordinary was extraordinary and the commonplace was commonplace. Jesus, the carpenter who lived down the street, was common. Because he was common—just one of the folks—he couldn't be special, he couldn't be the Messiah—and he couldn't have a halo.

But where do halos come from? Halos are rings of golden light that we tend to selectively put around holy people and things. We invest the sacred with special importance; we set it aside, and then we believe in it. Graced with our self-imposed halo, we have "faith" in it, and as a result sometimes miracles flow from it. Since we are always in search of what is special, we tend to bypass the daily marvels of our lives. What if **all** of creation were sacred? Could we paint a halo around the whole earth?

Many years ago, while on a pilgrimage to the East, I had the privilege to journey into the Sinai Desert. I had gone there to climb Mt. Sinai, the mountain where Moses met God face to face. Having spent the night at a monastery halfway up the mountain, the other pilgrims and I were awakened at three in the morning so that we could climb to the top of the mountain in time for the sunrise. I can remember how special, how "sacred," was that sunrise. I was rapt in wonder as the sunrise spread out across the mountains and desert of the Sinai. It was one of the most holy experiences of my pilgrimage. But isn't the sunrise over Syracuse or Cincinnati just as holy as the sunrise over Mt. Sinai? Yet how often do we get up before dawn and walk to the top of the nearest hill to sit in prayerfulness and watch the sun rise.

If we are to "pray always," it will be necessary to take up our brushes and gold paint and go about our lives making halos! We should try to see a halo around the stranger at the door, our marriage partner, our children or parents. Try it and see the marvelous and miraculous difference it makes in your life. God has not created a world of walls where the sacred and ordinary are nicely separated. Rather, God has invested the wonder of the divine presence into all of creation. God is indeed among us.

Without such a special halo-making kit, however, we will find it difficult to pray always. And without such a special vision of what is common-yet-sacred, the Nazareth Syndrome will prevent our lives from overflowing with miracles.

19 **Solar Wonder Day**. Pause today in wonder that our star, the sun, emits more energy in one second than humanity has consumed in all of history! That one second is thirteen million times the annual mean consumption of energy in the U.S. The vastness of the power of even one small star among the two hundred billion in our galaxy provides a storehouse of prayerful wonder. Let the brightness of the sunshine enlighten you today to the sacred miracle of life spread out through all creation.

20 **Summer Cool-Off Day**. In 1630 in Paris, one of the classic drinks of summer, lemonade, was created. May delighting in this wonderful way to cool off be an opportunity to toast all cool summer drinks, and all ways to beat the summer heat.

21 **Garrett Morgan Day**. In 1923 Garrett Morgan invented the automatic traffic light. Celebrate Garrett Morgan Day by falling in love with his yellow light. A day to slow down before you stop or complete a task. Take "yellow" or caution time today to slow down the merry-go-round of your life.

GARRETT MORGAN'S GIFT

The first black man to own a car in Cleveland was Garrett Morgan, but he is also known for something more important. In 1923 he invented the automatic traffic light. Even today his invention remains the most successful, efficient and democratic way to handle busy traffic at an intersection. No doubt, each of us at times has cursed Garrett Morgan, even if we didn't know his name! We've been late for an appointment and been forced to stop and wait until the light changed from red to green. But Morgan's invention insures that each person has a proper turn at the right of way regardless of race, creed or bank account. The only exceptions to this are those driving emergency vehicles and funeral processions—we honor the dead by giving them the right of way.

But traffic lights can also be a blessing in the face of the demands of daily life and a wonderful reminder of how life should be lived. Every red light is a prophet if we can see it as such. And meeting a red light is also a good time for a short devotional prayer, like:

O God, I pause because the light is red.
May I, by frequent stops, to peace be led.

If we could see ourselves from outside our culture, we might be surprised at how silly we look as we speed through life. We race from event to event, rushing from home to work and back again, and we speed through many human encounters as well. If we could view our lives honestly, we might call upon the ghost of Garrett Morgan to invent little traffic lights for our homes. They would be protective devices as life-preserving as smoke detectors! Located at the table, in the bedroom and throughout our homes, such automatic traffic lights would first flash yellow as we begin to rush about our homes and start to miss the enjoyment of life. The red light would flash on whenever our rushing about began to endanger our home's environment of love and affection or when we needed to pray. When they flashed red we would have to come to a complete stop. These small domestic traffic lights would be cause for us to do what we all do at every red light: we look around. We look at who is in the cars around us. We look at the houses and lawns and the lush summer trees. In short, we see clearly what otherwise is only a blur as we speed from one commitment to the next.

Our loves and our life's beauties at home are often only blurs to us as well. May the ghost of Garrett Morgan strategically place little automatic traffic lights throughout our lives. May those yellow lights slow us down, and the red ones bring us to a dead stop. If we are lucky, we will make numerous dead stops before we are dead. We will stop to pray, to make love and to drink deeply from the gift of life that God has given us.

The next time you watch a funeral procession pass readily through a red light, ask God for the blessing to stop dead before it's too late to stop.

International Day to Check for Symptoms of a Nervous Breakdown. Bertrand Russell (1872-1970) once said, "One of the symptoms of an approaching nervous breakdown is the belief that one's work is terribly important." Protect your health and your **life**: call in sick today and enjoy some time in the sun.

22

THE LIFEGUARD

Summer and swimming go together like coffee and cream. And whether you are on the beach at Atlantic City or in a swimming pool in Topeka, the one person who is always present is the lifeguard. A frequent summer sound is the lifeguard's whistle, warning swimmers that they are in danger or correcting some behavior in the pool. The function of the lifeguard is simply what the name implies, the guardianship of life.

Water itself is a living symbol of life. Water holds great gifts and potential for us beyond recreation. As we swim and splash around, our most ancient memories are awakened. These primal memories go back to our earliest ancestors emerging dripping wet from oceans and lakes to stand on dry land. Water also symbolically and literally washes away our cares. And touched by the sun and the healing movement of water, we can relax our perpetual defense systems and begin to play. But in that process we can forget to care for that most precious and fragile of all gifts: life! The lifeguard's voice or whistle calls us back to the reality that in water there is also death. Within the essence of water is a twin force that creates life and causes death. The presence of a lifeguard reminds us of that fact of life.

Perhaps we could also use lifeguards at other places in our daily lives. Imagine a lifeguard, sitting on a high white stand, at some busy intersection, watching over people as they crossed the street. Or picture a lifeguard overlooking an assembly line to ensure the safety of the workers. It's not hard to imagine many other life situations that might call for a lifeguard's presence. The next time, for example, that you decide to bypass your prayers or meditation because you are too busy, a whistle would sound. Danger: you are forgetting the wondrous marvel of life, forgetting to respond to that marvel with the gratitude of a prayerful response. This inner lifeguard would warn you, "Caution, friend, a piece of your life is dying. Be careful, you are **too** busy."

The next time you turn down an invitation to go to a party because you have too much work to do, the inner lifeguard's whistle would blow to warn you, "Be careful, friend, the water is getting too deep. Remember that the ancient Jews believed that water was a sign of chaos. When you are not free to enjoy life, your life is becoming chaotic. Move to a place where more humane patterns are possible."

The next time you are in a huge department store and you begin to buy something that will put you in debt for months to come, you would hear the whistle and the warning, "Be cautious, friend, as you acquire this desired object. You will also lose the ability to buy a new dress, have an evening out on the town or give a gift to someone in need. Do you really have to have this thing? Is it a possession worth all the other possibilities for life that you will give up because you went into debt to buy it? Loan offices, like deep water, are places where you can lose your life."

When you are being honored for some achievement and the crowd is applauding, the whistle of the inner lifeguard would go off: "Well, friend, was it really worth it? Was it worth all the time you had to spend to achieve this honor, time that you could have spent with your children, family and friends or engaged in activities you really enjoy? What about those experiences that didn't happen because you simply didn't have time for them? Be careful, you've lost some life already, and you are in danger of losing more." The next time you are busy labeling parts of your life as important and others as unimportant, the inner lifeguard's whistle would sound in the background, cautioning you, "How accurately, friend, can you judge what is of value and what is not? Be careful about placing yourself in the deadly position of focusing your energies on 'matters of grave importance' and forgetting about the little things of life, little things like healthy eating and sleeping, having fun, fishing, visiting with neighbors or simply sitting and appreciating a summer sunset?" We risk our life whenever we use the wrong scale of values. But the inner lifeguard's whistle would blow to warn us that most of the things we think important are not really so central to life, and the things we often think of as unimportant are among the truly valuable things of life. Happy are they who are attuned to hear that whistle.

23 **Contraceptives Introduced** in Egypt in 2032 B.C. Birth control was a-chieved by inserting a mixture of crocodile dung and honey into the vagina. The acidity of the dung altered the pH environment necessary for conception. Since then, men and women, for a multitude of reasons, have developed and chosen to use a variety of contraceptives. Take time today to reflect on the world's oldest contraceptive, the expression, "I can't." This and other statements of the inner critic, such as, "It can't be done, you've tried it before," are mixtures of honey and dung that limit life and prevent the birth of creative deeds.

WHOSE VOICE IS IT?

We have within us a lifeguard far more effective than any you might find at the beach or pool, and its name is conscience. Our silent inner voice of the spirit is responsible for guarding our precious gift of life. That voice is formed by many influences, including our parents, society and religious beliefs. But for the voice of our inner lifeguard to ring true, it must come from deep within. And that's where the practice of daily meditation or the prayer of centering comes in. As we find the center of our being, we begin to see clearly those things that are harmful to the quality of life. Such an insight comes from being close to the divine ground of our being. The Kingdom of God is within and when we approach the very core of our being, we can experience not only the presence of God but the wisdom of God as well.

But the voice of the lifeguard that dwells in the shrine of the heart needs to be distinguished from the voice of our inner critic. The inner critic is not the same as our conscience. Instead of originating from our center, it is merely a combination of parental figures and social pressures. The inner critic judges our behavior as good or bad not to guard life but rather to protect reputation. Such a voice warns, "Don't wear that dress, it looks too young for you. If you don't go to the gathering, people will talk. If you fail once more, no one will like you." The intent of the lifeguard, on the other hand, is not to box in behavior according to what is "proper," but rather to keep us free to respond to Life. It warns us when our deeds begin to close us off from the possibility of loving God or others with a full heart. The inner critic has its office in our head while the lifeguard resides in our heart. We should attempt to tune out the inner critic while attending to the lifeguard. For the lifeguard is so finely tuned to the Spirit that it is alert to those things that outwardly appear as good but inwardly are only destructive to a true enjoyment of life.

When we are attuned to our inner lifeguard, we can swim safely and freely in the waters of life. Perhaps the best way to keep one ear open and sensitive to the inner lifeguard is through regular prayer. If we pray daily, we can truly play in the world. It is not "saying prayers" but the quiet prayer of stillness that provides this freedom to playfully enjoy life. And this freedom comes because in stillness we can let go of fear. As St. John told us, "Perfect love casts out fear" (1 Jn. 5: 18). By daily spending time sitting with Perfect Love, we will find that we are able to approach life with trust rather than out of fear. And trusting in the ever-vigilant watchfulness of our inner lifeguard, we once again become children of our Primal Mother, the earth and the sea, and our Heavenly Father.

Commemoration of the Three Hundred Holy Martyrs who received their victory crown during the reign of Valerian in the year 253. Ordered to offer incense to the god Jupiter, they refused. As a consequence they were thrown into a pit filled with lime and were reduced to dust. As you celebrate this feast day, remember the words of George Bernard Shaw, "The purpose

24

of saints is not to edify us but to shame us." Do something today that requires the courage and conviction that flows from a love of God.

25 **Gas Mask Day**. In 291 B.C. in China, there occurred the first use of poison gas in warfare. Since the gas mask hadn't been invented yet, it must have been equally dangerous for its users. Whenever we release the poisonous gas of discrimination and hatred, we, like the victims, are also poisoned.

26 **Celebration of Toilet Paper**. The Chinese first invented toilet paper in 580 A.D., but it took over a thousand years to reach the West. It was first sold in a roll in 1871. In a relatively short time it has become a necessity in our culture, although it is still considered a luxury item by three-fourths of the world's population. Besides this humble aid to a clean environment, are there any other luxuries in your life that you take for granted?

DOWN-RIVER MENTALITY

Daily, we are told, over twenty-two billion gallons of sewage waste is col-
lected in the United States. That amounts to about one hundred gallons daily
for each one of us! With so much to dispose of, we seek the easiest and
cheapest way to do it. So if there's a river flowing through our town, we
are inclined to dump waste in it. Such an attitude is called "down-river men-
tality." We don't care about those who live down-river from us, we only
want to get rid of our waste as easily as possible.

Jesus spoke of rivers when he said, "From within the one who believes
in me, rivers of living water shall flow" (Jn. 4: 14). The inspired author
tells us that Jesus was referring to the Spirit which he was to give to those
who believe in him. It's an interesting image of the Holy Spirit: a river of
"living waters."

Not all rivers flow with "living" water, as environmentalists or those who
fish in rivers or who live beside them will tell you! Since ancient times people have used rivers as their sewers. In medieval London, people dumped
their waste in the Thames. Monasteries near the river complained that the
stench of the river was stronger than their incense and "caused the death
of many brethren." As late as the mid-1800's the stench of the Thames River,
the great sewer of London, was sufficient to prompt discussion of moving
Parliament from its buildings along the river. Because of the river's foul smell,
the windows of Parliament had not been opened in years!

When you and I fail to keep a careful environmental control over our
thoughts, there flows out of us not a river of living water but a stinking sewer
worse than the Thames. Our speech, actions and presence form a river flowing through the lives of countless people. It is our sacred duty to exercise
control by means of daily prayer.

By daily silent sitting in meditation or prayer of the heart, we keep watch
over the river of our consciousness. By desiring with all our hearts to be
a source of living water, we forbid that river from being the "dump" for
petty, judgmental, vicious, angry thoughts or for negative self-criticism and

personal fears. These and other evil impulses pollute the River of the Spirit that flows through and from each of us.

The first name given to the great Mississippi River by the Spanish explorers was a beautiful one. Ponce de Leon named the river that flows through the heart of our nation "The River of the Holy Spirit." A river as big and power-ful as the Mississippi flows out of us. If that river of life is to be beautiful, fertile and life-giving, then we must monitor daily what goes into our minds and out of our mouths.

This sacred environmental work is never completed; we must "pray always." But once we have acquired the habit of allowing "No Dumping" of any spiritual sewage, it is amazing how much easier and more effortless this lifelong labor of love becomes.

Environmental Restoration Day. In 2189 the world's forests destroyed by fire and acid rain in the late twentieth century are finally restored to their full beauty. Nature takes time to heal herself; be patient too as your nature heals itself from the pollution of thoughtless thoughts and behavior—and do your best to prevent pollution.

27

Birthday of St. Elizabeth Seton in 1774 in New York City. The first American-born saint, she was canonized in 1975. After becoming a widow, she dedicated herself to the care of the poor and teaching young children. She was the founder of the Sisters of Charity and was called the mother of the parochial school system. The world needs more American saints. Do not hesitate to choose that as your lifework. And become your own saint rather than copying the saintliness of others. Be a saint who would look out of place on a pedestal—learn from your mistakes.

28

HIGHER EDUCATION

Today most of us acquire a high school education. Some then go on to study in college. A lesser number continue their studies and receive a master's degree, and a few move beyond that to obtain a doctorate. These latter have the right to place before their names the title "Doctor" as a sign of their achievement and their degree of knowledge.

My father did not go to high school, but the scope of his knowledge and wisdom exceeded that of many persons I know who have advanced degrees. My father was self-taught; it was the kind of ongoing process that should be embraced by everyone. While I studied formally for eight years after high school in my preparation for the priesthood, I have neither a master's nor a doctor's degree from the seminary. But I am well on my way to a doctor's degree from U.M. of which I am very proud. U.M. doesn't stand for the University of Missouri, Mississippi, Massachusetts, Montana, Minnesota or Michigan, but rather for the University of Mistakes.

All over the country at this time of year people are again preparing to begin their studies at various levels of education. As we or our children, grand-children or friends go off to school, it's also time for you and me to go back to the classrooms of "good ole" U. of M. In fact, there's no way we can play hooky from that school. But we *can* sleep through class! We are truant when we try to hide our mistakes or pretend that we don't make them. I find that the mistakes in my life have a habit of repeating themselves. The first time I make a mistake, I learn a valuable lesson. If I make the same mistake, that lesson is more deeply impressed in my mind. There is nothing to be ashamed about for making such errors in daily life. They are part of attending the most famous university in the world, the Self-taught School of Higher Education. The third time, however, is "test time." If I repeat the mistake after two lessons, then I flunk.

Even though the greatest minds, the most creative geniuses, are all alumni or alumnae of U. of M., why is it that most of us attempt to cover up the fact that we are students there? Perhaps it is because when we were beginners in school we were the object of laughter when we made a mistake. The shame that accompanies such experiences is the shadow of our mistakes, often causing us to avoid new activities that are pregnant with the possibility of making another mistake.

Jesus was well aware that life and mistakes go hand in hand. When we make an error that is the result of failing to love ourselves, our neighbors or God correctly, that mistake is called a sin. In the famous prayer that Jesus gave us, he included an important lesson for all who attend the U. of M. "Forgive us our mistakes as we forgive those who make mistakes that cause us pain or shame." Those who are unable to embrace their own errors in life, who hide their mistakes and are unable to forgive themselves, will find it almost impossible to forgive others freely.

As yellow school buses once again travel the country roads and city streets, let us proudly return to our studies at the U. of M. To be middle-aged and still in school is nothing to be ashamed of. I hope that when death's angel comes for me, it will find me still in class at U.M.

29 **Feast of the Beheading of the Prophet, John the Baptist**. After lashing out against King Herod's morals, the Baptizer loses his head for speaking his mind. He is the patron of those who speak out fearlessly against the immoral injustices of our times. A day to reflect on our times of self-protective silence.

30 **First Home TV Reception** in 1930 on this date. Today the average American watches seventeen hours of television a week. While the new electronic window screen has shrunk the world into the space of our living rooms, has it conversely caused the human heart to grow larger in compassion and care for the world?

A YELLOW SIGN OF YOUTH

As summer draws to a close, school opens once again. We are properly reminded to take special notice of those yellow road signs which show an image of a boy and girl carrying books. Those signs mean **Slow Down, School Zone**. Such yellow school signs can also be *life signs* for us. They can remind us not only to reduce the speed of our cars, but also that learning is not just the business of children between the ages of six and eighteen! To be a student is a lifetime vocation for each of us. We attend school for several years not so much to acquire knowledge as to learn how to love to learn—to fall in love with knowledge.

Those yellow school-zone signs should remind us to ask ourselves, "Am I still a student? Am I still a person who enjoys learning new things?" Henry Ford once said, "Anyone who stops learning is old, whether at twenty or eighty. Anyone who keeps learning stays young. The greatest thing in life is to keep your mind young."

Students are recognized, as we see on those school signs, as persons who have a book in hand. While there are many ways to learn, books are often the best teachers. Unlike television, books allow students to pause, ponder and integrate the new knowledge into their mental storehouse. While classroom teachers and television open wonderful possibilities, they usually do not allow us to stop the flow of information in order to reflect upon, or germinate, some novel idea or insight. A book allows us to move at our own personal pace and welcomes reflection.

To have a book frequently in your hands is a very good way to stay young. But we also need the other ingredient expressed in the yellow school signs. Those signs present us with a most needed admonition for the end of the twentieth century: "SLOW DOWN!" All true learning requires leisure. In fact, our English word "school" comes from the Greek word for leisure. The lack of leisure in our society is one of the primary reasons why we are becoming an "old" people. So many of us do not understand that we remain youthful not so much by the use of oils, creams and physical exercise as by continuing to be students all our lives—which in turn requires the cultivation of leisure time.

The homework of our student days should have taught us that our homes should always be our primary schools. New learning leads to new frontiers for our minds and hearts; it is always hard work to extend boundaries and push outward. Doing homework means that we will not become old and stale but will continue to grow and will remain youthful till death.

The next time you see a yellow school-zone sign, slow down for the students, but also remind yourself to ease the pressure in your life, to create the leisure essential for learning. I promise you that if you can do that, you will die a happier, wiser and younger person.

Student-Teacher Day. As schools open their doors across the country, it is a good day to ponder the Hindu proverb, "When the student is ready, the teacher will appear." Regardless of your age, do all that is necessary today to make yourself ready for **the** teacher.

31

September

1

The First American Woman Telephone Operator, Emma M. Nutt, begins her job in Boston in 1878. If you use an operator today when using your telephone, wish her or him a "Happy Emma Nutt Day." And break through to new ground in your work today.

A LABOR DAY SONG

Back in 1932, in the midst of the Great Depression, a song by Jay Gorney and E. Harburg swept America, "Brother, Can You Spare a Dime?" In case you're too young to remember it, here are a few lines from that once popular song:

> They used to tell me I was building a dream.
> When there was earth to plow or guns to bear,
> I was always there, right on the job.
> Why should I be standing in line just waiting for bread.
>
> Once I built a railroad, made it run.
> Made it race against time.
> Once I built a railroad, now it's done.
> Brother, can you spare a dime?

This Labor Day we have an obligation to reflect not only on the dignity of labor but also on our duty to those who helped to make the American Dream come true. It's easy to avoid seeing the millions in our land who once built our cars or made our clothes but today stand in line waiting for bread.

How quickly we blind ourselves to any sense of obligation toward those who, not that long ago, labored for what we enjoy today. How casually we can think, "Well, that's their tough luck" when we see them dressed in the shame of unemployment. "It's everyone for him/herself in this dog-eat-dog world" is the easy response to those who ask, "Brother, can you spare a dime?"

How readily this attitude overlaps all of life, not simply toward those who once worked on an assembly line but also toward those who once worked at another dream, the building up of the Kingdom. Bishops, pastors, directors of religious education and teachers all come and go. When, for various reasons—from old age and retirement to illness or resignation—they move on, do we feel a sense of gratitude for their having labored among us? And because others are always there to take their place, how easily we forget them. Do we take the time to be grateful to them and to God?

An unsung song surrounds these people who labored with such zeal and love in our midst:

> Brother, sister, can you spare the time?
> Once I taught you how to pray.
> I unraveled what the Gospels say.
> I called you to love, come what may,
> to social justice and to the Way.
> And now God sings,
> "Brother, sister, can you spare the time?"

The British Calendar Act, which adopted the Gregorian Calendar correction, went into effect on this day in 1752 in Great Britain and the American colonies. Because of the change, September 2 became September 14. Rioting broke out in the streets as people demanded the twelve days back. This act also made January 1, instead of March 25, New Year's Day. **2**

Birthday of Prudence Crandall on this day in 1803. This American teacher's school was boycotted because she admitted a black girl. A Quaker, she was a pioneer in education for black children. Celebrate this date by determining to be a lifetime student. The best way to stay vital and youthful is to never stop learning. Do not boycott studenthood. **3**

All in the Name Feast. This day in 1871 marks the founding of a city in California, El Pueblo de Nuestra Senora La Reina de Los Angeles de Porcuincula. It is known today simply as Los Angeles. Give your home a colorful name today. **4**

SOPHOMORE SPIRITUALITY

September is the back to school month, and in the names we have given to the different classes of students is hidden a truth about our journey to God. Freshmen are, of course, those who enter high school or college for their first year; it is easy to see how the name originated. This is likewise true with Seniors, who are in their last year, as well as Juniors, who are in the class beneath Seniors. But the remaining class of students, those in their second year of studies, has a name that isn't as easily understood: the Sophomores. The name is a combination of two Greek words meaning "wise fools." No doubt parents and teachers of sophomores will nod in agreement with this definition.

Though it may sound like a joke, we are all called to a Sophomore

Spirituality. Everyone has a spirituality, for spirituality is the lifestyle that flows out of what we believe. It is more than prayer or certain religious exercises, it is an entire way of thinking and acting. If we believe that money is the most important thing in this life, then our daily lives will reflect that belief in countless ways. If we believe in God and in the words of Jesus Christ, then our entire life should express that belief. But why should we as Christians have a sophomore, a "wise fool," spirituality? What is foolish about loving God and living that love out in my daily life? St. Paul says to us, "We are fools for Christ's sake, while you are such sensible Christians" (1 Cor. 4: 10). Paul went on to list the hardships of his life and ministry, telling how he tasted distress and disgrace, how he was cursed and persecuted for his attempt to live out his faith.

Are we sensible Christians or foolish ones? We may appear foolish if we attempt to live out the teachings of Jesus as a lifestyle. We may look foolish if we believe in peace instead of war, if, for example, we promote nuclear disarmament. We will likely be counted as fools if we think that giving money to someone in need is helping Christ. We risk being fools if we waste time daily on prayer, which most of the world believes doesn't change anything. Most will consider us fools if we trust more in God than in our bank accounts or our clever plans for the future. And we will surely appear foolish if we always return kindness for injury or abuse. But in these and any other attempts to live out the Gospel, we will be sophomores, wise fools.

Let us examine our daily lives to see if we are sensible Christians or if, like St. Paul, we are sophomore Christians.

5 **Feast of St. Cassian of Imola**, patron of afflicted teachers. He was a Christian school teacher who refused to sacrifice to the Roman gods. His punishment was to be handed over to his pupils, who stabbed their mentor to death with their iron pens.

6 **Random Target Day**. On September 6, 1901 Leon Czolgosz shot President William McKinley. Originally, Czolgosz did not set out to kill the president; he wanted to shoot a priest. But when he told a friend of his plan, the friend responded, "Why shoot a priest? There are so many priests." Czolgosz chose a more unique target. A day to reflect on how discriminating we are in the "shots" we take at others.

POT SHOTS

With the coming of autumn the sounds of gunfire will soon be heard across the countryside as the hunting season is under way. As every farmer knows, one of the favorite targets for city hunters are his signs that read "No Hunting or Trespassing." These, along with highway road signs and mail boxes, become an easy mark for frustrated hunters. Such easy shots are called "pot shots," since the target doesn't move.

Once upon a time a "pot shot" meant a shot taken by a hunter at some game in disregard for game laws, with only a desire to fill his cooking pot.

It was an easy shot at close range so that the animal didn't have a chance; there was no sport involved, only the intent to get the game. With time, "pot shot" also came to mean a criticism or verbal attack on someone.

Who hasn't been the target of such a pot shot at one time or another? Verbal pot shots are in disregard of the law of love which forbids all such ill-willed behavior. Unkind words only fill the pot of the attacker with a sense of "getting back" at others or "putting them in their place." Often the victims of such pot shots are indeed easy game, for they are not expecting an unkind remark or the cutting humor of the offending person. Sometimes the victims will simply fall silent with inner pain. More often, however, they will take a pot shot back—and then the feuding begins!

As we consider the marks of pot shots in the farmers' "No Hunting or Trespassing" signs, perhaps we can find another solution to our own common household sport. In the Lord's Prayer we pray, "...forgive us our trespasses as we forgive those who trespass against us." Those who tramp across the land of our hearts with their unkind words, disregarding our feelings, are indeed trespassers. Those who invade our personal affairs with questions about matters that are none of their business are also trespassers. But perhaps instead of responding with anger, we could graciously forgive them.

The next time you are the target of a painful pot shot or find someone trespassing in the terrain of your heart, try giving them absolution. You might invisibly trace the sign of the cross and inwardly say, as a priest says in the confessional, "I absolve you in the name of the Father, the Son and the Holy Spirit." This act of forgiveness can, of course, leave you vulnerable to another easy shot, but it can also have a surprisingly disarming effect on the other. It often also takes several absolutions before we have truly forgiven and forgotten an injury. But it is important not to abandon the forgiving action, even at times when it seems difficult. The better the pot shot, the deeper the wound, and the greater the struggle with our pride to forgive the injury. But it is also at such times that great grace is available to help our forgiveness to hit the target—and for a little more peace to come into the world.

Celebration of the Ancient Persian Prophet Zoroaster who lived around 600 B.C. Zoroaster proclaimed a religion that worshiped one God, whom he called Ahura Mazda. His teachings are the basis of the Parsi religion in India. Parsi temples are called "fire temples" since a fire is kept burning in each temple as a symbol of the divine fire in the soul of everyone. The Parsis believe that a person who does not love to study is no longer a servant of God. Celebrate this birth of the prophet by dedicating yourself to being a lifelong student.

7

Feast of the Birth of Mary, the Mother of God. This is the traditional day in Europe for bringing the cattle down from the mountains into the pastures. A festival day to conclude the joys of summer and prepare for the delights of Indian summer and autumn.

8

Feast of Saints Dorotheus and Gorgonius, holy martyrs in 290, during the reign of Diocletian. They were lacerated with whips, had the skin torn

9

from their bodies and vinegar and salt poured over them. They were then burned on a gridiron and finally strangled. Choose, today, to endure mild torments for the sake of peace rather than being violent or vengeful. It's a holy call to become a martyr for peace in the world.

10 **Festival of Ludwig Roselius** who discovered decaffeinated coffee in 1900. His father had been a coffee taster, and Roselius believed that his father's early death was caused by caffeine. Today, all decaffeinated coffee drinkers should toast Ludwig Roselius.

11 **Gift to Christian Lips Day**. In 1058 coffee was first brewed by Moslem Arabs. When it finally reached Europe in the late sixteenth century, the Italian clergy opposed the use of the new beverage because it was "the drink of the Infidels." Also, the orthodox clergy banned coffee as an intoxicating drink. But Pope Clement VIII tasted it and proclaimed, "Fit for Christian lips!"

GOD BLESS CLEMENT VIII

The next time you have a cup of coffee, you might raise it up in a toast: "God bless good Pope Clement VIII!" Why such a toast? Well, if it had not been for Clement, we might not be enjoying that wondrous dark beverage which awakens us in the morning and is the perfect conclusion to a good dinner.

Coffee originated in Ethiopia in a province called Kaffa, from which comes its name. It is a gift to the world from the Arabs, who first made it into a beverage in the eleventh century. It was used as a religious drink to keep worshipers awake during long Islamic prayer vigils. When coffee appeared in Europe in the sixteenth century, it was pronounced "the devil's drink," since it came from a pagan pot. Many clergy and "good Christians" loudly opposed the use of coffee on the grounds that it was the beverage of infidels. But good Pope Clement tasted it and pronounced, "Ah, fit for Christian lips!" Thank goodness that Clement was a "catholic," that his vision and his taste buds were global. Of course he was only a good son of Holy Mother Church, who over the centuries has not hesitated to take pagan practices and baptize them for her own use.

The Church borrowed freely from the pagan religions of Greece and Rome, just as her mother, Israel, appropriated practices from her neighbors, such as the rituals of circumcision and the slaughter of the Passover lamb (the ritual slaughter of a lamb at springtime). The early Christian communities came from a Jewish background which strictly prohibited any images or statues, yet the Church borrowed and "baptized" the use of them from the pagan religions of Greece and Rome.

Church bells are also a borrowed pagan practice. They were used to call worshipers to the temples of the gods and goddesses. Prayer beads were part of Buddhist tradition a thousand years before they appeared in the hands of Christians. The organ, which became **the** sound of Christian worship, was once a pagan instrument. Even the name "Easter" for the feast of the Resurrection is taken from the ancient Teutonic festival of spring called "Eostre." From coffee to Christmas trees, a long list of our religious practices and the dates of our feasts are baptized former pagan customs. The Church has always looked to see if a thing was good and useful in providing a way to God; only secondly did she look at its origins.

Today, that process of wholesome incorporation continues, as Christians have adopted such Eastern religious practices as yoga and meditation and have glimpsed "the ray of divine truth" in the words of the saints of other religions. The Second Vatican Council, in fact, has called upon Christians not only to respect but to preserve, protect and promote all that is true and holy in non-Christian religions.

Let us learn a lesson from our Mother the Church. In all things let us have a catholic, a global, attitude. Let us, like good Pope Clement VIII, be open in our personal lives to any spiritual truth or practice that might aid us in our journey to God and in our expansion of life. As Deng Xiaoping is fond of saying in regard to China's use of capitalistic ideas, "A cat of any color is good if it catches mice!"

Respect for the Spiritual Tradition of Others Day. An old Hindu prayer says, "All different streams having different sources and wanderings, crooked or straight, all reach the sea. So, Lord, the different paths which people take, guided by their different tendencies, all lead to Thee." A good day also to reflect on how those streams can intersect along the way, serving each other's way Home.

12

THE PARABLE OF THE CLOTHING STORE

Once upon a time, there was a man who was dissatisfied with his clothing store. For several generations his family had shopped at the same store, but even as a teenager he found that nothing offered there seemed to fit him well. The only sizes available were small, medium, large and extra-large. He was not an average size. Is anyone? If he purchased a shirt, it might fit perfectly in the shoulders, but the sleeves would be too short. And there was the problem of style. The store offered only a limited selection of designs from which to choose. While he dreamed of different styles that would fit his personality, the store's unimaginative assortment forced him to dress like everyone else.

His frustration reached such a point that he decided to change clothing stores. Against the strong objections of his family he went to another store. At first he felt out of place walking into a different store, but his years of disappointment outweighed his anxieties. While the style of clothing there delighted him, the new store also offered only regular sizes.

Over the years he went from store to store seeking one that would fit his unique needs, but he found each of them to be basically the same. Finally he decided to reject all stores, concluding that he would only be satisfied by making his own clothes. So he went to the library and obtained books on tailoring; he bought a sewing machine and bolts of cloth and sat down to work.

And work it was, since he had no experience and had to make everything—not simply shirts and pants, but socks, underwear and shoes. It required so much time and energy to make his own clothing that he had room in his life for nothing else. And so, he was once again frustrated. And considering the fact that his homemade clothes were rather crudely designed and put together, he sought another alternative. Reflecting on his dilemma, he chose what seemed a perfect solution: "I shall join a nudist colony!" So, he gave away all his clothing and finally found relief in being free of all garments.

But alas, he wasn't completely happy, for he really enjoyed wearing clothes. And there were those special occasions in his life when he wanted to dress up and celebrate, but he had nothing to wear!

***

Who among us can afford a personal tailor or a religion that fits perfectly? So St. Paul proposes a wardrobe that can fit everyone and every occasion: "Put on the Lord Jesus Christ..." (Rom. 13: 14). "Clothe yourselves with heartfelt mercy, with kindness, humility, meekness and patience" (Col. 3: 12).

13
Am I on the Right Path Day. Which religious way is the right way? Today ponder the Persian prayer, "Whatever road I take joins the highway that leads to Thee." A good day to focus more on the Beloved than on the way to the Beloved.

14
Death of Dante Alighieri on this day in 1321. This deeply spiritual Italian poet hastened the Renaissance and was one of the most influential thinkers of his time. The title of his great epic *The Divine Comedy* is an excellent description of life. Though the path involves its share of trials, woe to those who can't laugh or at least smile today at the humorous aspects of human life.

15
Cross-Fertilization Day. In 2500 B.C. the Aryan people invaded India, bringing their language, which evolved into Sanskrit, and their world-affirming religion. The cross-fertilization with the existing nature religion of the native people of India produced Hinduism. Today, join your prayers to those of the millions who practice that ancient religion and with all those who have benefited from the deeply contemplative spirituality of India.

WITCH OR SAINT?

The story of Saint Joan of Arc becoming the patron saint of France is an unlikely—and inspiring—one. In the fifteenth century, as a teenage girl, she heard "voices" in the midst of her prayers, calling her to lead the armies of France against the English invaders. Her visions and voices also directed her to have Charles VII crowned as King of France. Charles was a weak man who was losing badly at the hands of the English troops. In desperation, he gave to this young teenage girl, who could neither read nor write, full command of the French army. St. Joan, dressed in full soldier's uniform, led the armies of France to stunning victories, using a military genius that both amazed and embarrassed the French and English generals.

After St. Joan had seen Charles crowned as king, she quietly retired to her life as a farm girl, her "voices" now silent. But the king was eager for more victories and coaxed her back again into battle against British troops. In May of 1430 she was captured by the English, who had her tried as a heretic and a witch. The Church court condemned her, and at the age of nineteen she was burned at the stake in the city of Rouen on May 30, 1431. Her ashes were refused Christian burial and were thrown by the English into the Seine River. In 1456, Pope Calixtus III pronounced her innocent of the charges of the ecclesiastical trial that had condemned her as an enemy of God and the Church.

George Bernard Shaw, in his play *St. Joan*, wrote the lines, "Must then Christ perish in torment in every age to save those who have no imagination?" That sin of "no imagination" is not restricted to the fifteenth century or any age. One historian, speaking of our recent war in Vietnam, said that its tragedy was that the leaders of our armed forces and the nation failed to imagine the effect of saturation bombing and other inhuman practices on the Vietnamese people.

Again and again, as Shaw pointed out in his play, Christ is forced to die in torment in every age because of our lack of imagination. Christ suffers in our midst today because we are also unable to imagine a world, a society and a church other than those we have known. The verdict of the reverend judges at Joan of Arc's trial was muddied by both political and personal prejudice, which was at least partially responsible for its definite lack of imagination. It is possible for God to call anyone to take heroic and prophetic positions, even a teenager. But we still act as though it is beyond our imagination that God could call women to assume roles of leadership or to do work that only men have performed previously.

St. Joan would make an ideal patroness for the women's movement of our own day. She is an example of those women who seek to respond to the gifts that God has placed within them. But she can also be a patron for anyone, man or woman, who struggles to be faithful to the voices heard in the silence of prayer. St. Joan reminds us that such fidelity may cost us dearly and may even result in our being judged as enemies of Church and State. But she also reminds us that history gives the final verdict. St. Joan of Arc died a witch, a heretic, a disciple of the devil, a destroyer of public morals. But, today, both history and the Church call her a saint.

Death of Tomas de Torquemada on this day in 1498. As the Inquisitor General of Spain, he ordered the burning at the stake of more than 10,000 persons for heresy. The paradox, as true today as it was in earlier centuries, is that all witch hunts and attempts to blot out heresy, in the name of Gospel orthodoxy, are themselves heresy. **16**

Commemoration of the Saintly Rabbi Mordecai of Lekhovitz who died in 1811. Rabbi Mordecai taught that the whole body must pray. He said that one who prays should enter into each word so deeply that it arises from one's very heels upward. He was renowned for his great joy. An excellent day **17**

to make your heels the source of each of your prayers.

BUT I DON'T KNOW HOW TO PRAY

Perhaps one of today's most frequently heard spiritual laments is, "I don't know how to pray." A flood of books, tapes and conferences all address that contemporary problem. While many of us do pray, we feel that somehow we are doing it wrong, that there must be a better way. We often feel that we don't know the right method, that we lack the right prayers or that something prevents our prayers from possessing the quality we'd like in them.

Take heart if that is how you feel, for it's not merely a twentieth century problem. St. Paul himself felt that way, and he shared his problem in a letter to the Christians in the city of Rome: "...for we do not know how to pray as we ought" (Rom. 8: 26). But Paul gave us great cause for hope when he added, "...but the Spirit's very self makes intercession for us with groanings which cannot be expressed in speech." He went on to say that God who searches our hearts understands this mystical language of the Holy Spirit who transforms our aches and pains, our groanings and tears into divine prayerful poetry. The Spirit helps us in our weakness at prayer, so let us not be worried or anxious about "how" to pray.

Anyone who has struggled day after day to meditate and has had to face the fact that it seems impossible to hold the mind on one sacred point should find comfort in those words of St. Paul. Those who lament that their daily prayers seem a waste of time because the cares and problems of their lives pickpocket their morning and evening prayers of peace and contentment should find hope and promise in those few lines from the Epistle to the Romans.

What a gift to anyone who seeks to be a person of prayer is the Good News that the Spirit can take our tears, our groans and sighs and weave them into words that delight the heart of God. At the death of someone close to us, at the bedside of a sick child, after we have accomplished something wonderful or fallen in love, we want to pray but find that there are no words that can express to God the feelings of those sacred moments. Take heart and be glad, for it is at those times of great emotion that the Spirit makes music of great beauty from the deep stirrings of our hearts.

And not only at times of great emotion, but day in and day out, awake and asleep, the Spirit of the Holy is the Perpetual Pray-er within the sacred chapel of each of our hearts. This presence, however, does not excuse us from our efforts to pray and to make our prayers as full of love and devotion as possible. Nor does it grant us a dispensation from daily prayer. Rather, such knowledge should challenge us to pray even more earnestly since we need no longer worry that God finds our prayers to be boring or a numbed collection of distractions and daydreams. In fact, those efforts can not only more fully align us to the Spirit, they allow our prayer to arise from the core, the very ground, of our being, where the Spirit resides. Moreover, because we are in touch with the Spirit, our prayers tend to be lighter, less weighed down by the gravity of our concerns. And since we take ourselves less seriously, our prayers rise more freely to God.

If we believe in these comforting words of St. Paul, then perhaps even when we prepare to enter into personal prayer, we might begin with that liturgical expression, "Let US pray!"

Feast of St. Joseph of Cupertino who died in 1663. This Franciscan priest, when caught up in the ardor of his prayer, would float up to the ceiling of the chapel. His inability to predict and control these times of levitation led to his being placed under house arrest. He then was moved secretly at night from priory to priory. Furthermore, he was forbidden to celebrate Mass in public because of his mystic flights. Humorously, he was made the patron of aviators by Pope Pius XII during World War II. May your prayers today cause you to be free of the gravity of being too serious about your spiritual exercises or about life.

18

Prayer Energy Day. A prayer that is prayed with great devotion or a love-filled thought travels to the person remembered faster than the speed of light. Do not underestimate the power of this form of energy.

19

THE POWER OF PRAYER

Whenever the president of our country moves among a crowd, people reach out to touch him or shake his hand. To touch any famous person is a great honor and something that people remember for life. This is not a new desire, because since the earliest times people have sought to come into contact with "special" people. In the East, it is believed that even if you touch the robe of a holy person you will share in the power and life-giving energy that emanates from that person. And it is believed that your very person is enriched and enhanced by that physical contact. In the Gospels, for instance, we hear of the woman who had been sick for years and who reached out in a crowd to touch the hem of the robe of Jesus. We are told that she was healed at once as power went out from Jesus.

In the East it is also believed that coming into contact with an unauthentic spiritual guide, a pretender at prayer, will drain part of your life-force from you. Have you not heard, "I came away from church in worse shape than when I went in." But it is not just priests and ministers who must examine whether they are failing to be what they claim to be. For the mission of Christ is not limited to the ordained. All who are baptized are called to be ministers of the Gospel. Are we not all members of the royal priesthood of which St. Peter wrote? Are we not all called to be people of prayer?

The more we go inward in prayer and touch the mystery of God that lives deep within us, the more God's power flows out of us. Real power, real energy, radiates from a person of prayer. Even when we are unaware of it, in a crowded shopping center, at work or at play, the power of Christ flows out of us and touches others. If we are only "fake" disciples, if our daily lives are devoid of prayerful contact with God, then we can drain life from others and leave them less for having been in touch with us. Those who touch us, even in the most common of human contact, are either renewed by that contact or they are lessened.

St. Peter instructed us, "Clothe yourselves in humility" (1 Pt. 5: 5). Those persons who make daily prayer part of the fabric of their lives find that in time they are clothed not only in humility, but in a host of other holy qualities as well. Those who take time each day to pray find that even their clothing becomes radiant with graceful energy. And wherever such people go, power also flows out from them.

20 **Feast of the Virgin Fausta**. The Emperor Maximian ordered her head to be bored through and her body pierced with nails because she refused to worship idols. She was finally martyred by being burned to death on a flaming grill. Pray to St. Fausta when you are bored by a dull lecture or sermon.

21 **Neutrinos Awareness Day**. Pause today and be aware that every second, without your knowing it, one hundred million neutrinos are shooting through your body. Not one of your cells is aware of this either. These neutrinos are part of the sun's radiation which shines through us even at night. They are produced by a nuclear reaction deep in the sun's core, and, like Superman, they can travel through anything. Even during hours of darkness they penetrate the earth and zip unnoticed through you. What other sources of energy, present but hidden from your consciousness, may be circulating through you today?

22 **Birthday of the Ice Cream Cone**. In 1903 on this date, Italo Marchiony, an Italian immigrant, applied for a patent for his new creation. Marchiony's idea made possible the consumption of both the ice cream and its container. A good day to reflect on how you can help the ecology by recycling as many containers as possible. While the problem of "throw-aways" seems bigger than Mount Everest, remember that mountains can be leveled one handful at a time. Begin today to do your handful.

23 **Autumn Equinox**. In "flat world" terms, on this day the sun rises over the earth due east and sets due west, and daytime and night are of equal length. On this feast that marks the beginning of the sun's ebbing vitality in its journey toward winter, watch the sun "set" with reverence.

ALIEN TEARS

The visitor from outer space was delightful and charming, and, like every tourist, he wanted to see everything on that first day on Earth. The alien marveled at the beauty of our planet, its mountains and rivers, its vast rolling prairies and lush green vegetation. The official delegation who escorted the extraterrestrial visitor took pride in his obvious fascination with Earth. As they toured the heartland of America, evening was approaching, and they became absorbed in one of the Midwest's typically magnificent sunsets.

All of a sudden the visitor from another planet began to weep and sob, all to the dismay of his official guides. "What's wrong? Have we said something to offend you?" they inquired.

Through his sobs the visitor replied, "Oh, look, your beautiful sun is dying. How can you not grieve?''

The guides looked at one another in amusement, and one of them spoke reassuringly, ''Don't be sad, sir, the sun isn't dying. This happens every day. We don't mourn, because we know that the sun will appear again tomorrow morning.''

The alien only shook his head. ''How can that be? Look, it has almost disappeared, and all the light is fading! What faith you Earth-people have to believe that it will ever appear again.''

This small story awakens us to how strange it would be for someone to weep over the daily disappearance of the sun. We are able to watch a sunset and see its beauty because we believe in sunrises. That faith is supported by the fact that the sun has never disappointed us; it always reappears in the morning.

The Autumn Equinox is a perfect time to reflect on how our lives are filled with sunsets; this day initiates the sunset of the year as all of creation begins its annual decline toward the death of winter. But we also experience sunsets in our relationships which end as the persons we love die or move away, in projects that run their course and are no longer needed and in each of the stages of our lives that pass. We are also in the midst of a number of painful sunsets in our Church: parishes are closing or being combined because of a shortage of priests; parish schools are shutting down because of a lack of funds or teachers; institutions that once carried great influence are now only ghosts; old customs and traditions are fading away.

We can look upon our many personal, social and sacred sunsets as terrible events that call for tears or regret, or we can see them with eyes that are filled with faith. Does anything really cease to exist, or does all life move through a constant rhythm of sunsets and sunrises? If someone we love dies, is that person gone forever? If one form of religious life, parish, school or pious devotion concludes, does it mean that the spirit of that expression is gone forever and will never reappear?

The central truth of our Christian faith lies in the mystery of the death and resurrection of Jesus. If we truly believe in that mystery, then we can live out our trust, witnessing any sunset event in our lives with the same feelings of joy and hope that come as we watch the glory of the setting sun at the end of each day.

Invention of False Teeth, 500 B.C. If you have artificial teeth, be grateful today that you can smile without being ashamed. The Empress Josephine, Napoleon's wife, often carried a rose which she would raise to her lips when smiling. Very sensitive about her bad teeth, she used the rose to hide them. A day to be aware of when it's a good idea to keep your mouth shut.

24

Festival of Giving Advice. Reflect, today, on the adage, ''Those who give advice when advice has not been requested, need advice.'' Or as Confucius said, ''Do not teach a ripe person, for it is a waste of person. Do not teach a person who is not yet ripe; it's a waste of words.''

25

IF I WERE YOU

One of the healing ministries of great value that is open to every Christian is that of compassionate listening. In everyone's life there exist difficulties and also decisions that must be made. The need to share our heart's burdens with someone we trust is essential to good emotional, physical and even spiritual health. And what a holy, prayerful and healing action it is to listen to another person's concerns.

But if there is one enemy that prevents this exchange from being healing, it surely must be our human compulsion to give advice. For when advice is given without it being requested, it is "a-vice." Hidden beneath the expression, "If I were you..." is a soft form of domination, a hidden sense of superiority. Indeed, if our opinion is requested, it may be of real service to give it. But usually when someone drops by for a cup of coffee and starts talking, he or she is not seeking advice but rather a listening and non-judgmental heart.

Set a guard over that desire to tell others how to get their marriages, children or business back in order and simply sit back and listen—and perhaps put yourself in a prayerful inner attitude. As people hear themselves expressing what's inside them, they may be surprised. For it is often simply in the "talking out" of an issue that they discover and clarify their own feelings or, as is sometimes happily the case, the escape route from their problem.

A frequently heard complaint from parents is that their teenage children do not share their problems with them. The reasons could be many for such a reluctance on the part of young people, but parents can ask themselves if they listen to the burdens of their children—if they truly listen. Or do they feel that the role of parents is to give advice or even to unilaterally dictate behavior? It is not surprising that most young people seek elsewhere for a listener.

We all need good listeners to help us hear ourselves and to assist us in finding relief from the inner burdens we carry—especially if that person is a praying listener. But the next time a friend stops by "just for a cup of coffee," remember a word of wisdom from the Orient, "People who give advice when it is not requested, need advice."

26 **Birthday of Johnny Appleseed** on this day in 1774. This American folk hero turned a hobby into a vocation. He planted apple trees across America and was a zealous preacher of Scripture. He was even revered by Native Americans who looked upon him as a medicine man. Besides his planting, his practice was to tear out a page from the bible he carried along on his travels, a page containing a passage which fit the situation of the family with whom he spent the night. He would leave the page with the family for their reflection. What page of Scripture do you think you need to reflect upon today?

27 **New Horizon Day**. Vasco Nunez de Balboa, Spanish conquistador, became the first European to see the Pacific Ocean on this day in 1513. Go for a walk today and act as if you were seeing some aspect of your local geography for the first time. Be a discoverer of the uncommon hiding in the common.

Feast of St. Wenceslaus, Duke of Bohemia, the national hero and patron saint of Czechoslovakia. A devout and prayerful man, he was murdered in 929 by his own stepbrother at the door of the church he was about to enter. Today, reinvest your prayers with devotion. Pray each day as Wenceslaus did, as if you would meet your death that day. If you pray that way every day, you will never have to fear being surprised by death.

28

Feast of St. Michael and All the Angels. "Angels can fly," said G.K. Chesterton, "because they take themselves lightly." A good occasion to lighten up a little and be more angelic. Avoid, today, the trap of thinking that sanctity is serious business.

29

A NEW PAPAL SCANDAL

A past issue of *Time* magazine carried a brief article about Pope John Paul's vacation in the mountains of Italy. The article included photos of the Pope dressed in slacks and a sports shirt instead of his white cassock. These photos of a pope in casual clothing have to be a first. To many observers such snapshots seem shocking, if not scandalous. And even the idea of a pope taking the day off stuns some people who might ask, "What's next? Will the next headlines read, 'Pope vacations in Las Vegas' or 'Pope rides motorcycle on his day off'?"

While we all probably agree that the Pope should have a day off, we are inclined to add under our breath, "Now and then," or "Oh yes, but not a long vacation like other people take—and certainly not an exciting one!" Those photographs of John Paul in "civilian" dress might have produced a real scandal in years past. Can we picture any of the popes in the past century enjoying a vacation at the beach or at a casino?

Kings, queens, presidents and popes often have what is called a summer residence. We do not like to think of them as going on a "real" vacation in those places but rather that they are working as usual, only with a bit of a change in environment. Why is it so difficult to think of a pope enjoying himself on a vacation or even having a regular weekly day off?

Perhaps part of the reason lies in the title "Holy Father." Fathers and mothers are not supposed to have a day off either, not a real day off from their responsibilities and duties, right? But here again we really need to ask, "Why not?" Doesn't it only make good sense in these times of great tension, of heavy responsibilities and demands to allow time "free" from all responsibilities to refresh and renew parents? The same is true for each of us. We would return to our duties much better suited to perform them if we had a refreshing break from them.

It was *risky* for Pope John Paul to release those photos of himself relaxing in civilian clothes because we still carry piously puritanical notions about what the behavior of our religious leaders should be. To have fun smacks of sin. To have a day off from religious duties implies doing something non-religious. The **Holy** Father should wear only holy clothes, do only holy things and above all keep up the ancient image of someone above such human needs as having time off.

What is true for a pope is true for a bishop, priest, minister or any religious. And, again, it is true for the "holy" father and mother of every family as well. Two thousand years ago, Jesus worked only a six day week. As a good Jew he would seriously keep the spirit of Saturday as a day of **no** work. Today, when a five day workweek is common, shouldn't Pope John Paul take two days a week off, like other people?

If you would like to give a beautiful gift to either your pastor or your parents, applaud long and loudly the next time that you need them and are told, "I'm sorry but they're not here; it's their day off."

30 Rest Day Festival.

The Council of Rouen in 650 issues the law of complete rest from servile work on Sundays. This obligation, originally confined to France, slowly spreads to the rest of the Church. As early as 361, the Council of Laodicea had decreed some form of rest on Sundays "as far as possible." In these days when both husband and wife usually work, the weekends are often times of household tasks and other labors. We need to recall the words of St. Augustine in 431 about "otium cordis," rest of the heart. If we must work on Sundays, let us go about it with a different attitude, with our hearts peaceful, approaching whatever must be done with a sense of joy.

October

Don't Give Up the Ship Day. This day in 1781 marks the birthday of James Lawrence, the American naval officer who, while under attack by a British frigate on June 1, 1813, cried out to his men, "Don't give up the ship!" Today, if the ship you're on is in danger of sinking, whether it's an institution, a marriage or your spiritual life, hold fast with a heart filled with courage. Don't abandon ship till it's no longer possible to stay with it, and spend your time now trying to save it.

1

BEHOLD, THE GUINEA PIG OF GOD

In the cathedral of Cuzco in Peru there is a painting of the Last Supper by a Cuzqueno artist. In the platter on the table before Jesus and his apostles the painting portrays a guinea pig instead of a lamb! While the lamb is the ritual meat of the Jewish Passover, the Peruvians regard the guinea pig as a delicacy. Such cultural changing of symbols is not unusual in the history of religious art. But while the image of a guinea pig on the table of the Last Supper might seem strange to us, it might also hold some hidden insights.

We use the term "guinea pig" for animals or persons used in scientific and medical experiments, or for anyone upon whom something new is tried. Was Christ a guinea pig in a medical experiment—the healing of a sick world? And if we believe that his experiment of the cross, of total surrender to the will of God, was successful, should we not then be willing to undergo that same process?

At the Last Supper Jesus gave us the commandment, "Do this in memory of me" (Lk. 22: 19). He was not simply calling his disciples to perform a religious ritual. He was calling each of them to surrender themselves totally to the will of God in an act that heals the world. Each time we join with the priest as a concelebrant in the Liturgy of the Holy Eucharist that commitment as a disciple of Christ should be understood. The ritual of the Last Supper which we repeat is meant to challenge us to "Do this..." in our marriages, in our service to others, throughout our daily lives.

With faith in God's promise of eternal life, Jesus submitted himself to the agony of suffering and death. While we believe that he triumphed over death in his resurrection, each time we surrender totally, we too are like guinea pigs. The solution of Christ to the evil and sin of the world, strangely speaking, must be embraced at every occasion as a radical and sublimely foolish experiment. To be nonviolent in speech and action when we are angry, to try to respond only with love, is truly to be a guinea pig in an experiment for peace. It is an effort to awaken the God-seed in both ourselves and our enemies. As the American writer Theodore Rosak once said, "People try nonviolence for a week, and when it doesn't work, they go back to violence, which hasn't worked for centuries."

Perhaps we might feel more comfortable in our efforts to repeat that love-filled sacrifice of Christ if the paintings of the Last Supper in our homes and churches, like the one in Peru, showed a guinea pig as the victim of the Passover sacrifice instead of a lamb!

2

Birthday of Mahatma Gandhi, man of peace and non-violence, on this day in 1869. He summed up his spirit in this statement, "Our armaments have failed already. Let us now be in search of something new; let us try the force of love and God which is truth. When we have got that we shall want nothing else." On this birthday of Gandhi, when you find yourself in some situation that seems to require force, try the force of love instead.

3

First Woman U.S. Senator, 1922. Will it be 2022 before the first woman president becomes a possibility? Or perhaps it will take until 2122 before some of us can let go of the deep-seated biases that prevent real equality. A good day to reflect on what qualities we do consider essential in our elected officials.

GOOD GUYS WEAR WHITE HATS

As election day draws near, we are saturated by advertisements about the virtues of the candidates seeking elected office. Recently the news media has been zealous in its attempts to uncover the vices of those seeking election. These news stories deal not only with the vices of the candidates but also with disclosures about members of their families. We have seen more than one candidate withdrawing from the race because of a lack of the purity considered necessary for someone holding public office. As a result of our demand for high virtue and no vices, and the zeal of the news media, the American electoral process has begun to resemble Rome's canonization process.

The attempt of political press agents to "market" their candidates as persons of great integrity and valor isn't new; in fact, it's time-worn. Our term candidate comes from the Latin word "candidatus," meaning clothed in white. In ancient Rome, it was the custom of those seeking public office to wear loose-fitting white robes. The robes were loose so that the candidates might show people their battle scars, and white since that was the color of fidelity, humility and purity.

Indeed, those whom we elect to office should be persons of the highest virtue. But we are electing public servants not saints! If we continue to demand that the personal lives of those who serve in public office be completely free of any moral failure, of any misconduct in their past lives, who will we have to lead us? Will we not merely have careful candidates with whitewashed images? And if we also demand that the members of the candidates' families be as white as snow, who will even desire to seek public office?

As we prepare to exercise our important duty as citizens, we need to look not so much at private virtues and vices as at public virtues that would make a good leader. We need to examine the candidates' public records, their social and global proposals more than their private lives. As Christian citizens we have an obligation to examine carefully whether a candidate's position reflects a genuine concern for the poor, the unemployed, the sick, the homeless and others in our society without a power base, as well as the candidate's commitment to a peace that is based on more than vested interests.

In the old black and white cowboy movies, the good guys and the bad guys were always easy to pick out. Tom Mix and the other heroes always wore white hats. But life isn't as simple as in those old movies. Perhaps the day will soon come when we can see past the superficial image of the candidates and elect to office people who will be instruments of true social justice and peace in the world, even if they happen to be wearing black hats!

Feast of St. Francis of Assisi, the great reformer who was called the first Protestant. Born Giovanni Francesco Bernadone in 1181, he died on this day in 1226. By living the Gospel in its simplest and most direct way, Francis had a profound effect upon the religion, poetry, art and life attitudes of the thirteenth century. He even invented the Christmas crib. Celebrate the feast of Francis by investing your life with great joy in God and joy in your communion with creation.

Also, the **Birthday of the Space Age** in 1957 on this day. The first successful launch of an earth-made satellite, Sputnik (fellow traveler of earth), from the U.S.S.R. began the exploration of space.

Calendar Celebration Day. On this day in 1582 the Gregorian Calendar was introduced. It is the order of days that we are presently following, having made a twelve day correction in the Julian calendar. The use of calendars was once reserved for shamans and priests who alone knew the secrets of the seasons, solstices and equinoxes. Today, remember that when you observe the changing of the seasons, the new and full moons and the other events of the cosmic calendar you are living in harmony with the universe. Celebrating the calendar is an excellent prayer.

Birthday of Charles Stilwell, the inventor of the brown paper bag, in 1845 in Fremont, Ohio. He called his flat-bottom, pleated-sides invention "S.O.S.," for "Self-opening sack." Pause today to give thanks to Charlie Stilwell whose modest invention makes taking your groceries home from the supermarket easier. And, of course, it also makes a convenient receptacle for your garbage at home.

A FLOATING PARABLE

Along with their comic roles in the movies, the Marx Brothers also often appeared on stage. Each enjoyed throwing ad-lib lines into a scene to see how his brothers would respond. In one play, Groucho was in the midst of a passionate love scene when his brothers opened the door and shouted, "The garbage man is here!" To which Groucho replied instantly, "Tell him we don't want any today!"

In 1987 the news media told and re-told the sad tale of a New York tugboat towing a barge full of garbage that numerous states and three foreign countries refused to allow it to unload. Like Groucho in his ad-lib line, no one wants anyone else's garbage today; they have enough of their own to handle.

The plight of the unwanted garbage barge is really a floating parable about each one of us. The other day I went into a small, privately owned store. The owner did not have the material I was seeking, but he immediately began bemoaning about how terrible his last three employees had been. He listed a series of complaints, from how they consistently had been late for work to the poor quality of their work. Without pausing to catch his breath, he then grumbled about some of his customers: how they lacked common sense, always wanted him to lower the price of his goods, and on and on.

I listened for a while, nodding in agreement, but gradually edged my way toward the door. I had a counseling appointment to keep and waited for a pause in his unending monologue of complaints. Thanking him for his assistance, I escaped from his store onto the sidewalk. But as I drove off, I thought about that barge full of garbage that nobody wanted and about the man in the store whose heart was full of garbage. And I wondered if I should have stayed and listened.

The store owner may have been an extreme case, but he is not an isolated one. The lives of many people today are full of troubles, worries and pain. They look for someone to listen with love and understanding to their problems and difficulties. There's a real priestly ministry in such listening, and anyone who has room to carry another's difficulties can apply. But because so many of us live isolated from a sense of community, family and neighborhood, this deeply human need is largely left unanswered.

Simply to listen to another, without offering advice (unless asked), provides a relief from the distress. Nothing needs to be said other than acknowledging a person's pain—and perhaps prayerfully holding it in the shrine of the heart. Simply knowing that another feels compassion helps free us from the burden of our distress. Sometimes the relief comes when we have released the anger or pain, freeing us to move on and let the issue be. In other cases, we suddenly discover a solution in the simple telling of our troubles. Indeed, inside each of us are the answers to our problems.

A listening ear is a holy ear. Such compassionate listening is one way we put flesh and bone on our prayers and worship. For by a willingness to take upon ourselves the trials and troubles of others, we are graced with one of the beautiful ministries of Christ in our modern world. It is also a humbling act of love because each of us has occasions when we need someone to listen to our garbage. By remembering our times of healing and grace, we will more easily be able to respond like Christ when that knock comes at our door. And when the voice announces, "The garbage man is here!" we can reply, "Tell him to come right on in!"

Birthday of the Bathtub in England on this day in 1828. After arguments by medical authorities concerning both the hazards and benefits of bathing, the bathtub was banned in Boston in 1845. But in 1851, President Millard Fillmore had one of the new contraptions installed in the White House. Relax today in a hot tub, let your cares float away and rejoice that Boston's ban didn't become a national prohibition.

7

Great Chicago Fire on this day in 1871. According to legend, Mrs. O'Leary's cow kicked over a lantern, starting a fire which destroyed most of Chicago. A fire in Peshtigo, Wisconsin on the very same day burned across six counties, killing more than three times the number of people lost in the Chicago fire. A good day to check the batteries in your smoke detectors.

8

Birthday of Benjamin Banneker in 1736. Banneker was called the fist black man of science. Besides being an astronomer, mathematician and surveyor, he was the author of an almanac. As you observe the birth date of this great African-American, check your heart to see if there are any left-over discriminations.

9

Month of the Harvest Moon Feast. When the moon is full this month, be full of joy and gratitude. Hold a moon party with apple cider and other fruits of this year's harvest.

10

OUR LADY OF SILENCE

Like Assumption which is a harvest feast, a summertime Thanksgiving, mid-October gives us another opportunity for a harvest festival honoring the Virgin Mother of God. But perhaps we might change this autumn feast's orientation a bit, reverencing Mary as Our Lady of Silence.

Mythologies, the stories of gods and goddesses of early peoples, are the sacred scriptures, the old and new testaments, of the covenant of Noah. In that first divine covenant, after the great flood, God promised to be with *all* peoples of the earth. In a way, then, the mythologies of the Greeks, Romans and even of American Indians are sacred writings that prepared the way for the Gospels. As such, they certainly have something to say to us.

For example, the Greek god Harpokrates, who was borrowed from the Egyptians, is the god of silence. He is usually depicted as a baby, nude and sitting on his mother's lap. She offers him her breast as he sucks his thumb. Perhaps in this scene of a Greek god is hidden a sign and message for us.

Part of the hidden message this myth holds lies in the fact that Harpokrates is in a child's form. For the prayer of silence holds the power to renew us, to make us children again. Silence calls us to that domain of dreams and visions, to a return to that pre-verbal period of our childhood. In that return we are made aware of how inadequate speech can be. Silence also strips us of our defenses, makes us naked of those cardboard defenses we so often employ. Slowly, if we allow it, silence strips away our need to engage in those arguments in which we insist that we are right. Times of silence cleanly cut through the constant flow of the words, rituals and worship of religion that so often keep God at a "safe" distance.

Silence carefully places us in our Mother's lap where Our Lady of Silence can feed us with the milk of heaven. The image of Harpokrates sitting on his mother's lap is very much like the hundreds of paintings and icons of the Virgin Mother with the infant Jesus on her lap. Viewing those sacred images through the image of Harpokrates opens new insights into the prayer of silence and perhaps even into the act of sucking one's thumb! The image does suggest the childlike contemplative prayer of being **absorbed** in God!

11

Feast of the Motherhood of God. Today in 431 the Council of Ephesus gave Mary the title of the Mother of God since she was the mother of Jesus Christ, the Son of God. This is an autumn Mother's Day, a feast to remember every mother who has borne a child of God.

12

Columbus Day. On this day in 1492 Columbus lands on the Bahamian island of Guanahani, which he renames El Salvador. The natives he finds there are called Arawak and are very gentle and friendly. As a result of harsh treatment and slavery they would later all perish. They left behind only one word, "hammock." This unique bed would be introduced by Columbus to Europe and would soon be used on ships crossing the Atlantic and other seas. A good day to consider if the arrival of technology may also kill off your culture. Resist the temptation today to purchase some new electric wonder simply because it's the latest.

13

Feast of St. Edward, the Confessor, 1003-1066. Also the **Birthday of Molly Pitcher** whose real name was Mary Hays McCauley. She was a water carrier in the American Revolutionary War battle of Monmouth. After her husband, John Hays, was wounded, she took over loading and firing a cannon against the British. General Washington honored her by naming her a noncommissioned officer. The name Edward is a compound word meaning a warden or guardian of wealth and happiness. Like Mary Hays McCauley, be prepared to jump in and do something bold if your happiness is threatened.

14

Japanese Quarrel Festival. People carrying burdens jostle one another on this day to demonstrate their skill and balance in handling their burdens. A good day to celebrate your skill at balancing your cross and burdens, a day to gracefully dance through your disagreements.

NO LOSERS

A coyote who was newly married lived near a river. One day his bride asked him for a meal of fish. He promised to bring some fish home even though he didn't know how to swim. He crept quietly down to the river and discovered two otters who were struggling over a huge fish they had just caught. After killing the fish, the two began to fight about how to divide it. "I saw it first; I should have the larger portion," said one. "But, said the other, "I saved you when you almost drowned while catching the fish!"

They continued to bicker until the coyote walked up to them and offered to settle the argument. The two otters agreed to abide by his decision in the case. He cut the fish into three pieces. To the one otter he gave the head and to the other the tail. "The middle," said the coyote, "belongs to the judge." He walked away happily, saying aloud, "Fighting always leads to losers."

The real moral of this story can easily be lost by those who too readily see the legal profession in the character of the coyote. Often those who preside over an argument do make a profit, but that fact does not detract from the central meaning. The story shows how fighting leaves those involved in the fight as the real losers. But, while we know that fighting does lead to losses on both sides, we need to be reminded of it frequently.

In the holy book of China, the *Tao Te Ching*, there is a saying: "A good person does not argue; the one who argues is not a good person." Fighting with words instead of hands or other weapons is still a form of fighting. When we are caught up in a quarrel, squabble or spat, everyone walks away like the two otters—as losers. St. Paul, writing to the Colossians, said, "You must put aside now all the anger, quick temper, malice..." (Col. 3: 8). The statement, "A good person does not argue" doesn't mean that a good person doesn't have misunderstandings. But these common difficulties are not an occasion to prove oneself right; they are opportunities to find a solution that respects both parties. Both sides should win, neither should "lose face" or be humiliated. This way of handling a misunderstanding may take twice as long as a good old-fashioned argument, but when it is over no one is a loser.

They say that in Japan a riot between students and the police takes a long time because it is most important that each side have the opportunity to win. Since it is a social evil to "lose face," the police allow the rioters proper time to demonstrate—then the rioters allow the police time to control the riot! Neither side "loses face." Both sides, in the words of the *Tao Te Ching*, are "good."

The next time you find yourself on the slippery side of a misunderstanding and are racing toward an argument, recall the tale of the coyote and the two otters, and make sure that all parties involved are able to walk away as winners. As you practice this attitude, you may find, to your surprise, that as St. Paul said to the Colossians, you have "put on" the garment of love.

Birthday of the Handshake. In 2800 B.C. there occurred the first recorded use of the handshake as a sacred sign of the transfer of power from a

15

god to an earthly ruler. Each New Year's Day in Babylonia, as early as 1800 B.C., the great ritual of the day involved the king shaking hands with the statue of Marduk, the nation's greatest god. As time passed, this once royal and sacred gesture became a token of goodwill as people extended to one another the hand in which they would ordinarily carry their weapon. By this sacred gesture the hand became an instrument of peace rather than war.

16

Dictionary Day. Birthday of Noah Webster in 1758. He was the author of Webster's Dictionary. Take some time today to explore the wonderful world of words and their origins.

17

Birthday of Writing. In 3000 B.C. the Sumerians in Mesopotamia invented writing. Egyptians evolved hieroglyphic (sacred signs) writing in 2800 B.C. Once a skill reserved for scribes and priests, this sacred art is now practiced by all. Write your name today and marvel that you are performing a priestly magical art.

18

Feast of St. Luke, patron saint of doctors, artists and writers. A physician and author of the third Gospel and the *Acts of the Apostles*, he creatively used his hands to both write sacred words and to heal. A good day to reflect on how well you use the great gift of your hands.

HOLY HANDS

From the Maidu Indians of what today is California comes the following creation story.

God the Earthmaker took some red clay, mixed it with water and carefully shaped man and woman. They were beautiful but unfinished, for they lacked hands. Earthmaker asked the other creatures what kind of hands they should have. The turtle said, "Like mine, so they can swim." And the coyote spoke up, "No, like mine, so they can run fast." Earthmaker thought and thought and then said, "Thank you all, but I have decided to make their hands like mine so that they can make things." Since Earthmaker's hands were the pattern for human hands, women and men became the most beautiful of all creatures because they could create things with their hands.

In the Catholic tradition, the hands of the priest are considered to be sacred, as they are anointed at ordination. But look down at your hands; are they not also sacred? The Maidu Indians knew what we have to remember. Our hands are godly in design and so should be busy making as God makes. They should not be hands that hold others back or down, "heavy" hands that prevent freedom, even the freedom to make mistakes. They should be hands busy with making peace—not clenched in anger, but waving away injury in movements of pardon that say, "No problem, don't think a thing about it." As Earthmaker's hands left the fingerprints of beauty on all creation, our hands should be busy making our surroundings beautiful, clean and delightful. Our hands should also be busy "making" prayer as we fold them or raise them up as a sign of openness and surrender to God's will. Our hands continue to mirror the divine pattern when we use them to "make" compassionate deeds. Such hands are different, unlike those who refuse to "lift a hand" to help or who "throw up their hands" in despair. But most of all, our hands are truly godlike when they are daily busy "making love" with hamburgers, dirty laundry, work at the office or shop and with acts of affection.

Perhaps we should ask ourselves a question: "Are my hands, like those of a priest, holy enough to hold the Body of Christ at Communion time?" Another question may help us to answer the first one: "What have I been making with my hands?"

Feast of the Fork. Dinner forks appeared in Italy in 1098. The clergy condemned them as contrary to nature since God had created human fingers to touch God's bounty. Before forks, nobility used three fingers when eating, commoners used five. For centuries only the very rich used forks. They were considered an "excessive sign of refinement" and did not become common till the late eighteenth century. Celebrate, this day, by using your hands to eat your food. It may be a bit messy, but it will also heighten your appreciation for the "unnatural" invention, the fork.

19

Anti-Discrimination Day for Left-Handers. Celebrate, today, history's great left-handers. Among them are: Alexander the Great, Hans Holbein, Leonardo da Vinci, Michelangelo, C.P.E. Bach, Jimi Hendrix, Picasso and Babe Ruth. Then there is the sinister (Latin for left) Thomas Skorupa, the left-handed editor of this book. Be compassionate today toward your left-handed friends, since most common tools, such as scissors, can openers, gear shifts and golf clubs are designed for right-handers. PS: All polar bears are left-handed!

20

Thomas Edison Invents the Electric Light on this day in 1879. Because of this marvel which required years of patient experimentation, night can be like day. Tonight, turn on an electric light with a heart full of prayerful gratitude that you can have light all the time. And perhaps each time you turn on one of these wondrous servant inventions you can let its light remind you of your call to **pray** always.

21

WANTED: A WATCHMAN

There is a tale among the Jewish Hasidim about Rabbi Naftali from the town of Roptchitz. It was the custom of rich people whose homes were isolated on the outskirts of the town to hire men to watch over their property at night. Late one evening Rabbi Naftali was out for a walk, and he met one such watchman walking back and forth. The rabbi asked, "For whom do you work?"

The man told him and then asked, "And for whom do you work, Rabbi?"

The words of the watchman struck at the heart of the rabbi, who replied, "I am not sure whether I work for anyone or not!" The rabbi walked beside the watchman for some time in silence. Then he asked, "Will you come and work for me?"

"I should like to be your servant, Rabbi," the watchman answered, "but what would be my duties?"

And Rabbi Naftali answered quietly, "To remind me."

This Hasidic parable can speak to us on several levels, but one level is certainly that of prayer. The function of daily prayer is to "remind" us. Daily prayer is our lookout, our watchman, who reminds us that God is in charge. We easily forget that we are God's creatures, and prayer reminds us of our spiritual poverty and re-minds us that all in life is gift. Prayers are times of returning to the truth that, while we may have timetables for our concerns—even if our concerns revolve around the coming of justice and peace—the fruit of our work is in the hands of God, who may not be in as big a hurry as we are.

Prayer can happen anywhere at any time, but prayer-places in our homes, churches—or even the sight of a church—can remind us of our necessity for worship and prayer. A room or corner in our living quarters set aside for prayer is a constant watchman, a servant that shouts, "Aren't you going to pray this morning?" Like Rabbi Naftali, we need help if we are to remember whom it is that we "work for." If you presently lack such a watchman, today might be a good time to "hire" one. The cost is minimal: a small space, a few quiet moments and a dedicated heart.

22

End of the World Day. In 1844 on this day, the followers of William Miller, the founder of Millerism, await the end of the world. Mark this day with as many celebrations as the untimely end of the world has been predicted before and since William Miller. A good day not to take gloom and doom seriously.

Also on this day in 1938, Chester Carlson produces the world's **First Successful Xerographic Copy**. Twenty other giant corporations look the other way, seeing little future in his copying machine, calling it a "child's toy printing machine." It would not be until 1959 that Xerox would produce the "914." Raise a flag and fire a "canon" for Chester Carlson today.

23

Feast of St. John of Capistrano who died of the plague on this day in 1456 in Italy. In his honor, the swallows depart each year on October 23 from the old mission of San Juan Capistrano in California. Watch for patterns in nature in your part of the world and enjoy living in communion with creation's cycles. And watch for patterns in your heart which might prevent that communion.

TRASH IN THE TABERNACLE

If you were a bishop, how would you respond if someone reported that a certain pastor kept trash in the tabernacle of his church—and when you investigated, you found that the tabernacle indeed held not only the Blessed Sacrament but also all sorts of trash? What course of action would you take?

Some of you might propose compassion, for surely such a sacrilege must be the result of senility or mental imbalance. Others might insist upon the immediate dismissal of such a disrespectful or careless priest from that position of responsibility. But before you proceed any further with this puzzle-parable, think about whether that negligent priestly caretaker of the sacred shrine might be **you**!

All our hearts are tabernacles for the presence of the Divine Mystery. God dwells within each one of us, and our hearts are the awesome shrine of that Presence. Yet, while just about all of us believe that truth, don't we also allow trash to accumulate in our hearts? Haven't we all felt—and sometimes housed—anger, jealousy and indifference toward others within the temple of our hearts?

Certainly such sacrilegious carelessness is not new. Jesus was fully aware of what poor custodians of the divine shrine we are. Speaking of that failing, he tells us in Mark's Gospel, "Wicked designs come from the deep recesses of the heart: acts of fornication, theft, murder, adulterous conduct, greed, maliciousness, deceit, sensuality, envy, blasphemy, arrogance..." (Mk. 7: 21). These are only a few of the trashy things that can reside in our heart-tabernacles.

The tabernacles that occupy places of great honor and reverence in our churches have only a front door, but our heart-tabernacles also have a back door. If we do not stay alert, the ugly things of which Jesus spoke can slip through the unguarded rear door. If we are not to be guilty of the same sacrilege as the priest in the parable-puzzle, we will have to inspect our inner shrines constantly.

When we preform the ritual act of genuflection in our churches, as we enter and leave the presence of the Blessed Sacrament, we should do so with reverential mindfulness. And we might also add a quiet inner prayer to that wordless prayer of the body. Touching a hand to our heart, we could pray, "O God, may my heart be only a shrine for you and for thoughts which are worthy to be in your presence." When we pray with such devotion and mindfulness, we then become responsible custodians of the sacred shrine of the heart.

Rabindranath Tagore, the saintly Hindu poet, expressed all this beautifully when he wrote,

> I shall ever try
> to drive all evil away from my heart
> and keep my love in flower,
> knowing that you have your seat
> in the inmost shrine of my heart.

Birthday of the United Nations in 1945 on this day. The first at least partially successful effort to create a world government to ensure peace and harmony among the peoples of planet Earth. Support as best you can all such efforts to bring about planetary unity. And especially keep your heart a place where peace and harmony can thrive.

24

---

25 Birthday of Pablo Picasso

Birthday of Pablo Picasso born in Malaga, Spain in 1881. "Painting," he said, "is a form of magic designed as a mediator between this strange hostile world and us, a way of seizing the power by giving form to our terrors as well as our desires." Each of us is an artist who should strive to give form to our desires and fears and so be able to harness and balance their energy. Don't say, "But I'm no artist," for there are ten thousand ways to artistically practice Picasso's magic.

THE FEAST OF ALL SINNERS

Soon we will celebrate a beautiful feast, the feast of All Saints. But perhaps the Church needs another feast, one that is similar and yet may seem quite strange: the feast of All Sinners! It could come sometime in October, before the early-November honoring of the unnamed as well as the famous saints of the Church. Such a feast of All Sinners would help us better understand the mystery of the body of Christ, the mystical community which is not simply a gathering of the good, the beautiful and the holy, but the weak and sinful as well. The whole body of Christ includes the strong and the weak, sinners and saints. And so it seems fitting to prayerfully be in communion with sinners, the part of the body in which all of us share because of our struggle with sin.

At Holy Communion we take into our hands the living presence of the Body of Christ, to which we respond, "Amen." But do we say "Amen" to the whole body, which includes members who are spiritually infirm as well as those who are spiritually strong? Only when we are able to say "Amen" to the dark side, the sinful side of ourselves, can we say "Amen" to the full mystery of Christ and of the Church.

To enter into the communion of sinners would have some rather interesting implications in our daily lives. It would mean coming into communion with those who make mistakes, who commit errors in their work and who forget to do things they need to do. We would be one with those who by a lapse of memory cause us to be inconvenienced or who cost us money or time. When someone with whom we live or work makes a mistake, we have basically two choices—to become angry or to become one with them. If we believe in the communion of sinners, we will be less likely to condemn others for such a "sin." Instead, we might be inclined to **carry** that sin as we try to lessen the embarrassment, the shame or the failure. By such a communion we would not deny the fault or sin. Rather, by an act of personal communion we would identify ourselves as fully as possible with the person who is guilty.

If we are in communion with a person who is responsible for a mistake, sin or crime against us, we will be more disposed to reduce the other's pain rather than to demand an apology or desire revenge. Such communion is not easy, especially when we have been kept waiting for an hour or had some soup spilled in our laps.

But why would anyone want to "own" another's sin or mistake? Such an attitude might come out of an awareness that we each bear not only the effects of our own actions, but also share in the good and evil of the whole human family. Such an "ownership" of another's sins organically begins with being merciful to ourselves in our times of weakness and pain by opening to divine mercy. In turn we can become more open to graciously forgive those around us for their little crimes and mistakes. Such a radical communion first takes root within our own family and then with courage moves outward to embrace the sins of all people.

The Perils of Predicting Day. Chinese royal court astronomers Ho and Hsi were beheaded four days after failing to accurately predict an eclipse of the sun on October 22, 2137 B.C. Their failure caused great panic among the Chinese people. With a precise prediction the population could have prepared properly by enacting rituals of drum-beating and firing arrows into the sky. Death was the punishment for the sin of failing to predict such a cosmic event. **26**

THE SINS OF THE WORLD

The ability to hold the sins of the world in our hands, as Christ did, will be difficult if our hands are filled with our own sins. If we are unable to open our hands to God's absolution and to forgive ourselves, we will not be able to be compassionate with others. Unless we are able to gladly admit our own absent-mindedness, our own occasional clumsiness, anger or hurt, then we will find it most difficult to "handle" other's sins. If we are ashamed of our weaknesses, then we will find it necessary to point out the failings and sins of others so that our sins will look small in comparison. We must first take our own sins into our hands and open those hands to radical forgiveness. Then we will be free to "handle" other's failings as part of our failings.

"Behold the Lamb of God who takes away the sins of the world." As disciples of the Lamb (we might call ourselves "Lambites"), we should desire to take away the sins of the world by making them our own, just as Jesus has embraced our sins. Jesus, the Lamb of God, never denied sin, but instead of condemning the sinner, he turned his attention to the need for encouragement and radical affirmation. Blame or accusation are not creative tools in the development of a new heart or a new person. Christ practiced compassionate communion with sinners, which explains why sinners, spiritually weak people and moral outcasts were magnetically drawn to the humble carpenter rabbi.

Perhaps the sinners and tax collectors of Jesus' day experienced what a criminal recently found with a Christian community. An Indianapolis church was burglarized twice by a robber who stole some canned goods and then even took a bath in the baptistery! After the second break-in, the thief left a note that read, "I'm desperate and hungry with nothing to eat and no place to sleep. Please forgive me. Joe." The pastor, in response, left this note: "Dear Joe, We're very much concerned about you and want to help in any way we can. No one in this church is angry at you because you robbed our place of worship. If you come again, please call us at the following number and we will try to help.'' When Joe, the thief, came again, he found the pastor's note and called the number. The congregation found him a job and obtained clothing and housing for him. As a result, he began a new life.

When we are compassionate, we are in communion with others. We have the ability to share their feelings and fears, and from such "holy" communion comes the power for new life.

The next time you prepare to receive Holy Communion, as you stand with open hands, ready to receive the Body of Christ, you might reflect on whether you have a desire to take the whole and holy body of Christ into your hands and heart. Can you receive not only the Risen Christ into your hands but also the mistakes and sins of the members of Christ's body, along with their graceful service, holy deeds and love? Only by such a full communion can we touch the whole Christ. We should "handle with care" such a daily communion of saints and sinners, aware that in this communion the world is indeed healed—and you and I with it.

---

27 **First Use of Lead Pencils** in England in 1492. An October day to honor that most useful piece of writing equipment. A good pencil always has an eraser since none of us is infallible.

A SECOND CHANCE

Once there was a small Midwestern town in the country where the hardware store was the local gathering place. Charlie, the owner, could usually be seen playing checkers with one of the townsfolk while others stood around watching and visiting. One rainy day, Mike, a farmer, was Charlie's checkers partner. Standing nearby, the old parish priest looked on, smoking his pipe. He was concerned about Mike because he never came to Mass, not even on Christmas or Easter. Mike was known in the community as a man living on the edge, living two lives, if not three. The old priest was a gentle and kind man. And so, although he was concerned about Mike, he avoided mentioning religion or questioning Mike's lifestyle or behavior.

Mike made a bad move in the game, one that put him at risk of losing. He said to Charlie, "I wasn't thinking when I made that move. Give me a second chance; let me take it back and do it again." Charlie agreed to let him make a different play. Later in the game, however, Mike made another thoughtless move and again asked to take it back. But this time Charlie wouldn't let him replay it, and soon the game was over.

The old priest leaned over and whispered in Mike's ear, "Michael, you're a lucky lad. It's a good thing you're not playing the Game of Life with Charlie!" Between the lines was a message about God's willingness to always give another chance. The priest looked at him with great affection, then turned and walked out of the hardware store.

In that moment a fire of God's love was kindled in Mike's heart. The next Sunday he was back in church.

Birthday of the Statue of Liberty, dedicated on this day in 1886. Frederic Auguste Bartholdi's creation is a symbol of freedom around the world. On her birthday, take time to reflect on the state of your liberty.

28

Sausage Celebration. Today, thank Julius Caesar who in 48 B.C. introduced to Rome the Gaulic art of making pork sausages. The hot dog actually appeared in 1500 B.C. in Babylon before it became a favorite dish at the Roman feast of Lupercalia, which also included sexual initiation rites. Since the Romans tended to play with the food of this feast, the early Church outlawed Lupercalia and made eating sausages a sin. The Emperor Constantine in the fourth century totally banned sausage consumption throughout the Roman Empire. But as with other ''forbidden, sinful and illegal delights,'' people bootlegged sausage until it finally became acceptable.

29

War of the Worlds Day. In 1939 on October 30, Orson Welles creates panic with his radio show, ''War of the Worlds.'' A good reminder that not everything one hears on radio or television may be true.

30

FAKES AND FORGERIES

In 1974, the Cleveland Museum of Art acquired what was believed to be one of the greatest masterpieces of the sixteenth century German artist, Matthias Grunewald. The painting was purchased at the cost of one million dollars. The museum was understandably proud of having such an acclaimed work of art in its gallery, until it was discovered that it was really only a well-crafted forgery! It was actually a skillful imitation of the original done by a German artist who made his living producing clever art forgeries. The museum now had a worthless fake canvas on its hands—and was minus a million dollars. But it did find a purpose for the forgery. The painting is now examined to give clues in detecting imitation masterpieces.

This is Halloween week, when streets and sidewalks will be crowded with imitation witches, ghosts and monsters. Fake skeletons and other forgeries of the fearful will knock at your door, shouting, ''Trick or Treat!'' It isn't hard to see at once that they are not genuine ghosts, only playful imitations pretending to be what they are not.

Jesus had harsh words for mask-wearers and pretenders. He called them by the word used for an actor who wore a mask in the Greek theater: ''hypocrite.'' He said that one who pretends to be good—who wears a pious face, but is not really devout inside—is like that Grunewald painting the Cleveland Museum purchased: a forgery! Jesus preferred a sinful saint to a saintly-looking sinner. He called us not to imitate great saints, but to be originals—to become the unique saints that God designed us to be.

The Gospels show us clearly that Jesus loved originals, even if they were flawed with imperfections and sins. He judged people's spiritual state not by how they kept religious laws, by their external prayers or their fidelity in worship, but by how they loved. A tree that looks like an apple tree, smells like an apple tree, but lacks good apples is a hypocrite, a hollow imitation.

But an apple tree struggling to bear good fruit, ashamed many times because of its poor crop to even call itself an apple tree, was dear to Christ's heart. And it was with such struggling, sinful saints that Jesus chose to associate, rather than pious, judgmental, simulated saints.

Each time we pray the Hail Mary, we end with the petition of flawed people: "pray for us sinners." We are a sinful and flawed Church, and we would do well to keep such an identity before us at all times. And while we may pray devoutly and attempt to do good in our lives, who among us is good enough to sit in judgment upon the deeds and lives of others?

On the day after Halloween we celebrate our future holy day, the feast of All Saints. After a lifetime of struggle with our flaws and imperfections, our attempts to be trees that bear at least a few good apples, we will all stand naked before our God. Let us pledge this Halloween-All Saints week to go through life simply being ourselves, not playing any role or attempting to imitate someone we are not. For while we all need to be aware of our numerous flaws, we also need to be aware that God loves us for who we are. To be loved so totally, so unconditionally, should call forth a response from us, just as it did from those whom Jesus loved and refused to judge. Such a love invites a response of humble gratitude. It should also encourage a continuous effort to remove from our own trees as many bad apples as possible. As we struggle to do that, let us also remind ourselves that an original spiritual masterpiece, a saint—even if badly flawed—is priceless. Such an original Master's piece is worth more than a hundred times a million dollars.

---

31 **Ancient Druid Feast of Samhain, Sacred Fire**, on the eve of their new year. At this feast spirits from the other world and the dead are free to roam the earth. Today, on the feast of the eve of All Hallows, All Saints, we become aware of how small children are the "museum keepers," the custodians of the ancient rituals of pre-Christian religions.

Also on this day in 1517, **Martin Luther Nails His Ninty-Five Theses**, denouncing the selling of papal indulgences, among other things, to the door of the Wittenburg Palace Church. This decisive act begins the Reformation in Germany.

November

Feast of All Saints. A day to celebrate all the saints, including the unknown saints whose names are not mentioned in the Holy Hall of Fame of the Church. A day to recall that we are all called to be holy. Pray today that someday in the future this will be your feast day too.

1

CHINESE CANONIZATION

The Chinese have a story about a man who asked a hunter to teach him how to shoot birds. The hunter agreed, but his pupil not only failed to shoot a bird in flight, he could not even hit a stationary bird! Finally, as a last resort, the hunter sent the poor man home and told him to fire his gun at a piece of blank cardboard. The hunter said, "Just concentrate on firing at the cardboard. When you have finished, you can draw a bird around each hole."

This Chinese story holds much food for reflection as we celebrate the annual festival in honor of the saints of the Church. The feast of All Saints also remembers the saints of our own families whose blood flows in our veins today. We, the unknown, unnamed saints of the end of the twentieth century, will be honored in centuries to come. We may not feel like saints today. In fact, we may feel much like the poor shot in the Chinese parable. Even when we try to be holy or to pray, we miss the mark.

Rather than giving up or forgetting about being a saint, we need to do something that's within the range of our capabilities. And we must not evaluate our efforts. The first and cardinal law of all efforts to be a saint or to pray is "Thou shalt not judge." Do not assess the value of your prayer, for you are totally unqualified to do so! How do you know what kind of prayer is cherished by God? Does not a parent take heavenly delight in the stumbling, inarticulate attempts of an infant to speak?

Like the man in the Chinese story, let us take aim at holiness, even if the spiritual labor we take up isn't the work of a master. We can draw the halo around it later—or better yet, let God draw the circle of light around our feeble effort. We don't have to color it as holy or prayerful, but just as our own small attempt, done with love. If we could try for sainthood in this humble style, our world would blossom with blessedness.

2 **Feast of All the Holy Dead**. A day to remember those you love who have passed through the doorway of death. Take time today to prayerfully recall those family members, friends and significant people in your life who have died.

3 **Do-It-Yourself Canonization Day**. Before the twelfth century when the lengthy process of the official canonization of saints by the Catholic Church began, the people pronounced the holy deceased in their midst to be saints by common acclaim. Take some time today to place among the ranks of the saints those who touched you by their faith-filled lives and holy deeds; your parents, friends or teachers. May these saints be holy guides and sources of inspiration for you.

FAITH: A LIFESTYLE OR A CREED?

A story is told about Queen Elizabeth of Belgium who made a state visit to Communist Warsaw in 1956. She was assigned a Polish protocol officer to accompany her to Mass. As they traveled to the church, she asked him, ''Are you a Catholic?''

''Believing but not practicing,'' he replied.

''I see,'' she said. ''Then you must be a Communist.''

''Practicing, your majesty,'' he said, ''but not believing.''

I expect that the officer's reply to the queen strikes a chord for most of us. Are we not a lot like the Polish protocol officer; do we not also believe things that we fail to practice? And do we not also practice things we no longer believe? The expressions of our faith often become habits and ritual routines. As outward signs of belief, they have long since died and are only empty shells. And because of fear we do not practice or express some things in which we do believe.

November is a month in which we remember the saints of the Church. Saints are simply those who practice what they believe and believe what they practice. In contemporary slang, ''They've got it together,'' which is a good definition of holiness. Such a ''together'' lifestyle, however, requires both faith and honesty.

Conviction is the virtue by which we are stubborn in a saintly way about what our heart says is true. It sometimes requires great courage, as in the case of Joan of Arc. Conviction is a 90% belief which is comfortable with the missing 10%, since it knows that a dash of doubt flavors faith. Sometimes compensation appears as conviction, a 110%+ belief which is the mark of a fanatic and often an expression of a deep but unaccepted lack of faith. Like barking dogs, such believers' bark is to convince themselves as much as to frighten others. But more people are bitten by silent dogs than by barking ones!

The honesty that leads to holiness is not simply a profound love affair with truth, the refusal to lie; it is also the willingness to **be** what you believe. Saints are not fanatical believers; they are ''be-ers'' of what they believe.

They celebrate the sacred wedding of lifestyle and belief. May the twin feasts which opened the door of this month call each of us to look at our lifestyles and see what beliefs they proclaim.

Festival of Where Did I Put It. Today is a holiday for everyone who has misplaced something. Don't be too critical of yourself. Take heart, for Beatrix Potter estimated that 50% of the time squirrels forget where they buried their nuts! And the U.S. Department of Defense reports that in 1984 the Pentagon misplaced items valued at $1,021,876,000! But it also found items valued at $1,031,697,000. Good luck finding your lost item today.

4

Feast of the Sandwich. John Montague, the Fourth Earl of Sandwich, was an addicted gambler. In a twenty-four hour long gambling session on this day in 1762 he decided not to stop for a meal. He simply ordered slices of meat and cheese between two pieces of bread. Salute England's First Lord of Admiralty today and enjoy your favorite sandwich.

5

Which Direction to Be Buried Day. In the Middle Ages it was the custom to bury people facing east, the direction from which it was believed Christ would come on Judgment Day. On that last day, people would rise facing the Cosmic Judge's glorious arrival. Priests, however, were buried facing west so that they would rise in a position to read their judgment to their people. A November day to reflect that regardless of the direction of our tombs or graves, we shall all read our judgment in the eyes of our friends and neighbors, especially our neighbors in need.

6

THE MOST BEAUTIFUL TOMB

These days of November provide an appropriate time to think about where we wish to be entombed. And it would help in making that decision to reflect for a bit on the nature of tombs.

The tombs of the rich and famous are well-known to us. Among those that come readily to mind are Grant's Tomb in New York City, Napoleon's in Paris and the Taj Mahal in Agra, India. This latter tomb, built by the Shah Jahan for his favorite wife Mumtazi-i-Mahal, required the labor of twenty thousand workers between the years of 1632 and 1653.

A tomb is actually a house for the dead that is above ground and is therefore different from a grave. Tombs, like the pyramids of Egypt, are intended to be permanent reminders of the great ones buried within them. Yet one of the greatest men of all times lacks not only a tomb but even a headstone for his grave. And in his death and burial lies some meaning for each of us.

Moses, who was so intimate with God, who was the source of the Law, a prophet, liberator and wonder-worker, died before he was able to enter the Promised Land. He was buried in an unmarked grave. But in spite of this fact, his tomb is among the greatest in the world. For Moses is buried in the hearts of his people, Israel, and in ours, as those who share the fulfillment of his mission from God.

All of us, by our lives, similarly construct our own tombs; they are located in the hearts of those whose lives we touch. Pause for a moment and look inside your own heart to see those who are entombed there, in a memory that is both blessed and beautiful. Within the living memory of our hearts are parents, teachers, friends and lovers. If we wish to be remembered, that is the place for us to be buried—not in a magnificent tomb of marble or gold. John Kenneth Galbraith once remarked, "The Turkish Sayyids built their fine domed tombs for their future repose before they died. It was possible that they foresaw that no one would think well enough of them to do so afterward."

While we will all be buried somewhere, the physical location is not what is really essential. Mindful of Moses—whose physical grave cannot be visited, honored or venerated—let us recognize that our grave site is not as important as where our memory is entombed. As we savor the autumn life of this November, let us reflect on whom we have loved and served. That reflection will also tell us where we will be entombed in splendor.

---

7 **Feast of St. Leonard,** patron saint of Prisoners. This fifth century French saint was given a forest by a king whose sick wife he cured. Leonard converted it into a home for escaped and freed prisoners. A day to be mindful of the overcrowded conditions in our prisons. Be in solidarity today with all who are justly or unjustly imprisoned.

Also join with the citizens of the U.S.S.R. as they celebrate the anniversary of the **1917 Socialist Revolution**.

---

8 **Birthday of Dorothy Day,** holy woman of the *Anawim*, the disenfranchised, on this day in 1897. She was instrumental in the Catholic Worker movement which provides houses of hospitality for the poor and the homeless. Today, celebrate her birthday by sharing some of your good things with the needy.

---

9 **Torch Day**. In 50,000 B.C. Neanderthals begin to bury their dead with flowers, food and hunting weapons. Their burial sites also have evidence of torches. Later, the ancient Romans used flaming funeral torches to guide the departed to their eternal resting place. Our word "funeral" comes from the Latin *fumus*, "torch." Regardless of your age or health, this is a November day to think about your Torch Day.

GIFTS FROM THE GRAVE

As the cold winds of November swirl around us, we reflect on this month of remembrance of the holy dead of our families. We have remembered in prayer and in our hearts those persons with whom we have shared life, and who have so richly shared life with us. Perhaps a story can help us reflect on and appreciate some of the gifts we have received from our departed loved ones.

A true story can hold the same power as a parable, and so I'd like to relate what happened to a certain British actress named Sarah Allgood. She moved to the United States in 1940 after having nursed back to health a friend who had been famous in the role of Eliza Doolittle in Shaw's play *Pygmalion*. When they parted, the recovered actress gave Sarah Allgood a token of her appreciation. It was a watercolor painting of a graceful heron.

Sarah took the painting with her to her new home in Hollywood. In the first dream she had there, her actress friend appeared, saying, "Have you found my gift to you from the grave? Look behind the painting." Sarah was puzzled by the dream, as she had no reason to believe that her friend was not alive. But she removed the cardboard back and looked behind the picture. There she found a drawing of her famous friend, Sir Max Beerbohm. The drawing was worth thousands of dollars at the time. Later, Sarah Allgood learned that her friend had died in France the very day of her mysterious dream in Hollywood.

We proclaim the mystery of our faith, our belief in the Communion of Saints, when we open ourselves to be gifted by the saints we have loved. That Communion of Saints is the community of those who have died in the loving embrace of God. They now live in that inexhaustible life which is beyond our present knowledge, but our living faith assures us that we are still in communion with them. Our rational minds balk at such a possibility, and our twentieth century sophistication objects to such an unscientific reality. Yet our faith says it is possible for those who love us in life to continue to love us even after they have passed through the door of death.

In the summertime, if we wish to feel the breeze, we must open our windows. How easily we close the windows of our hearts and minds by cold logic and reason. How easily we shut out the possibilities of being guided by our parents or friends who have died and are no longer physically with us. If we believe in the Communion of Saints, and if our inner doors and windows are open, can we not feel the grace and guidance that comes from those who have loved us?

Behind the symbols of our family heirlooms—an old photograph, a rosary, a prayer book, chair or dish—is a gift, just as there was behind Sarah Allgood's watercolor painting. We who stumble along the path to holiness need only prayerfully open ourselves to whatever gifts those who always loved us in life wish to send us from beyond the grave.

Birthday of Martin Luther, the great reformer, on this day in 1483. Luther said, "Faith, like light, should always be simple and unbending; while love, like warmth, should beam forth on every side, and bend to every necessity of our brethren." 10

Feast of St. Martin of Tours (330-397). This feast was called Martinmas and became a Medieval Thanksgiving Day, with a goose as its main supper dish. Martin, one of the most popular saints of the Middle Ages, is the patron saint of France, of beggars, the poor and the homeless. Like Martin, see if you can transform other's troubles, today, into a cause for thanksgiving. 11

IF I AM CURED

"When the devil was sick, the devil a monk would be; when the devil got well, the devil a monk *was* he." This old adage hits a homer for each one of us, for it says, in effect, that when we are sick or in some danger we make pious resolutions but forget them as soon as the danger is past. Sickness and extreme danger hold great power to help us remember the end and the purpose of our lives. But we easily forget this insight when the crisis is over and we are up and about, feeling strong and unthreatened by death. While neither death nor danger should be courted, they do help us to see things that we are not so inclined to see under normal circumstances.

The concerns and pleasures of daily life can easily blind us to the ultimate reason for why we are alive. We might intellectually admit that our purpose here is to know, love and serve God, a lesson learned in the first book of our religious education. But we generally find it difficult to live that out fully. Oh, we may indeed pay our religious dues by attending church on Sundays, and we may even say grace at the beginning of meals, but it is quite another thing to translate the words of prayer into living acts.

The old adage quoted at the beginning of this essay tells us that even the devil—Ole Nick himself—would be ready to reform if he were sick. But surely we do not need to be flattened on a "bed of pain" before being ready to live what we believe. Must we see a person without legs to be thankful for the gift of legs and the ability to daily walk and dance? Do we need to see pictures of those who are dying of hunger in Africa before we are truly grateful for the daily bread and butter that is ours?

While pain, sickness and grave danger can forcibly open our understanding to the purpose of life, thanksgiving is the gentle key that opens the door to a deeper involvement with God. Frequent and short blessings of gratitude hold the power to awaken us to a loving response of service and prayer to our generous and loving creator. If our eyes were constantly open to the multitude of gifts and pleasures that surround us, we would pour out our gratitude to God with every breath. And as we thank God, we might find that prayer, service to others and acts of charity come as naturally as we breathe. Indeed, may sickness and danger be far from you, and may the shower of divine gifts on you always be the cause for your change of heart.

12 **Festival of the Missing Birds**. Have the songbirds migrated south in preparation for winter, or have they become extinct? Today only 0.01% of all life forms known to have existed are still alive! This sobering fact from the book *Microcosmos* by Margulis and D. Sagan is made even more somber by the fact that, according to a Harris survey, 74% of Americans believe that science and technology will soon make humans extinct.

13 **Month of the Dead Reflection** taken from a tombstone in Middlefield, Massachusetts:

> Old Thomas Mulvaney lies here.
> His mouth ran from ear to ear.
> Reader, tread lightly on this wonder.
> For if he yawns you're gone to thunder.

TIME TO GET DRUNK

This is the month of the Holy Dead, and as such it provides an annual opportunity to reflect on the mystery of death. The poetry of the Hindu mystic Rabindranath Tagore provides a good starting point for such a reflection:

> In the heart of thunder plays the melody,
> to its rhythm I awake!
> I get drunk with that life
> hidden in the core of death;
> to the sound of the tempest's roar
> my heart dances with joy.
> Tear me away from the lap of ease,
> plunge me into the depths
> where majestic Peace reigns
> in the midst of restlessness.

For Tagore as well as other mystics, life and death are not enemies but rather companions in the mystery of the divine. When we fear death and run away from it, we also limit our capacity to live. Those who have come close to death sense that at its core is the secret of life. Instead of cutting ourselves off from the process of death in its countless forms—in aging, illness, the ending of relationships, the diminishing of abilities and strengths—let us learn to live with death in a loving way.

When pain and suffering enter our lives, let us learn how to plunge into their depths instead of shrinking from them. The peace of Christ is not found in the absence of war, turmoil and stress, but rather in living profoundly in the presence of Christ in the midst of the struggles and troubles of life. How easily we crawl up in the lap of ease; yet it is too much comfort, too much ease that is the real enemy of the Spirit. The Greek writer Nikos Kazantzakis said that the adversary of the Spirit is not the atheist or even the oppressor of religion but rather **lard**! The spirit-life is slowly smothered to death by excessive luxury and ease.

November, then, is a great time to get drunk with life—to feel the chill of the autumn wind on our faces, to plunge into the intoxicating joy of being alive, even if it means opening our arms wide to the suffering present in our lives. As the tempests of our lives crash and roar around us, let us not complain or pity ourselves; instead, let us learn how to dance in joy.

For what possible reason would we want to dance with suffering and death? Because, as Jesus taught and Tagore knew so well, it is in such storms that saints are made.

Birthday of Astrid Lindgren, Swedish storybook writer who originally wrote tales about Pippi Longstocking for her daughter. Soon, however, they became best-sellers. If you are a parent or a friend of children, keep alive the art of reading stories to children. According to Tom Biracree's book *How You Rate Women*, 40% of American parents never read to their children! **14**

15 **Feast of Shichi-Go-San.** A day for small children in Japan to visit shrines to pray for good health and fortune. Visit the shrine in your heart today and awaken the child within you.

16 **Dying Words** of Sadi, Persian poet, 1291, "Better is the sinner who hath thoughts about God than the saint who hath only the show of sanctity."

WHAT TO WEAR TO YOUR FUNERAL

How would you like to be dressed when you are buried? In ancient times the dead were laid to rest in clothing that represented their station in life, together with flowers, food and weapons for their journey to the next world. Royalty were placed in their tombs in splendid clothing and adorned with precious jewels, golden crowns and symbols of their power. Often they were accompanied into the grave by guardian soldiers and even servants to care for their needs. And it was the custom of some peoples, especially the Jews of old, to be buried in a special garment, a shroud. So instead of being buried in our functional clothing, even our best suit or dress, perhaps the custom of *special* burial attire should be revived.

I would like to propose a new special funeral clothing that would have great symbolic value for us: to be buried in our pajamas, nightgown or whatever we wear to bed each night. This could present a bit of a problem for wakes, since a recent survey revealed that 50% of men and 31% of women sleep in their birthday suits. But that could be solved easily by having a closed casket service.

My reason for this rather immodest proposal is that being buried in our sleep-wear would be a powerful sign that we take with us to death only what we take to bed each night. For who among us takes to bed at night a billfold, checking and savings account books, property deeds or any of our possessions? No, we go to bed naked of everything that we own.

Regardless of what you wear—or don't wear—when you go to bed, that's the way you go to the next life. Yet while "you can't take it with you" is a folk saying full of holy wisdom, we do not leave this world completely empty-handed. Each one of us takes into death whatever we hold in our hearts when we retire to sleep.

No one should go to bed with a heart filled with negative, angry or hostile thoughts about others. We should be dressed for sleep with a clean conscience, with peace of mind and hearts full of gratitude to God for all the many gifts and blessings that are ours. A wonderful night prayer is to fall asleep polishing our loves, blessings and the memories of those we cherish.

Those who surround themselves each night with love, with their friendships and the treasures of their heart will at their death be buried in a wealth far greater than any Egyptian pharaoh. And they need never fear that when they come to the gates of heaven they will find them locked.

17 **Feast of Different Clothing.** Pope Celestine I in the year 431 admonishes the clergy and religious of the Church, "We should not be set apart from

others by our dress but by our conversation and by the style of our lives."
A day for all clerics and religious who wear "different" clothing to pause
and reflect on the wisdom of Celestine.

Birthday of Mickey Mouse, created on this day in 1928 by Walt Disney, an international hero who is known and loved by all. Hitler began to rid the Reich of "dangerous" foreigners in 1933 and so considered it important to ban Mickey Mouse. He was also banned in the Soviet Union in 1936 and in Italy by Mussolini in 1938. Are you also a mouse hater? See if you can look with love today on all rodents, even if they appear destructive and cause fear.

18

THE HOLIDAY SEASON

Soon the holidays will be upon us. The holiday season begins in many ways with Thanksgiving and continues until Epiphany. It is a season filled with expectations and the richness of tradition. Our word holiday is but another spelling of "holy day." The idea of combining religious celebration and relaxation from work goes back to the origin of holy days. These were days of both attending church and freedom from work—because rest itself was considered holy. The British still call their vacation time a holiday, and we call such weekends as Labor Day and Memorial Day holiday weekends.

We need more holidays! We need those days when we can pull out of the fast lane and rest a bit on the side of the racetrack of daily life. Long ago, Sundays were such days of rest from the labor of the week. They were observed with the same attitude as was the Jewish Sabbath, when even the beasts of burden were forbidden to labor. Today, such days of complete relaxation and rest are few and far between.

We each need to honor holidays or free days when we exercise the discipline of closing our eyes to the mess in the garage or to the closet that needs to be straightened, and just relax. Such days are holy days even if they fall on a Saturday, or some other day, and even if we are the only ones observing them. We need such days of freedom if we are to be holy and whole.

Part of our religious tradition is the keeping holy of the Sabbath. The requirement of abstaining from work was to be a weekly celebration for the Jews of their liberation from slavery in Egypt. Slaves don't have days off; so to have one free day out of every seven was a powerful statement about who the Jews were and who they were not. How easily we become enslaved to a host of masters who keep us "on the go" seven days a week. If it isn't one master who is cracking the whip, then it's another. They have names like efficiency, tidiness, success, achievement; as well as others we know so well: the boss, the business, the job.

In addition, marriage, friendship and health all prosper when they are given holidays and free times. And if our commitments are such that we consider an entire day an impossible reality in our week, then at least there is always the holy hour or "holihours." We can fence off a certain time each day to be free, to relax, and so become more holy. An entire holiday is better, but as the old saying goes, "A half a loaf is better than no loaf at all." And loafing is what holidays and Sundays are really all about, even if we have misplaced their original purpose.

As we begin to prepare for the coming holiday season, we could apply some discipline this year to our agendas about what "should" be done. While decorating, purchasing gifts, writing cards, cooking grand feasts and attending parties is indeed part of the tradition of the holidays, so is loafing. Perhaps the best way to begin to prepare for the great holy days of this season is to put on your loafers and have a holiday or holihour today.

19

'Tis the Season to Be Thankful, the celebration of the feast of Thanksgiving. Because it is a movable feast, check your calendar for the precise date of this year's celebration. The first American Thanksgiving was in 1621. The invited guests included Chief Massasoit and ninety men of the Wampanoag tribe, along with fifty-six white settlers. The meal was prepared by four Pilgrim women and two teenage girls! Perhaps this is one of the reasons why the Pilgrims did not regularly celebrate Thanksgiving.

HALF-BAKED THANKSGIVING

The other day I read about a newspaper food editor who on the day before Thanksgiving received a telephone call from a youthful sounding woman. The woman asked how long it takes to roast a 19½ pound turkey. "Just a minute," said the food editor as she turned to consult a chart on the wall in her office. "Thanks a lot!" said the caller as she hung up.

That young cook must have served a Thanksgiving feast fit for wild animals. To believe that a turkey that large could be cooked in one minute is a sign of our times. What once took days, now takes only minutes, whether developing a photograph, preparing food or calculating math problems. But some things, like a 19½ pound turkey, still require time.

Friendship takes time, education takes time, meals that are truly holy and wholesome take time—and so does prayer. We Americans are a people who suffer from a great poverty of time. We are always short of time: to write letters, to visit old friends, to enjoy life. And the near future, especially for middle-class Americans, will find our clocks running faster and faster. With husbands and wives both working, numerous commitments to the parish, school and community and with children involved in numerous extracurricular activities, we are left with less and less quality time within the family. Consequently, we can expect to see, in the coming years, more instant foods and quick worship services.

But just as a 19½ pound turkey baked only for a minute will be a disaster dinner, so will prayers dashed off "on the run." The soul, like the body, knows hunger, and it will not easily be able to digest even a half-baked prayer, let alone some kind of "minute meditation." Delicious prayer, like a properly baked turkey, requires the same first step: the oven must first be preheated to about 450 degrees. One way to preheat the ovens of our hearts to the proper prayer temperature is with the fire of thoughts of devotion and love for God. Failure to do so may result in properly recited but chilly prayers.

Next, you need to stuff your prayer, before placing it in the oven of the heart, with generous handfuls of gratitude, seasoned with humility and a dash of awareness of your creaturehood to remind you of who God is. Frequently baste your prayer with the fullness of attention, by bringing your mind back again and again from its constant wanderings. And regarding the correct cooking time, allow at least twenty to twenty-five minutes per pound if you want a feast fit for a king or queen.

Anniversary of the 1910 Mexican Revolution, led by Francisco Madero. Have a revolution of your own today against the money spent on military weapons. Redirecting just one-fifth of the annual military weapon expenditures could abolish world hunger in ten years! Take a stand against hunger in the world and do something about it. **20**

First Flight Day. Frenchmen Jean Rozier and Francis d'Arlandes were the first men to fly. They ascended in a hot-air balloon in 1783 and flew for about twenty-five minutes over the city of Paris. And so the Space Age began. A day to do something that defies gravity; be lighthearted! **21**

Feast of St. Cecilia, a Roman virgin martyr of the third century, patron saint of music and musicians. In her honor, play or listen to some beautiful music. Music has the power to quiet the heart and inspire the soul. It's prayer for the ears. **22**

Birthday of Billy the Kid, 1859. He was shot to death on July 14, 1881 in New Mexico. Few, if any, mourned the passing of this notorious thief of the Old West. Reflect, today, on the words of St. Ambrose, "The bread which the rich eat belongs to others more than to them. They live on stolen goods... . Who is wise? The one who shows compassion to the poor, who sees the poor as natural members of one's family." **23**

AMNESIA—THE GOAT DISEASE

Hearing of a person who suffers from amnesia can cause us to shudder. To forget one's identity, to lose memory of oneself, and all that we associate with self, is truly a terrible affliction. We are aware that amnesia is produced by a shock, psychological disturbance, brain injury or illness, but it is less commonly known that it is a goat disease!

We suffer from a form of amnesia whenever we are unable to identify ourselves with the poor and suffering. While most of us feel sad that people are homeless, jobless and living in dire poverty, we find it difficult, even impossible, to identify ourselves with them. This inability to recognize ourselves in the faces of the suffering is a common affliction and is not merely a modern problem. Recall the images Jesus used in his story about the Last Judgment. The saints were separated from the sinners on the basis of amnesia. Those who suffered from that affliction he called goats, placing them on his left and finally sending them off to their reward—hell! They failed to see him, and themselves, in the naked, the hungry and the imprisoned.

If you and I are not to suffer from the goat disease, amnesia about our true and corporate identity, we must first learn how to see Christ in ourselves. When we look in the bathroom mirror as we put on our makeup, brush our teeth or shave in the morning, whom do we see? If we cannot see Christ in ourselves, how can we see Christ in the poor and the homeless?

Without the discipline of daily personal prayer it is not likely that we will see anyone but ourselves when we look in a mirror. Our primal vocation in this life is learning to know who we are—including our corporate identity— and loving ourselves with all our hearts, souls and bodies. That is no easy task, considering how widespread and contagious is the goat disease. A good preventative prescription for this illness is to keep our relationship with the Divine Healer constantly before us as we go about even the most ordinary task.

24 **Festival of the Forgotten Name of God.** Every typewriter has a sacred key which prints one of the most ancient symbols for the reality of God, the "*." The asterisk was the first Sumerian pictograph for God, being a five-thousand-year-old symbol for the sun. If you wish to sacramentalize a letter, you might type an asterisk after the date or elsewhere on the page to help you and the friend you're writing to remember the divine presence.

25 **Birthday of Pope John XXIII**, born Angelo Roncalli in Sotte il Monte, Italy in 1881. Elected Pope in 1958, he called into session the great reform movement of the Second Vatican Council before his death in 1963. In his document *Peace on Earth* he said, "Those who claim their own rights, yet altogether forget or neglect to carry out their respective duties, are people who build with one hand and destroy with the other." A good day to ask if you know what your other hand is doing.

26 **Birthday of Karl Benz** in 1844 in Karlsruhe, Germany. In 1885 Benz invented an internal combustion vehicle, a three-wheeled car which reached speeds of ten miles an hour. A German newspaper reported the event by saying, "Who is interested in such a contrivance as long as there are horses for sale?" Reflect, today, on the difficulty of humans to embrace the new and different. Ask yourself if that is one of your inclinations.

27 **Festival of the Handkerchief**, introduced into France in 1499 by French sailors who had seen Chinese field workers wearing lightweight linen cloths on their heads as sun protectors. Thus came the name "Couvrechef," meaning "covering for the head." Originally carried as a fashionable sign of social standing, only later was it used for the nose. Erasmus of Rotterdam wrote in 1530, "To wipe your nose with your sleeve is boorish. The hand kerchief is correct, I assure you." In more recent times handkerchiefs have been used by sports fans to rally support or show appreciation or even to show disapproval, and others have used them to wave hello or farewell. Look, today, upon the linen cloth you carry and celebrate its long use for various purposes.

GOODBYE

News item: "On April 14, 1959, Bruce Campbell and his wife drove from their home in Massachusetts to visit their son. On their way the couple stopped at a motel in Jacksonville, Illinois, where Mrs. Campbell awoke the next morning to find her husband gone. His clothes, wallet, belongings and car were left behind, but Campbell himself was never found."

How casually and halfheartedly we say "good night" or "goodbye" to one another! Such expressions are among the numerous daily rituals of life. Like so many other common acts in which we are involved, they can easily become lifeless and hollow. How much *good* is there in "good night" or "goodbye"? How often do we fail to invest them with goodness and true feeling because we live in the perpetual illusion that we will surely see those we speak to again? How easily such expressions of love become empty box-cars that once held or could hold great stores of goodness! When Mrs. Campbell said "good night" to her husband on that April 14th as they fell asleep, she fully expected that she would awake with him beside her the next morning. If she had known the truth, I expect that her "good night" would have been filled with *good.*

The month of November, in our religious tradition, is a month of reflection upon the mystery of death. We tend to avoid and deny that absolute reality of life because it is so awesome to deal with daily. The funeral of a friend or family member has the power to bring us temporarily in touch with the truth of death's reality, but usually we quickly slip back into the slumber of illusion. That illusion says, "Life is forever; tomorrow will always come. Later I will speak of my love with full meaning."

Those who seek the spiritual path, who are pilgrims of the Way, should travel with a guardian angel, the angel of death. Such a companion would guard us from empty "goodbyes" and casual "good nights." To travel daily with the angel of death is to be on the cutting edge of life. To be aware of that dark angel leads one to a life of prayer, to a perpetual attitude of turning to God. And those who creatively engage the angel of death are given a happy death, for their lives have been lived fully, with no regrets.

The ritual parting expression, "goodbye," was originally an expression of prayer, for it is a contraction of the old blessing, "God be with you." Yet we need not return to its original form for it to remain prayer; we have only to invest it with as much goodness, love and meaning as possible. Then, truly, God will go with those we love.

Feast of Farewells. A day to reflect on the last words of Lawrence Oates who was born in 1880. He died on an ill-fated expedition to the South Pole in 1912. Believing that he was a burden to his companions, he left the tent in the middle of a blizzard, saying, "I am just going outside and may be gone for some time." He proceeded to wander out into the snow-covered waste of the polar region and was never seen again.

28

Frozen Americans Day. According to *Trans Time* of Oakland, thirteen Americans are presently frozen in hope of one day coming back to life!

29

Why wait to come alive? The season of Advent is a winter thawing of frozen hearts by prayer, charity to the poor and needy and an awakening of a love for God. There is perhaps no more certain way to come back to life.

THE ADVENT QUESTION

If an alien from outer space were to visit America in the first weeks of December, he or she would likely be impressed by what a religious people we are. Shopping malls, stores, streets and homes are all richly decorated for a religious feast, as spiritual carols fill the winter air from giant loudspeakers. The poor and homeless who are usually overlooked throughout the year are cared for with charity and generosity. The religious feast of Christmas, and all that is connected with it, saturates our society in this time before December 25.

But if that space visitor were to report back that Americans are a church-going people, it would not be totally accurate. According to a recent Gallup survey, slightly over half of Americans regularly attended church over a six-month period, other than for special religious holidays, weddings or funerals. Of those who do not go to church, 48% are providing religious education for their children, 63% believe that the bible is the word of God, 31% say that religion is "very important" in their lives. 58% believe in life after death, and 75% revealed that they occasionally pray to God. Considering these rather high percentages of religious feelings and attitudes, they were asked why they did not attend church.

Most responded that they did not feel any hostility toward religion, but they felt that churches were not living up to their responsibilities! This season of Advent is a good time for those of us who attend church to ask ourselves, "What indeed are our responsibilities? What is it that those who do not go to church see us failing to perform?"

Being a professed believer and member of any church must require responsibilities beyond financial support and attending church services, beyond prayer and supporting action against immoral practices. But what exactly is missing? A good Advent exercise would be to take a few minutes, right now, to seek an answer to that question. Living answers are required from each one of us if Advent is indeed to be a time of reform and renewal of our faith life.

30 **Birthday of Samuel Clemens**—pen name, Mark Twain—in 1835 in Florida, Missouri. Twain once said, "Most people are bothered by those passages in Scripture which they cannot understand; but as for me, I always notice that the passages in Scripture which trouble me most are those which I do understand."

December

Advent Veiling Days. Between now and Christmas you might try veiling all the pictures and images of Christ in your home. Moslems rarely depict saints of their religious tradition in art. And whenever Mohammed is pictured, the artist always covers the prophet's face with a veil. If we covered the face of Christ in our home and church art with a veil, we would be less tempted to "know" what Christ looks like. Advent is a season to look into every face—man, woman, black, brown, yellow, red, rich or poor—and ask ourselves, "Is this the face of Christ?"

1

THE FIRE OF ADVENT

Advent, like its cousin Lent, is a season for prayer and reformation of our hearts. Since it comes at winter time, fire is a fitting sign to help us celebrate Advent. It is also a symbol well-suited to this season because a patron saint of Advent, the cousin of Christ, John the Baptist, was a fiery saint.

John, an intensely zealous mystic, called for the fire that creates a new heart as a prerequisite for the coming of the Divine Fire, the very life of God, into the world. Coming from a wealthy, priestly caste, John was singularly dedicated since his birth to a holy madness. He was a charismatic prophet living on a diet of bugs and honey, his home the desert wasteland, his clothing the skins of animals. His tongue was a machine gun rattling out damnation upon the pious and righteous, the religious pretenders of his culture. His mystical message was equally practical, advising his crowd of social outcasts, tax collectors and soldiers not to cheat, to be honest, to share their goods with one another and to refrain from rough stuff with the poor and weak. But the heart of his message was the creation of a new heart and the need for fire. He is that Voice of God that in every age calls people away from their frigid prayer and worship.

Each age has its energy crisis, and for too long we have all felt the chill in the chapel, the cathedral and the parish church. It is the common cold of worship life for which authorities have sought an all too common cure:

new programs, visual aids, guitar music. But the message of God through John is simple: the chill in our lives can only be removed by fire.

What is missing in our prayers and spiritual life is **life**! We essentially know what will happen to us in our parish church—no surprises. We know that when we go to worship, nothing will happen—at least nothing will happen to our souls! What does our attendance at a religious service mean? Is it merely a community social event, or is it an outpouring of the soul, a transformation of the spirit?

Our chapels are usually tidy, clean and neat—perhaps an air of tranquility prevails. But can it be that in this climate-controlled atmosphere, our souls are dying in silent agony? If prayer becomes for us an empty gesture, a chilly, calm, unemotional echo of our uncertainties about God, then the ardor of our intimate relationship with the Divine Mystery fades.

If Christ is to come more fully into our lives this Christmas, if God is to become really incarnate for us, then fire will have to be present in our prayer. Our worship and devotion will have to stoke the kind of fire in our souls that can truly change our hearts. Ours is a great responsibility not to waste this Advent time.

2

Feast of St. Isaiah who around 742 B.C. said, "They shall beat their swords into plowshares and their spears into pruning hooks. Nation shall not lift up sword against nation, neither shall they learn war any more" (Is. 2: 4). Isaiah along with John the Baptist, two patron saints of Advent, call us today not to teach war by thoughts, words or deeds that are intended to injure others.

3

Beat Your Taxes into Plowshares Day. The average citizen today doesn't have a sword to pound into an instrument of peace and plenty for a starving world. But there is a way you can be true to Isaiah's prophecy. Consider the following fact from the Military Spending Research Services. In 1986 the percentage of your individual income tax that was spent on military programs was an astounding 51.4%! If you take God's word spoken through Isaiah seriously, then take the hammer of political power and the ballot box and begin pounding away this Advent day.

THE SILENT "O"

We hear it at every turn: "Have a good day." That expression, complete with those buttons showing a round face with a broad up-turned smile, abounds in this land of the Great American Dream. That parting wish, which concludes telephone conversations and business transactions, is based on our belief that we are a people in pursuit of the "good life." And we can be rightly proud of the achievements of our country in providing those things necessary for its citizens to live the good life.

Central to the American value system is the belief in the right to happiness. Our national heritage also proclaims "liberty and justice for all" right alongside the right to "the pursuit of happiness." But both of these realities should be possible for everyone rather than reserved for just a privileged class. Is it not un-American then that a large portion of our people is unable to have a "good day" and to enjoy the "good life"? It would be rather cruel to say "Have a good day!" to one of the two million homeless of our land. And I, for one, would find it very difficult to have a "good day" if I were among the eight to ten million unemployed or the thirty-three million who, even by the government's standards, live in poverty.

In this holiday season, "Have a good day" is replaced by "Merry Christmas!" But this wish also implies that one has the necessities of life to make this Christmas, and the days that follow it, merry. Otherwise, Christmas becomes only a tiny island in a sea of suffering. I would like to propose that when we wish another a "good day," we make the third letter in the word "good" silent. Then the wish becomes "Have a God day."

Now, you may ask, "What's a God day?" Such a day would be one in which we are actively involved in the work of God, which is justice and peace. And such a greeting would imply more than a wish that the receiver enjoy her or his possibilities for a good day. It would also presuppose a commitment on our part to the work of achieving such a day for everyone in our society and in the world. Being concerned about the hungry and homeless at the holiday season has always been part of the American way. In fact, we are very generous to the less fortunate at Christmas and Thanksgiving. But they are only two days out of 365! What about the other 363?

Our Advent work is more than wrapping gift packages and decorating the Christmas tree. In the second letter of Peter we are told that we are not only to be holy in our conduct as we look for the coming of the day of God but that we are to hasten it! We hasten the day of God not only when we enflesh our prayers for the poor and homeless in gifts, donations and assistance that care for their immediate needs, but also when we say political prayers. The God day that the helpless long to see will come when we change the structures of our society that create the God-less day of suffering that millions experience today. The Prayer of the Ballot Box can help us to choose leaders who are truly concerned about the needs of all people, not simply a privileged few. Further, our letters to already elected officials strongly encouraging action on peace and justice issues and a political awareness that keeps such concerns in the public forefront are also political prayers.

The call of Advent is a radical one, for it challenges us to clear out of the way anything that prevents the path of God from being straight. What makes that path crooked are ideas, attitudes, institutions, structures and systems that are not aligned with peace and justice. Advent calls us to more than a change of heart; it also calls us to a change of society—and to the radical prayer that enables both. May you, then, in these days of Advent and everyday "have a God day."

Watch Your Diet Day. As the pre-Christmas season begins with its parties and feasting, don't forget your diet. Also remember as an Advent prayer that 75% of the world today, more than three billion people, does not have adequate nutrition or calorie intake, while the other 25% has enough or *too much* food!

4

5 **Hindu Advent Reflection**, "The narrow-minded ask, 'Is this person a stranger or one of our tribe?' But to those in whom love dwells, the whole world is but one family."

THE PAY-LESS SHOE GIFT SHOP

One of the patron saints of this Advent season is good old St. Nicholas whose feast is December 6. Legend tells that he was the holy bishop of a city in Asia Minor. He is the patron of children, sailors, young women who wish to be married and pawn brokers—an interesting collection of persons to have the same guardian. But we might also add one more to the list of clients for the patronage of this kindly and generous saint: holiday shoppers.

By every advertising means at hand, we are encouraged to buy gifts for our loved ones. Christmas is the time when we empty our bank accounts in an attempt to satisfy our desire to find the right gifts for all those we love. Clever minds create commercials telling us that the cost of the gift speaks of the depth of our love. Hassled, hurried and haggled, we crowd our way through stores attempting the impossible feat of balancing our affection with our bank accounts. And each year, as the cost of goods increases, we find it harder to give a gift that truly speaks of our love. Woe to those who struggle through purchaser's purgatory!

But then, in the midst of our depression, comes St. Nicholas with a solution that's nearly a miracle (for which he was well known on land and sea). And it is fitting that the feast of St. Nicholas comes at the beginning of Advent and the beginning of the shopper's season. As the patron saint of shoppers he proclaims, "Keep it simple!" Keep it simple enough to fit in a shoe (as you may recall, in Europe it is St. Nicholas who gives gifts to children, leaving presents in their shoes or stockings). True, a diamond ring or a gold watch could fit inside a shoe, but that's not quite the idea behind this St. Nicholas advice.

One gift that could fit in a wooden or leather shoe, or in a stocking hanging on the fireplace, is a note that speaks of one of our most precious gifts, the gift of time. Such a St. Nicholas note might read: "My gift to you, Mom, is an offer to dry the dishes every night for the next three months." Or, "The gift I give you, dear, is half an hour of quality conversation each night right after the dishes are done." We can appreciate the value of such a gift if we keep in mind that according to a recent sociological survey, the average married couple in America has only thirty minutes a week of communication outside of exchanges that take place at the family table. And that thirty minutes a week even includes arguments! As you can see, the possibilities are almost unlimited for these St. Nicholas shoe gifts. Such love gifts imply that what you hide in the shoes of your loved one is yourself.

Come, St. Nicholas, patron of shoppers and gift-seekers, and make Christmas this year fun, creative and love-filled!

6 **Feast of Saint Nicholas**, Bishop of Myra in Asia Minor in the fourth century, patron of children, pawnbrokers and sailors. Nicholas, known for his generosity, is also the patron saint of Greece, Russia and Sicily. Today in many European countries this Dutch Sinter Klaus, or Santa Claus, gives gifts of fruit, candy and sweets. Pray today for the heart of a child so as to enjoy this magical and mystical season of Christmastide.

HOBBIT GIFTS

In J.R.R. Tolkien's wonderful trilogy, *The Lord of the Rings*, we are introduced to a delightful group of little creatures called hobbits. These easy-living, gentle people who inhabited Middle Earth can teach us much about gift-giving at Christmas time.

Among the customs of the hobbits was to give new gifts only to new friends. Old friends were given old gifts such as family heirlooms. The older the friendship, the more ancient the gift. What happened naturally was a sort of perpetual gift exchange. Prized possessions, rare and beautiful things, simply flowed back and forth among them. This custom of giving away a gift that you yourself had once received might strike us as being impolite. But if the gift is a symbol of love, should not the love be shared—passed around?

This practice of the hobbits expresses a good theology about what we, as Christians, should be doing at Christmas time. Just because a gift is old, well worn and perhaps out of style does not take away from its symbolic value: perhaps it adds to it! For the longer we have a valued possession, the more affection we will have had a chance to invest in it and the more of our loving energy it will have absorbed. Our friends the hobbits could remind us that all gifts are really symbolic. They are magic reminders that we ourselves are the real gifts that are exchanged with others. This central and sacred concept that gifts are intended to be signs is often forgotten in the blitzkrieg blizzard of business advertising. We become more concerned about the size, shape and price tag than with the meaning invested in the gift.

May the hobbit's simple but sincere gift-giving tradition temper our usual holiday excesses and free us to give gifts that are true expressions of the heart.

Celebration of an X-Rated Holiday. A day to recall the anti-Christmas movement. As early as 1583 the Puritans banned Christmas. In 1644 they made it a day of fast and penance. Any celebration was outlawed under pain of severe punishment by an act of the English Parliament in 1647. Until 1856, December 25 was an ordinary work day in Boston, and in as late as 1870 the public schools of Boston had classes on Christmas. But as with so many other forbidden things that people love, Christmas escaped the law. And, of course, it is alive and well today. This has been largely due to the influence of nineteenth century immigrants to the United States from Catholic Europe. Be grateful, today, if you love Christmas, that it wasn't outlawed.

7

Feast of the Immaculate Conception of Mary, the Mother of God. Mother Mary, Advent patroness, help us today to give birth to the God-seed that lies hidden within each one of us. Today, pause to pray in solidarity with all unmarried pregnant women that Mary of Nazareth, who knew the feeling so well, will be at their side this Advent day.

8

Also celebrated in Japan, the **Feast of the Enlightenment of Buddha Under the Bo Tree**. Buddha, who sat in stillness for forty days and nights until deep understanding broke through into his consciousness, taught that "All that we are is the result of what we have thought. What we think, we become."

A feast to appreciate the silence out of which peace comes into the world.

ADVENT: LISTENING TIME

One of the prayers inherent in this season of Advent is the prayer of stillness. It was the prayer of Mary, the Mother of God. In her silent prayer she heard the voice of God telling her of the Great Mystery which had been planted within her womb. But listening is hard work. Full listening demands an openness to communication through our eyes as well as our ears. Indeed, messages are received through all the senses. Communications come by way of another's voice, eyes, posture, dress, attitudes, and it comes in most concentrated form in silence.

To hear another, we must be very still. Not only do we need to be still exteriorly, but we must be free of hearing only ourselves and our needs. Prayer purifies us. The prayer of stillness continually brings us back to the present moment. It brings us back to "what's happening here." And if we are aware of what's really happening, then something **real** is likely to happen! Our awareness opens out into caring, into concern externalized. Such prayerful listening shifts our center from self to God. And being one with God, we gracefully begin to act like God. We become compassionate; we become caring persons in the Gospel spirit.

Such divine manifestations are just as necessary today as they were in the days of Christ. Who cares? Truly, who cares about you? Who cares about what happens to you, to what you're feeling? Our first response, and the response we often hear in song and prayerful talk, might be: "Well, naturally, God cares about you!" If that is true and if we are one with God, then we must care for those who stand within the circle of our lives. It is thus that social action flows out of, is supported and nourished by prayer. Such action or concern is alive; it is miraculous. Such caring is graceful because it flows naturally from the divine heart rather than out of a sense of duty or guilt. How often have we acted to assist another not because it was heartfelt, but because we were "supposed" to act that way.

To prepare oneself for social reformation by spending the time and effort necessary on the difficult road of daily meditation is hard work. It is much easier to run into the street and immediately try to "do good." But most "do-gooders" usually grow tired by the noontime of their apostolic kindness. By supper time they become disillusioned because of the ingratitude of those who were helped or the meager financial rewards. And by nightfall, they are often convinced that they can't change the system. Tomorrow, they will stay indoors and watch television.

True spiritual social action is a result of true hearing. It flows out of good listening that has now come full circle. The process usually begins with a struggle to move away from hearing only ourselves, our problems, our needs and our inner turmoils to truly listening to another's words. At some point we go beyond hearing words to hearing the Author of the words. The paradox is that having found a oneness with God in the discipline of listening, we begin to hear a cry of need as our **own** cry! We begin to hear others with a knowledge of the heart, we "know" what it's like when another is hungry or in need of liberation. Because of being one with the Divine Mystery, we come back to the place from which we started. We are again listening to ourselves, but now it is not the little I; it is the big I that hears the cry of my/another's need.

Beware of Advent Clip Joints Day. As you rush from store to store, doing your Christmas gift shopping, beware of pickpockets. In the seventeenth century the watch chain was invented as an anti-crime device to prevent pickpockets from stealing pocket watches. But thieves created small metal snips to "clip" the chain and thus easily detach the watch. Those gathering places that were visited by disreputable gypsies and other thieves were called "clip joints." Beware that your addiction to consumerism doesn't clip you and pickpocket your heart this shopping season.

9

Birthday of Emily Dickinson on this date in 1830. This American poet wrote, "Parting is all we know of heaven, and all we need of hell." Reflect today on the wisdom of not taking "partings" lightly lest you become guilty of the *presumption* that you will see your loved ones alive again! Invest your goodbyes with as much love and meaning as possible. (See p. 185.)

10

Feast of the Christmas Card. They were originally homemade, but in 1843 in England John Horsley designed a card for sale; its message read, "Merry Christmas and a Happy New Year to you." A good day not to let signing and sending the greeting cards of this season be an assembly line production. Write notes and mail all your cards with love so that your wishes to those you love will come true.

11

A CHRISTMAS CARD TO OUTER SPACE

Christmas is the season for greetings, for messages of love, concern and peace. A unique message was sent by U.S. scientists several years ago—a Christmas greeting, we might say, from the entire earth. Beamed into space from the troubled third planet of our solar system, the radio message sent from a giant radio tower located on the island of Puerto Rico constituted an act of faith on behalf of all humanity. It expressed the conviction that we on Planet Earth are not alone, that the joy and the struggle of intelligent life is not an isolated accident of creation found only on this planet, but that throughout the giant cosmic sweep of the universe there is life!

The communication was brief: a three-minute transmission in a mathematical code describing the make-up of our solar system, the inhabitants of Earth and the present population of this world. The target of this signal was a cluster of some 300,000 stars located on the remote fringe of the Milky

Way, a cluster called Messier 13. The message was addressed simply to "Occupants" of any planets that might be orbiting Messier 13. Earth's Christmas signal, traveling at the speed of light, 186,000 miles per second, will not reach the star cluster for 25,000 earth years! If anyone is listening and cares to answer it, it will take at least as long to reply. But nonetheless, a response to our greeting is requested by Christmas of the year 51,974 A.D.

We await the sunrise, the dawn of the feast of Christmas, as have our Christian ancestors for almost 2000 years. We look for the coming of Light as an act of faith. We await the message God sent to earth, a signal beamed from the divine heart 2000 years ago to Bethlehem of Judea! Christmas celebrates that beautiful message from God to this troubled planet. As the transmission that left earth a few years ago told those in the fringe space of our galaxy about who we are, so the message beamed to earth at Bethlehem told us what God, the creator of our planet, is like! And just like our message to Messier 13, that divine transmission requested a reply!

Christmas is a celebration not of a radio transmission to this planet but rather of a communication of the "Word made flesh." God's message was a human person, born of Mary and Joseph in a crude cave-barn-stable on the outskirts of the little town of Bethlehem. "And the Word was made flesh and dwelt among us" (Jn. 1: 14). All of us have heard the message from God, and each of us translates it according to the dictates of his or her heart. But the basic meaning is universal: the Divine Mystery—the Alpha and the Omega, the beginning and the end, whose names include Yahweh, Allah, Buddha, Vishnu, the Great Spirit and many, many more—that God is Love.

God is not a tyrant, a blindfolded judge of human behavior, nor some cosmic electric current of depersonalized energy. God is kindness, concern and providence enfleshed. God is all we mean and experience in the beauties of human love and much more. But the joy of the divine message to us is that it is also true that the goal of love is always union with its object. The true end for all creation is union with the divine. And in man and woman this end has become conscious and appreciated.

Jesus, the son of Joseph and Mary, was and is the ultimate expression in flesh and blood, a living message, that God and all creation are One! To be spiritually alive, to find real contentment and peace in our lives, we must be conscious of that unity with the Divine Mystery. "Every moment," wrote Dom John Chapman, "is a message from God; every external event, everything outside us, and every involuntary thought and feeling within us is God's own touch." As our radio message to Messier 13, the distant cluster of stars, was an act of faith, so to be conscious each day that everything within and around us is an expression of God demands real faith.

This meditation began by saying that Christmas is a celebration of the Divine Signal in human form which has been given to us, and that a reply is requested. While our earth message was sent in a mathematical code, we rejoice that God's message was not coded, but is clear, understandable, knowable and as plain as the nose on our face—and on the face of Jesus. If we find it difficult to live out this profound sense of unity with God in every aspect of our daily lives, it is largely because the extremely simple message of Christmas, "And the Word was made flesh" (Jn. 1: 14), has been lost in theological algebra over the centuries. And as with the radio transmission from earth, the message takes a long time to hit home.

Feast of Our Lady of Guadalupe, patroness of the Americas. As the patron saint of Mexico, she appeared in 1531 as a young Aztec maiden. This is a festival of the Mother of God whose skin is brown, red and yellow as well as white. A day to celebrate our rainbow-colored God. **12**

Feast of St. Lucia, a festival of candles and lights in European countries and among Americans whose immigrant ancestors carried on the tradition. This is a feast day of light in the midst of the darkness of approaching winter. Light a candle today in honor of St. Lucia, a beacon of hope and of hospitality to holy pilgrims. **13**

DECK THE HALLS WITH ANTS AND HOLLY

The holiday season is a time to rejoice at the presence of guests in our homes. It gives us an opportunity to practice the holy sacrament of hospitality. We can find a pattern for our service as ministers of this sacred ritual in the scriptures of the Hopi Indians of the Southwest.

According to the Hopi holy tradition, God became displeased when the children of earth forgot to sing songs of praise and thanksgiving to their creator. God thus destroyed the world, not once, as in our scriptures, but several times. Those who still praised God, however, were spared each time.

Now, on the occasion when the earth was destroyed by fire, the faithful were taken underground to live with the ants. After the rain of fire ended, the time for the earth to cool took longer than anyone had imagined. Therefore, the food supplies of the ant hosts began to run out, and so the ants gave their share of the food to the Indians. As a result, the ants had to keep pulling in their belts as they grew skinnier and skinnier! When the earth was cool enough for humans to live on, the Hopi came up out of their temporary ant homes. But to this day the ants have never regained their normal waistlines. As a sign of respect and remembrance of how they were sheltered and fed by the ants, the Hopi, even now, are reluctant to step on or kill an ant. So goes the beautiful story about who comes first in true hospitality.

As we approach our religious observance of Christmas, we should be aware that entertaining others, being hospitable, is an important aspect of our celebration. Generous service to Christ in attending to strangers as well as family and friends may be as central to Christmas as gifts under the tree. It's too bad that ants are usually not around at Christmas time. They would be a great symbol for the season. The sight of ants in our houses could be an occasion not to reach for a can of insect spray but rather to reach out with kindness and love to those who seek warmth and hospitality under our roof. This season of Christmas has many wonderful traditions that are familiar to each of us. Alongside the holly, mistletoe and candles burning in the window, we might also place the lowly ant with its narrow waistline. The ant would call us to practice true hospitality and to remember that by such kindness we continue to sing the song of praise and gratitude to God.

14 **The South Pole Discovered** in 1911 by Roald Amundsen. A good day for you to discover that in all the traditions and trimmings of this season is hidden the sacred. Look inside all the decorations and customs of Christmas time for messages about your spirit quest. See them as sacred signs and colorful prayers.

15 **Halcyon Festival.** Traditionally seven days before and after the Winter Solstice, this feast was believed by ancients to be a time of great peace and calm. It was named after the halcyon bird who was said to calm the winds and waves. In these hectic days before Christmas, may the halcyon fly over your house.

WHICH WAY TO BETHLEHEM?

Each year we rejoice in this marvelous season of Christmas. It is a time for celebration, gift-giving and remembering with cards, letters and parties. The reason, of course, for all the music and lights, the festive spirit and good feelings, is an event that happened in a small Palestinian village where the Jewish prophets had foretold that the Messiah would be born. When the birth took place, it seemed that no one remembered the ancient prophecy, and so people were looking for Emmanuel in other places. Perhaps they were too busy to remember the words of the holy visionaries. And we need to ask ourselves the question, "Does history repeat itself?"

Jesus as prophet said, "Again, I tell you...where two or three are gathered in my name, there I am in their midst" (Mt. 18: 20). We should tattoo these words on the back of our hands so that they might be constantly before us. For taken in their fullness, without the dust of centuries or the cobwebs of spiritual slumber, they contain the most radical of truths. Where two or three are united in prayer, in love, in justice, hope, affection and work, that place can be called Bethlehem. It is a place where once again the Divine Presence becomes a reality, the birthplace of Emmanuel, God-among-us.

The idea of the Messiah coming into the world in the midst of sheep, goats and other animals in some stable-cave was unbelievable to the people at the time of Christ's birth. Is it any easier for us to believe that Jesus becomes a living reality in our kitchen, bedroom, automobile or workplace? Each Christmas we are reminded not to make the same mistake made by the people of Israel, even in Bethlehem.

Take time to be aware that in the very midst of our busy preparations for the celebration of Christ's birth in ancient Bethlehem, Christ is reborn in the Bethlehems of our homes and daily lives. Take time, slow down, be still, be awake to the Divine Mystery that looks so common and so ordinary yet is wondrously present. The old abbot of the monastery where I attended the seminary was fond of saying, "The devil is always the most active on the highest feast days." The supreme trick of Old Nick is to have us so busy decorating, preparing food, practicing music and cleaning in preparation for the feast of Christmas that we actually miss the coming of Christ. Hurt feelings, anger, impatience, injured egos—the list of clouds that busyness creates to blind us to the birth can be long, but it is familiar to all of us.

"Excuse me," said one ocean fish to another, "you are older and more experienced than I and will probably be able to help me. Tell me, where can I find this thing they call the ocean? I've been searching for it everywhere to no avail."

"The ocean," said the older fish, "is what you are swimming in now."

"Oh this? But this is just water. What I'm looking for is the ocean!" And the small fish, feeling disappointed, swam away to search elsewhere.

Little fish, stop searching for the ocean. There is nothing to look for. Instead, stop—be still—open your eyes and look. Which way is Bethlehem?

Posadas Celebration. In Mexico, and among Mexican-Americans, the celebration of Posadas, meaning "shelter," is a highlight of the pre-Christmas season. In imitation of Joseph and Mary's search for shelter, pilgrims knock on doors and ask for shelter on this night and every night until December 24. These are nights of parties and celebration in peoples' homes. Perform an Advent act of love for Christ today by doing something for all those who lack Posadas, the homeless of our time. Also a day to view all who come to your door as holy pilgrims.

16

The Wright Brothers' First Airplane Flight at Kitty Hawk in 1903. As we prepare for the birth of the Prince of Peace, let us recall that the Wright Brothers believed that the airplane would bring about world peace, for with airplanes nations could keep close watch on one another and so prevent surprise invasions. Moral for the day: no weapon can end war. Only non-weapons can end war. This is as true for individuals as for nations.

17

THE DIVINE RECALL

Careless words, once spoken, are like feathers cast in the wind. How can you ever call them back? That old folk saying is true—yet not always. Some words can be called back once they are spoken. Blessings are such words. Jesus instructed his friends and us about such a divine verbal recall when he said, "On entering any house, first say, 'Peace to this house.' If there are peaceable people there, your peace will rest upon them; if not, it will come back to you" (Lk. 10: 5).

Any blessing of peace is a sacred word and seems to possess the power to choose its dwelling place. This means that no prayer or blessing-wish for peace is ever wasted. When you wish someone God's peace (shalom, shanti, the divine presence), if he or she lacks a proper heart to be a shrine for the divine presence, it will return to you. Because it is a sacred expression, a blessing-wish of peace cannot share the same space as anger, resentment, greed or other such negative attitudes.

Frequently each of us is blessed with the peace of God in worship, on greeting cards and in farewells. Yet we do not often experience the fruit of such blessings: contentment, balance, wholeness and grace. Perhaps these blessings do not find the proper environment within our hearts. We all desire peace, but are we willing to pay the price of such a divine indwelling: humility, reconciliation, hope, a desire for the communal good rather than only our personal gain, a passion for unity and an abiding trust in the mystery of God's plan for us? And these are but a few of the requirements for hearts that wish to host the divine peace.

Perhaps all blessings of peace should be temporarily suspended. If a moratorium were declared, we might take the time to clean house and heart. And, of course, Advent is the perfect time to clear and prepare the Way. Advent is a winter training camp for those who desire peace. By reflection and prayer, by reading and meditation, we can make our hearts a place where a blessing of peace would desire to abide and where the birth of the Prince of Peace might take place.

Such a prayerful preparation does not mean abandoning the colorful celebration of the Christmas season. While writing greeting cards, cleaning house, baking special holiday foods and attending parties, we can keep a watchful eye over the environment of our hearts. Daily we can make an Advent examination. Are there any feelings of discrimination toward race, sex or religion? Is there a lingering resentment, an unforgiven injury living in our hearts? Do we look down upon others of lesser social standing or educational achievement? Are we generous with the gifts that have been given to us, seeing ourselves as their stewards and not their owners? Are we reverent of others, their ideas and needs, and of creation? These and other questions become Advent lights by which we may search the deep, dark corners of our hearts.

We have probably already begun receiving Christmas cards wishing us a blessed and peace-filled Christmas. If the good wishes of our friends are to find a resting place in us, we will have to create a prayerful space for these blessings. That was equally true for the whole earth when the first Christmas card was delivered by the angels as they swooped over the rolling hills around Bethlehem. That first blessing also contained a conditional clause about the divine recall—"Glory to God in high heaven, peace on earth to those on whom God's favor rests" (Lk. 2: 14). Peace to the hearts of those who have made their inner shrine a place pleasing to God.

18 **Ratification of the Thirteenth Amendment** to the U.S. Constitution on this day in 1865, abolishing slavery in America. An Advent day to be aware of whether anything—an idea, belief, habit or unforgiven injury—holds you in slavery today.

19 **World Census Day**. A 2020 census of the world's population reveals that only 16% of earth's people are white! Pray today that the ugly seeds of centuries of discrimination by white people against those of other skin colors will not reap a harvest of retribution in the twenty-first century. On this day, plant an Advent seed of non-discrimination toward any aliens or persons of another race.

Longest Night of the Year. An evening of enjoyment with candlelight, fire, feasting and storytelling. Let the ancient art of telling tall tales and family legends entertain you, your family and friends on this long, dark and mysterious night. Also spend some time in silent prayer on this night of nights, resting in the embrace of God's "dark-eyed daughter."

20

THE MYSTERY OF DARKNESS

In the northern hemisphere this is the season of the longest nights. Because of the tilt of the earth the sun seems far distant from us, and the hours of darkness are long. But in this darkness are hidden gifts of insight for those who wish to look.

Light and darkness have, over the centuries, been cast as enemies: light has become a sign of the holy and the good and darkness a symbol of evil and ignorance. Yet it was at night, in the surrounding intimacy of darkness, that some of the greatest religious events in our tradition occurred: the Passover meal, the birth of Jesus and his Last Supper. At the moment of his death darkness covered the earth, and since he was already absent from the tomb at dawn on Easter, Christ must have risen in darkness. We are told he went into the mountains to pray at night or before dawn, and these were the times of Jesus' most intimate communion with the Divine Mystery. This love of night by God should not surprise us, for is not night the time of lovers?

We need to appreciate darkness as the soft companion of prayer and love. With a gentle touch, darkness closes our eyes to the world of work, shrinks our cosmos to a close circle and produces an inner prayerful proportion. The mystery of night not only allows us to feel closer to each other but closer to God as well. Perhaps this is why night vigils are practiced by persons of all religious beliefs.

Jesus said, "I am the light of the world" (Jn. 9: 5). We would probably have more difficulty saying, "Jesus is the nighttime darkness," yet this is also true. Perhaps these final days of Advent could be a time of atonement for our failure to love night as we love the day, for our sin of prejudice against the darkness, for our failure to see how darkness and light play together in the circle of God's wholeness. And when our day is finished, our work at rest, with a sense of accomplishment and gratitude, we open our arms, as the French poet Peguy would say, to the embrace of God's dark-eyed daughter, night.

For darkness is more than the absence of light. As we consider the opening words of Scripture in the book of Genesis, we see that "the earth was a formless waste and darkness covered the abyss" (Gen. 1: 2). The darkness of space covered the earth. There was just darkness and God, intimate in their ageless embrace. And when God said, "Let there be light!" (Gen. 1: 3), from the very heart of darkness light appeared.

Advent is the ageless season of waiting for the birth of Emmanuel into the world. And it is appropriate, for those of us who live north of the Equator, that Advent comes at the darkest time of the year. For Advent's silent sister, the dark, holds the gift that allows us to wait quietly for the Light of Lights.

Let us use these Advent days around the Winter Solstice, earth's darkest day, to wait in open stillness for "the light that shone in the darkness" (Jn. 1: 5).

21

Winter Solstice, the festival of fire, love and friendship in the darkness of winter. On this day in 1620, the Mayflower landed at Plymouth Rock. As a pilgrim of the cosmos, celebrate this change of seasons in the annual pilgrimage around our great daystar, the sun. Celebrate the new season of winter by wearing or doing something new.

22

Pre-Christmas Home Cleaning Day. As we dust and clean our homes in preparation for Christmas, let us also sweep clean our hearts of anything that separates us from others and from God. A good day to go to confession to one another, asking pardon from anyone you may have injured. Pardon is the most beautiful gift you can give at Christmastide.

CHRISTMAS HOUSE CLEANING

A traditional part of Advent is the ritual of confession of sins as a sort of inner house cleaning to prepare for the great feast of Christmas. But perhaps confession and absolution are not enough! In St. Luke's Gospel, Jesus tells a story about a man who cleansed his house of an evil spirit. That spirit wandered about and finding nowhere else to live finally returned to find his old house clean and tidied. He then invited seven other spirits far worse than himself to come and live there with him.

At first reflection it might seem that Jesus was telling us not to cast out one evil habit lest seven worse ones come along. But actually it was a matter of not going far enough. Religion needs to be concerned with more than "Thou shalt nots." For if we only remove evil and do not fill the empty house with goodness, we have created a vacuum into which even greater evil can come.

Maria Montessori, the famous educator, once said, "The first idea the child must acquire in order to be actively disciplined is that of the difference between good and evil; and the task of the educator lies in seeing that the child doesn't confound good with immobility and evil with activity." So often we say to children, "Now sit still and be good," as if non-activity were the same as goodness. The spiritual life requires an active performance of good and not simply the removal of evil. Our thoughts of unkindness toward another person should not be removed but should be replaced by positive thoughts. Likewise, all vices need the seeds of virtues planted in their place. Spiritual poverty is not merely the absence or denial of some possession or desire, it implies an order of spiritual fullness. Celibacy, for example, is not the denial of love or the human gift of sexuality, it is rather the freedom to embrace a different way of loving.

Perhaps we need a new prayer form that would allow the confession and absolution of our faults to open us to filling our inner house with good activity. We might imagine the good coming into our lives, picture it in action and then taste the joy of its fruit. Such a new prayer would prevent undesirable guests from moving in after we had vacuumed the house.

It's really the same process that happens in homes all around us at this time of year. First, houses are cleaned for Christmas, and then they are decorated. Let us, this Christmas season, decorate our lives with goodness and charitable deeds.

Birthday of the Universe, 13,500 billion years ago. Celebrate, today, the Big Bang that birthed the galaxies 12,000 billion years ago with a festival of fire, light and feasting. You might even want to make a big bang as part of this cosmic celebration—with clanging pots and pans, a slammed door or a popped balloon or paper bag.

23

The Feast of Christmas Eve, and among Eastern Christians **The Feast of Adam and Eve**. Our first parents by their "happy fault" in the Garden of Eden made necessary the coming of Emmanuel. This evening, share an apple with friends and family at supper as a sign of sharing in each other's faults and sins. Remember that all sin is social. Christmas Eve is also a night of great magic and wonder. Every gift under the tree is but a symbol of God's love made flesh in Jesus Christ—and in each one of us.

24

MILLIONAIRE MEDICINE

The leader in the ever-skyrocketing cost of contemporary life is medicine. The cost of curing an affliction today, other than a mild headache, can be staggering. But there have also been other times when medical care has been very expensive.

For example, in 1534, Pope Clement VII, who was the patron of Michelangelo, Raphael and many other great artists of the Renaissance, became seriously ill. His physicians prescribed a very costly cure that may have actually been the death of him. Over a period of fourteen days the ailing Pope Clement swallowed over three million dollars worth of precious stones, including one very large diamond! The "practicing" physicians, however, were unable to save their papal patient.

The Renaissance was a time of expensive art *and* medicine. The most popular medicines were concoctions made up of crushed jewels. Indeed, the more expensive or rare the remedy, as with Clement's last pill, the more effective it was believed to be.

We are in the midst of a season that is meant to remind us just how truly expensive was that cure called salvation. And we are preparing to celebrate the feast that honors the most expensive and rarest of all medicines, our cure for selfishness. We sing carols rejoicing in the coming of our Savior, who is the source of the salvation of the world. The same mother-word that gives us *savior* also gives us *salve*, which means *healing*. As Native Americans would say, "Jesus is good medicine." In fact, he is **the cure**. And perhaps no more expensive and rare a jewel could be found than "he who was crushed for our sins" (Is. 53: 5), as Isaiah said. But Emmanuel is no pill. Emmanuel is therapy, a healing activity.

Most of us would prefer to pop a pill that would cure our tension, pains, physical-mental suffering and even being overweight. We want something fast, effortless and cheap. But Emmanuel therapy requires that we become part of an expensive cure, for we cannot simply swallow a savior. True healing comes from an active communion with our Cure. Indeed, our salvation is in Jesus, but we must engage ourselves in the daily therapy of giving away **our** body and blood, our very selves. The divine "good medicine" prescription is very clear: "Do this in memory of me" (Lk. 22: 19). This is not simply a recipe for a ritual but rather for the reality of becoming a part of the salvation of the world.

Christmas is the feast of joyfully giving gifts to one another. This act is a symbol for how the world will be cured of its sickness of selfishness, war, discrimination and exploitation. We give gifts because it is the feast of the Divine Gift. In each of us the Son of God, the Cosmic Divine Diamond, the Healing Salve, is waiting eagerly to become Emmanuel, "God-among-us," again. The birth of Emmanuel within us is the only effective medicine for our terminal illness.

May the gifts we give this Christmas become part of an addictive therapy that will lead us to the point of giving away all of ourselves as gift. As Jesus said at the Last Supper, "This is my blood, which shall be shed for you and for *all*" (Mk. 14: 24).

And a merry medical Christmas to you!

---

25 **Feast of the Birth of Jesus Christ, Christmas**. Let your family celebrations of this great feast not overshadow a sense of gratitude that the birth of Jesus Christ was the beginning of a new era of peace and justice for all people. Let Christ be born anew in you on this holy day. And may today not be the end but rather the beginning of celebrating in various ways the twelve holy and merry days of Christmas.

---

26 **Feast of St. Stephen**, first century deacon and patron saint of care for the poor. It's called Boxing Day in England where people box-up some of their Christmas gifts to give to the poor. What of your overflowing Christmas celebration can you share with the poor today?

THE FEAST OF ST. STEPHEN AND CHRISTMAS PIGGY BANKS *OR* SANTA CLAUS RIDES AGAIN!

Christmas gift-giving isn't restricted to December 25 but flows over, in true Christmas fashion, to the 26th, the feast of St. Stephen. In England the feast is called Boxing Day, when people box-up gifts for the needy. St. Stephen, the first deacon, was entrusted by the apostles with the task of caring for the poor among them. Since his feast is on the day after Christmas, it is fitting that it has become the traditional day of sharing one's surplus with the poor. And do we ever have a surplus on December 26!

But in our American society, the day after Christmas is not often one for remembering the hungry and poor. In our culture it's the great Gift Exchange Day at department stores, as well as the beginning of the post-Christmas sale season. Our thoughts are usually centered on ourselves and not on those who face a bleak future. As the number of needy in our country increases dramatically, why don't we reinstitute the ancient feast of St. Stephen and Christmas piggy banks?

Now, we usually don't associate piggy banks with Christmas, but at one time they were closely connected. On the day after Christmas in medieval England, merchants customarily presented their apprentices with money boxes shaped like pigs. And, of course, inside them were gifts of coin money.

A twentieth century celebration of the feast of St. Stephen could provide an opportunity for the poor to be less poor by our sharing of some of our Christmas gifts with them. If we feel uncomfortable passing on our gift from Aunt Nellie to the poor, we could give a Christmas piggy bank gift—a financial gift whose size would be measured by the richness of our gifts on the feast of the birth of Christ.

What child among us needs more toys? And what adults truly need 95% of the gifts they receive at Christmas, our lives already so full of gifts? The gifts we receive are tokens of love more than essentials needed for survival. But as we rejoice in even more gifts, all around us there are millions whose lives are devoid of even the essentials.

Mindful of this, Christians should always give gifts to one another with the understanding that the gift can continue to travel to yet another. To give away a Christmas present is not necessarily a sign that we don't care for it. In fact, to give away a Christmas gift in which we take great pleasure only adds to the value of the gift. If the gift was given in true love, then when we give it away to someone who truly needs it, that gift is twice-blessed by love.

The feast of St. Stephen on December 26 further allows us to play Santa Claus-a-la-Christ, who said that such deeds of justice and charity should be done without the left hand knowing what the right hand is doing. We may never see the persons who receive our St. Stephen's Day gift, and they may never know our identity. The result of being such an invisible gift-giver would be that "Santa Claus rides again!"

To so celebrate the day after Christmas can greatly add to our joy in this holiday season. Like drugs, joy is addictive. And we might find that we would turn every day into a St. Stephen's Day so as to taste again the joy of anonymous giving. And what better ritual for Christmas evening, after a day of feasting, than for children and parents to gather around the tree and its sea of gifts. Then after expressions of gratitude, all can decide together which of the gifts will go into a St. Stephen's box or what can be put into a Christmas piggy bank. Then all the family can rejoice together as "Santa Claus rides again!"

Feast of St. John the Apostle, Galilean fisherman and friend of Jesus. This is a traditional day to bless wine, in his honor, to be shared with friends and lovers. A feast day of friendship and love.

27

Feast of the Holy Innocents. This fourth day of Christmas commemorates the massacre of Israel's children by King Herod. It is an occasion to reflect on child abuse. The feast honors all holy innocents who today suffer from physical, mental and sexual abuse.

28

---

29 **Feast of St. Thomas Becket**, Bishop of Canterbury who was murdered in his cathedral in 1170. In T.S. Eliot's play about Becket, four tempters appear to Thomas. The fourth is the most dangerous, tempting Becket to do the right thing for the wrong reason, to give up his life in order to be acclaimed as a saint and martyr. A day to take stock of our motives in life.

CHRISTMAS GIFT WRAPPING, 100% OFF

The most joyful and festive of Christian feasts, Christmas, is over. And as stores offer Christmas cards and rolls of colorful wrapping paper at the annual after the holidays 50% sale price, we have an opportunity for a reflection on that important aspect of everyone's spiritual life, the sacrament of giving.

The goal of the spiritual quest is to become aware that we and God are united in a bond of love that is beyond our human comprehension. To give gifts without strings, to give gifts wrapped in unconditional love, is to attempt to love as God loves. Anyone who has tried to love another person unconditionally realizes at once that not only is such love very difficult, it is truly divine. Cervantes, the Spanish author of *Don Quixote*, said, "When God sends the dawn, he sends it for all." The splendor and blessing of the rising sun is a gift for saints and sinners alike. Cervantes only rephrased the words of Jesus that "God sends the rain upon the just and unjust alike" (Mt. 5: 45).

If you or I were God, we might be seriously tempted to give the gift of dawn or the refreshing rain only to good people who were daily grateful for them. We might be inclined to leave those who were sinful or ungrateful in an arid desert or in a chilling, never-ending night. As we struggle in our family life and at work to live and love as God does, we are gradually awakened to the vast untapped divine powers that sleep within us. The more we allow the light of our dawn to shine through the small clouds of others' irritations and insensitivities to our needs that usually cause us to withhold our love-light, the more we are transformed into beings of light. And the more our baptismal birthright of loving like God is exercised, the better our dawns can penetrate even the storms in our lives and the more grace can rain down through us. And who knows, perhaps one of these years, we will realize that we have died to our need to hold back our full love from those who hurt us. We may find that we don't have to wait till year-end holiday sales to give our love 100% off!

30 **Christmas Feast of Thanksgiving**. Take down this year's calendar, now useless for all practical purposes. Slowly turn the pages and reflect on what this old year contained for you as you go through the months. As the old year prepares to die, decide what you want to die in you. See what you can remove from your life because it is now old and no longer useful, so that you can be as new as the new year that is peaking just over the horizon.

31 **New Year's Eve Celebration**. Parties and festivities mark the death of the old year. A night to be with family or friends to rejoice in all the gifts of the past 365 days. It is the end of one complete pilgrimage journey around our daystar, the sun. As you prepare to begin another pilgrim's journey of 365 days, and our planet's journey of millions of miles, rejoice and be filled with grateful expectation for all that the new year will hold for you. Open your heart to all the experiences of the coming year that are hidden from you. Be thankful in anticipation of tasting all the pleasant ones and make a New Year's Eve intention to let the unpleasant and painful ones be sources of growth and wisdom.

NEW YEAR'S EVE

The poet Alfred Lord Tennyson captured well the spirit of New Year's Eve when he wrote:

> Ring out the old, ring in the new,
> Ring, happy bells, across the snow:
> The year is going, let him go;
> Ring out the false, ring in the true.

At each new year's beginning we are called to make resolutions about abandoning the false and choosing the true. But such personal reform isn't easy. As Somerset Maugham wrote, "The unfortunate thing about this world is that good habits are so much easier to give up than bad ones." For Maugham as for a good number of us, ringing out the false isn't as easy as Tennyson seemed to imply.

The paradox of life is that bad habits sneak up on us. When they begin, they are so weak and seemingly insignificant that we hardly even notice them. Gradually they become so strong that we find it almost impossible to break them. When they are so well-formed that they seem part of our personalities, we find it much simpler to own them than to change. And when our bad habits, the false impulses within us, are challenged, we can find ourselves replying, "That's who I am, take me or leave me!" But those aspects of our personalities that are unbecoming, that make it more difficult for people to love us and that cause pain are not the persons we really are.

New Year's Eve is like the whole season of Advent rolled up into a party. The season of Advent was also a call to reform, to make new resolutions about our lives that would "make straight the way of the Lord" (Mk. 1: 3). Now, after the splendor and wonder of Christmas, we are once again called to take stock of our habits and see if they reflect our true nature. Mindful that good habits are easier to give up, we must invest our new year's resolutions with sufficient energy to change the false, or there will be little that is new in this new year.

Regardless of how we celebrate the end of one year and the beginning of the next, whether quietly or at a party complete with paper hats, we can make a positive decision to remove at least one negative pattern from our lives. Such a positive resolution could be the focus of a small ritual with friends or family. For example, each person could write a bad habit on a small piece of paper; all the folded papers could be placed together in a basket or on a plate. Then, one by one, the old and false patterns that these papers contain could be symbolically burned away over a lighted candle or in a fireplace. Finally, a wish about how one desires to change could be written on a fresh sheet of paper. That intention, stated in a positive way, might be placed where it could be seen throughout the coming year. Such a family or personal ritual might also have time set aside for silent prayer as an expression of support and encouragement and as a means of deepening each person's intention to make the coming year really new and true. Regardless of what we are doing as the old year is rung out, may it find each of us desiring to be as new as the infant year!

Additional Readings
for
Movable
Sacred Seasons

A TOMBSTONE PRE-LENTEN EXERCISE

The Buddhists have a saying that the arrow that hits the bull's eye is the result of one hundred previous misses. Woe to those who give up after their ninety-ninth try, for they shall miss the reward of all their errors. The holy season of Lent is about to begin, and, if you are like the rest of us, you may also have a string of failures when it comes to how to spend those holy days of reform. So even if your previous Lents may have missed the mark, this may be **the** year for hitting the bull's eye!

Motivation is a key to making this Lent a success. And an excellent source of motivation is found on the first day of this season of reform. On Ash Wednesday we are reminded that we will die. We all know that it is necessary to frequently remind ourselves of that most basic of all truths. A sacramental reminder of our own deaths has the power to cleanse our inner eyes so that we can see more clearly the ultimate purpose of life.

We can help prepare ourselves for the feast of ashes and for the season of Lent by practicing a simple exercise. Take a few minutes to create the epitaph that you would like to have carved on your tombstone, a brief sentence or phrase that is the summation of your life. In a few words it expresses your deepest beliefs and how you would like to be remembered. This prayerful exercise can have added power during these coming Lenten days if you write your epitaph out and place it on your desk or on your bedroom dresser. Such a visual reminder will help motivate you to find the time to perform your various Lenten disciplines so that your epitaph will be a true expression of who you are. With it daily before your eyes, you will also be reminded to make the right choices about how you live and what to do with the limited time that is given to you.

One of the rich gifts of the tradition of our faith is that we have several new beginnings each year besides the civic New Year. The sacred seasons of Lent and Advent both call us to remember our mortality and to prepare our hearts so that we can truly live the life that Jesus promised us in its fullness. And a great obstacle to such wholehearted enjoyment of his gift is our self-inflicted blindness to our own deaths. This refusal to ponder death is a primary reason why we waste so much of life. It is the reason why we delay, put off till a better time, a host of activities that would enrich our lives and the lives of others.

On Ash Wednesday you might try silently repeating your tombstone epitaph as you come forward to receive the mark of death upon you. If you do, your chances of hitting the bull's eye in Lent this year are better than ever before.

A HOLY LUST

The author of the famous *Fellowship of the Rings* trilogy, J.R.R. Tolkien, who created the world of hobbits, once said, "All that is gold does not glitter. All those who wander are not lost." Each year as we enter into the season of Lent we are called to wander.

As Jesus went into the desert, we are called away from the daily chores of life to wander in the desert of God. Wandering is at the heart of a good Lenten experience. Israel, while wandering for forty years in the Sinai desert, experienced an intensity of love for God that was compared to a honeymoon. Time and time again the prophets called her back to that wandering desert experience for a renewal of devotion.

The Journey or Quest is the classic symbol for a life of prayer. Wandering is a special kind of journeying; it involves traveling freely and without haste, which makes it a sort of rambling. The desert is too hot a place to hurry, and we *wander* after God, mindful that it will take forty years—a lifetime—for the journey. The call is to be on the move, to wander instead of choosing a particular course—and without choosing to settle down. Settlers are wanderers who have dropped anchor, become stationary, stopped their quest. Many were the number of original pioneers who never made it to California, but who settled for something less hectic or demanding along the way. This is the eternal temptation of all who seek God—to stop and make camp, or even a permanent home, along the wayside.

Jesus entered the desert for his personal forty days of prayer to recapture that original spirit of Israel, to find again the original intimacy of the Divine Beloved, to face the faceless God, naked of all rituals, ceremonies and protective devices. Jesus entered the desert as the carpenter of Nazareth. He left the desert with a divine life's mission. The God with whom he left the desert was a broader God, at once more universal and more intimate than the God Jesus had known in the village synagogue of Nazareth. And because of that experience of forty days of wandering, Jesus became a perpetual wanderer.

In our worship and personal prayer we are called to venture into the unknown, to resist the temptation of routine prayers that can make us zombie disciples. Of course, it is always easier to pray the same way we did twenty years ago, to use the same words we did as children. It is much less trouble to live a religious life without constantly re-examining and redefining what we believe and how it should be lived.

How easily do you and I settle for our familiar, easy God? We often fail to understand or to embrace what worship of the mystery of God implies. God moves ahead of us constantly and calls us out of our personal Egypts or Nazareths to seek the Divine in the desert. Those who wish to be more than ordinary disciples, who seek to be more than "church-going" settlers, need more lust in their lives! This Lenten lust the Germans called *wanderlust*, the irresistible impulse to journey. Those who follow that path will be the travelers who meet Jesus on their own personal road to Emmaus.

LENT A LA SEQUOIA & PSALMANAZAR

The season of Lent is here again. If it is to be significant in our sacred journey, we must view it as more than just another Lent. One way to approach it in a creative and enterprising way would be to make it a Lent a la Sequoia & Psalmanazar!

The parables of Jesus contain his theology of the Age of God, the Kingdom, and they instruct us in how to live. Jesus' parable of the embezzling manager challenges us to be enterprising. The parable promotes a charlatan as our spiritual director for this Lent. The following stories of Sequoia and Psalmanazar recommend equally inventive Lenten guides.

Sequoia was the name chosen by an Englishman who posed as an American Indian in the 1890's in Britain. He toured England in a brilliant red coach, dressed in clothing made of animal hides, complete with a feathered headdress. Traveling with him were attendant "redskins," as the British called them, and a brass band. Sequoia was a traveling medicine man, a healer who sold natural remedies and removed teeth painlessly— at least so he claimed. Actually his brass band played so loudly that the screams of his patients were drowned out! Sequoia made a great fortune curing all manner of ills and aches with his Indian Oil and other medicines.

The second spiritual director for your Lenten consideration is the famous George Psalmanazar. He was French, but his real name is unknown to this day. He appeared in 1703 in London, claiming to be a native of Formosa. At that time almost nothing was known of that mysterious island in the Orient, so his stories were of great interest— and equally difficult to verify. The next year Psalmanazar published an account of Formosa together with a grammar of the native language. These were, from beginning to end, a pure fabrication—no small feat of creativity and effort.

Psalmanazar was lionized by the literary world of London, and its high society was taken in by his clever deceit. But after a time he was exposed as a fake when Catholic missionaries who had labored in Formosa came forward and exposed him as a charlatan. He confessed his guilt and then turned over a new leaf. He applied himself with vigor to the study of Hebrew, having a natural gift for language, and ended his life in 1763 as a man of some renown. He was even a personal friend of the famous Dr. Johnson.

Sequoia and Psalmanazar, like the manager in Jesus' parable, took great initiative to "make it" in the world. They used the gifts that God had given them, brass band included. And they guide us to look to the end of Jesus' parable when he asks a question which to my knowledge has never been answered: "Why aren't the disciples of the Kingdom of Life as clever, enterprising and crafty as the con men of this world (Lk. 16: 8)—can they not use their talents as inventively to bring about an Age of God?"

To that unanswered question another could be added. Why aren't we more crafty and clever in the ways we use these grace-soaked weeks of annual renewal called Lent?

THE INSIDE OF PRAYER

The saintly Rabbi Moshe of Kobryn often said, "When you pray even one word to God, enter into that word with all your body." One of his listeners objected, "Rabbi, how can a full-grown person enter bodily into a tiny word?" And the rabbi answered him, "Anyone who thinks himself greater than a word of prayer is not the kind of person we are talking about."

As we once again prepare to enter Holy Week, in which we remember the death and resurrection of Christ, we should take with us the words of Rabbi Moshe. For if Holy Week is to have significance, it must be a week of prayer. If we are unable for any reason to enter fully into the sacred liturgies of these holy days, we should find some ways to make this coming week as prayerful as possible. Those who allow the business of life to prevent them from spending this week differently are truly unfortunate in their loss. If we are to gain from the graces of this Holy Week, we must pray with the zeal and the passion which Rabbi Moshe spoke about. We will have to move beyond the mere recitation of words to invest each word we pray with all our body.

As Jesus reminded us, the love of God requires the total gift of ourselves. We are to love God with **all** our heart, body and soul. To enter prayer with such an intention makes us humble servants of the Divine Mystery. Such humble prayer allows us to climb inside each word of prayer, regardless of our personal size!

By his passion and death Jesus entered, body and blood, into the words of his prayer. Holy Week calls us beyond a habitual, mechanical repetition of "saying prayers" into the painful process of **becoming** prayer. Such a process focuses upon the quality of prayer rather than its quantity. And since, in the Kingdom of Jesus, daily life and religion are fused as one, when we enter bodily into each word of prayer all our words become full of our flesh, blood and spirit.

Our words often flow forth in daily conversation without much mindfulness. We are usually only half-present to what we say. As we struggle to fit inside every word we pray, we gradually begin to speak all words with greater meaning. Increasingly our daily use of terms like "friend," "beloved" or expressions like "I care," "I love you" or "I want to help" become more genuine and hold more power.

At the Last Supper, on that first Holy Thursday, Jesus put himself physically into his words of prayer and love. He said, "This is my body, this is my blood, given in love for you and for the world" (Mk. 14: 24). Those words which we repeat in loving memorial were truly spoken as Rabbi Moshe told his disciples to pray!

"Do this in memory of me" (Lk. 22: 19). Jesus called us in that final request to place our whole selves, body and soul, into our words of prayer—and into all the deeds and words of our daily lives.

REMEMBER

Good Friday is one of the most sacred and solemn days of the year. The traditions that surround it are numerous, as over the centuries we have paused in somber silence to remember the death day of Jesus Christ. While much merit and grace can be found in the prayerful remembrance of that first terrible Good Friday, the day offers other graces and calls us beyond a mere remembrance. As we consider how Jesus surrendered to the divine will and accepted death on a cross, we can reflect, "Am I ready and willing to surrender to the death God has arranged for me?"

No matter how busy our days are, we would do well to pause and reflect on a personal attitude of surrender to our own deaths. We might examine the death we fear the most: death by cancer or by fire, a slow death in a home for the aged, death that comes creeping over us as our mental faculties diminish, death surrounded by loneliness. As we prayerfully pause at each of these possibilities, we can inwardly search for the space to say with Jesus in the Garden of Gethsemani, "Yes, if that is your will" (Lk. 22: 42).

When we face death as a present reality for ourselves on Good Friday, making it a communion with the passion and death of Jesus, we become involved in a living faith. Such a dynamic faith finds a pattern for life. It is a source of energy and grace to live life fully in the events of Holy Week and in the weekly remembrance of the resurrection of Christ at the Sunday Eucharist.

Each Holy Week we look backwards, but only to be able to see with the eyes of faith the events, sufferings, pains and joys of our days. When we remember by means of tradition and ancient ritual, we project a pattern upon our lives. Like a dressmaker with a paper pattern for a new dress, we too know where to cut and where to pin, how to bring together the various pieces of our lives.

Without the aid of the patterns we are shown in the liturgies of Holy Week, and at other times of the year, all we have is a pile of pieces—bits of pain, threads of joy and seemingly unconnected events. As we hold up the life of Christ to our fragmented lives, we can begin to see how our sometimes seemingly insignificant lives are truly a precious part of the redemption of the world. "Remember," Christ says, "remember and be whole."

THE SCHOOL OF DEATH

Good Friday is the day when we not only remember the death of Jesus on the cross, it is also a day for us to come face to face with death. No one really wants to look into that face which stares at us daily from a thousand different directions. Yet our fear of death prevents our enjoyment of life, for one cannot reject death without reject- ing life as well. Persons who have embraced death are truly alive—and therefore very wealthy. They are also the bravest of heroes.

When a rebel army swept into a Korean village, everyone fled, even the monks in the Zen temple. The only one who remained was the abbot. The rebel general, his sword in hand, burst into the temple, angered that the abbot refused to bow before him and receive him as a conqueror. "Don't you know," sneered the general, "that you are looking at someone who can run you through without batting an eye?"

"And don't you know," returned the abbot in a calm voice, "that you are looking at someone who can be run through without batting an eye!" The general's haughty scowl was deflated. He simply bowed and left the temple.

How reminiscent is this story to the exchange which took place between the con- queror Pilate and Jesus. In both cases the one with the power of the sword, the power of death over others, acknowledges that the quiet, unarmed man before him is the true conqueror. The one who has overcome death holds the true power. Both Pilate and the Korean warlord recognized what we need to see.

And more to the point, we need a school to learn what the Zen abbot and Jesus knew. Perhaps Good Friday is such a school. For Good Friday calls us to do more than go to church or keep a fast; it calls us to learn the great lesson of Jesus' passion. Death holds power only over those who believe that it is stronger than love, that it has the power to separate lover from lover, friend from friend.

Fellow students, Good Friday is **not** a good day to skip school.

AN EASTER SURPRISE

Easter, like the other great feasts, holds many graceful insights. It holds so many that we take at least fifty days to explore them. These insights sometimes seem to be secrets, concealed from the casual glance, and they often appear as surprises. While it is hardly hidden to the careful eye, we may have overlooked one of Easter's eye openers. The first hint of this "secret" surprise can be found in the beginning of St. Matthew's Gospel, and there are many other clues sprinkled throughout the Gospels. The surprise of Easter is women! Surprising, even in these more liberated days, is the relationship that Jesus had with women.

St. Luke's Gospel tells us that Jesus journeyed throughout Israel accompanied by his disciples, among whom were "some women...who were assisting them out of their means'' (Lk. 8: 3). A "good" rabbi in those days did not travel about the country with women, for women of that culture were treated almost as non-persons. In the Hebrew tradition women were considered the property of their husbands or fathers. They lacked an identity outside of those two relationships. In the family trees of that time only one's male relatives were generally listed.

St. Matthew gave us a glimpse of the Easter surprise when he included the names of five women in the genealogy of Jesus. And it's interesting to look at who those five women are. Besides Mary, the Blessed Mother, we find the names of a prostitute, an adulteress and an unfaithful wife. The kingdom that Jesus came to proclaim was indeed to be a new Kingdom. It was to be a community where men and women were to be as one, received on a common, equal ground. Also, it was to be not only a community of good people, the righteous, but of sinners as well. Even after two thousand years we have not yet fully understood how radically different, how unorthodox, is this new Kingdom of Christ.

The newness of the Kingdom is strikingly revealed in the accounts of the resurrection of Jesus where we see that it was women who became the first apostles. An apostle is "one who is sent," and women were the first to bear the most important message in Scripture and in all of human history; "He is Risen!" It was not to men or to one of the twelve that the Risen Christ first appeared but to a woman, to Mary Magdalene. To her was given the divine commission, "Go and tell them" (Jn. 20: 17). And Mary rushed off to the apostles with that apostolic message. As we celebrate the feast of Easter, we have an opportunity to carefully examine that event to see some of its often overlooked implications. And the more deeply we go in that examination, the more we understand that, if we are to become Easter people, people of the new age of the Resurrection, we must re-examine our concepts of who belongs to the Community of Christ. We need to ask whether we view the Church as being only for good people or if we allow room among us for sinners, for those who have broken the Law of God and seek to be one with God. We also need to consider whether women are entitled to have an active and important role in the Christian community. We are slowly beginning to see women perform more and more functions once exercised only by priests or men. In the liturgy of the Church, in prayer and worship as well as in education, we find women as active ministers. This is not merely a concession to modern liberation movements; it is an attempt to live out the direction that God seems to have pointed out for the New Kingdom. Women's important roles as witnesses and "apostles" in the Gospels indicates that divine intention.

Perhaps women became the first witnesses to the Resurrection because they were in the right place at the right time. But was it really a divine accident or does it reveal a divine insight? Mary and the other women came to the tomb of Jesus to perform a service, to anoint the body. Perhaps at the heart of the hidden message is that if we seek an experience of the Risen Christ, we must seek out opportunities to be of service. Jesus proposed such humble service in his feet-washing sacrament at the Last Supper. Whenever we perform lowly tasks, what might be called "women's work," we place ourselves in the right place to be surprised by God. Such "women's work" implies caring, creativity, healing, encouraging and loving. When we do this kind of work, whether we are men or women, we open ourselves to the living presence of the Risen Christ, the Easter mystery.

Jesus' relationship with women, as in the case of the woman at the well in Samaria,

was new and startling for his day and his culture. It was difficult for most people—
including his apostles—to understand this break with tradition. Today, two thousand
years later, that difficulty does not seem to have lessened very much. It is difficult
for many to see women in active liturgical or pastoral roles. But if we are to call ourselves
true followers of Jesus, we must, with trust, open ourselves to the changing customs
and traditions of the Kingdom that were set in motion in the Gospels.

THE EASTER GIFT

One day when a holy man was speaking before a large group of people, someone who
was new to his teaching asked him a question. Gesturing to those who surrounded the
sage, listening to his every word, the man asked, "Are these people your disciples?"

The holy man answered, "No, not all of these are my disciples; they are rather my
audience. My disciples are few!"

As we rejoice in the annual celebration of Easter, we can reflect on this story and
ask, "Are we disciples of Jesus?" One way to answer that question would be to reflect
on how we use the Easter gift that Jesus gave his disciples. On Easter Sunday night,
the Risen Christ appeared to the disciples and forgave them. With the gift of peace
he absolved them of their failure to stand by him in his hour of defeat. He also gave
them the task and the power to forgive the sins of others.

The pages of the Gospels are filled with stories about how Jesus forgave sins and
called his disciples to forgive others. He said that we were to forgive each other seventy times seven times—or endlessly. Explore that challenge for a moment. How ready
are you, how willing and eager, to forgive another for the same injury?

To look at it logically, it would seem to be the sign of a fool to continuously forgive
without assurance that a real conversion or change were going to take place. To believe
that no one is ever beyond the possibility of changing his or her behavior demands
not only faith but also hope in the human heart. But to forgive another unconditionally
without any assurance that he or she will change requires even greater faith and hope.
Such hope and faith are beyond the natural; they are divine gifts. Easter is a feast of
hope and faith and an appropriate time to renew our dedication to the daily work of
disciples, the work of forgiving one another.

Often when we say that we forgive another, it really means that we "forgive" but
don't forget. The memory of the offense is kept alive and is frequently fed by bitterness.
To forgive other persons can also mean that we are only willing to tolerate their
weakness, carefully guarding ourselves against being hurt by them. Both of these types
of forgiveness imply that our way of relating to the other person is changed because
of the offense committed against us. Instead of acting, we are reacting to the other.
This is not the forgiveness of the disciples of the Risen Christ.

When we forgive another in the sense of giving that person absolution, we set the
other free from the consequences of his or her actions. A variety of consequences might
follow our being injured. We may no longer trust the other as much or at all. The offense may live a ghostly existence in our memory and on occasion may reappear in
conversation or in our actions. And if we act in a guarded manner, the other may in
turn build walls, making real communication—no less communion—very doubtful at
best. But when absolution is given, those reactions are no longer present. To absolve
people is to absorb them, their failings, their weaknesses—all of them. When we forgive

in this manner, we assimilate and incorporate the other person as a sponge soaks up water. In such a holy process we take upon ourselves the sins of the other and wipe away all the interpersonal consequences of the sin. In short, we truly forgive and forget. Only a forgiveness that contains absolution and absorption of the other leads to reconciliation—a full return of harmony.

"Forgive whatever grievances you have against one another" (Col. 3: 13), said St. Paul, echoing the call of Jesus to his disciples. We are to be ministers of reconciliation which means we are to forgive as we are to love—with all our hearts, minds and bodies. Truly only such forgiveness can heal the world. That is not only our Easter gift but also our Easter assignment as Christ's disciples. And this Easter question lingers in the air: are we disciples of Jesus or merely his audience?

ORDAINED TO BE WAITS

You are probably aware that we spend about one-third of our lives sleeping, but did you know that most of us spend five years of life just waiting? According to a recent study of human behavior, we spend that mass of time waiting for buses or planes, for traffic lights to change, for our turn at the check-out stand or for some event to begin. No wonder that impatience is such a common experience!

Washington Irving, in his sketch book which contained the stories of "Rip Van Winkle" and "The Legend of Sleepy Hollow," wrote, "I had scarcely got into bed when a strain of music seemed to break forth in the air just below the window. I listened, and found it proceeded from a band which I concluded to be the waits from some neighboring village." The watchmen of earlier times were called "waits," and they sounded a horn or played a tune to mark the top of the hour. Waits joined into a uniformed band for their town's civil or religious celebrations. Waits announced that the event or day for which people had been waiting had arrived.

The feast of Pentecost is one for which we wait fifty days after the passing of Easter. Pentecost celebrates the arrival of the Gift of God for which the early Church had prayerfully waited after Jesus' ascension. That gift of the Spirit which Jesus promised was also what the world had been waiting for, and waits for again today. The gift of God's Spirit is the gift of the Spirit of creation, of newness, the Spirit of the holy, the Spirit of unity. A splintered, divorced world hungers for unity and for peace, the sacred Siamese twin of unity.

As the world experiences the radical change of these days when old institutions are collapsing, she longs for the Spirit of a new creation and new life. Old and tired, she yearns for the perpetual youthfulness that is the gift of God's Spirit. The world is thirsty for dreams and visions of a new and better tomorrow, for she realizes the truth in the wisdom of the Book of Proverbs, "Where there is no vision, the people perish" (Pr. 29: 18).

Where there is no hope, vision perishes, for the heart is then blind to the good, the new and the fresh hidden in the midst of whatever burdens us. We must pray with hopeful hearts and have faith that, through us, God will send the Spirit to recreate the earth. We who have been anointed in the Spirit must constantly remind ourselves that it was with the oil of gladness that we were ordained to be "waits," the musician-announcers of the arrival of the Spirit.

By songs of joy and hope in our daily lives, we proclaim to our friends, our neighbors and to the world the Good News that Jesus has kept his promise of the gift of the Spirit. The Holy Spirit, who came as flaming tongues and a great wind, comes also as smiles and laughter. The presence of the Holy Spirit in this world is announced by those waits who find joy in their marriages and life commitments, joy in their work and joy in life. So, what are we waiting for—let's all make holy waiting our vocation!

AMPUTATED AMBITIONS

During the siege of Sebastopol, Czar Nicholas of Russia was once riding along the wall of the city when an enemy archer took aim at him. A Russian soldier who observed the incident shouted to the czar to watch out for his life. His scream startled the emperor's horse, causing it to swerve to one side. As a result the arrow missed its intended mark. The grateful czar later called the soldier before him and told him to ask for any favor he wished and it would be granted him. The soldier replied, ''My sergeant is a brutal man. He is always beating me and the other men. If only I could serve under another sergeant!''

''Fool!'' cried the czar. ''You should have asked to be a sergeant yourself!''

This story from old Russia is a good parable for each of us. We are like the poor soldier who could only ask to have his present petty needs met. The emperor of all Russia, in a token of gratitude, offered *any* favor, but the horizon of possibilities of the simple soldier prevented him from seeing beyond his limited experience. He could have asked to become a sergeant himself—or even a general! How often do we also ask only for our daily necessities instead of praying for great things?

As the feast of Pentecost draws closer, we are invited to ask for gifts from the Holy Spirit. We have access to the very Spirit of God. But what do we ask for—what are the limits of our horizons? The feast of the Holy Spirit is a wonderful opportunity for us to examine our prayer horizons, an occasion to search our dreams and hopes to see if they are limited by our immediate desires or our present problems.

The dynamic power of dreaming is borne out in the fact that people tend to become what they dream of becoming! Before we can truly celebrate a feast of the Spirit, we need to dream great dreams of becoming holy people! To become a saint is not far-fetched; it can happen to those who desire it with enough passion. To dream of becoming the best parent in the world, the most understanding marriage partner or the most compassionate servant of God is not daydreaming. It is rather giving substance to our prayers.

When you pray this Pentecost, can you ask for something better, wider and more dynamic? Can you pray for your heart's **true** desire?

COME, HOLY SPIRIT

News was given to Rabbi Moshe Leib that his best friend, the Rabbi of Berditchev, was seriously ill. On the Sabbath, Rabbi Leib said his friend's name over and over in his prayers for a full recovery (which, by the way, is a wonderful way to pray for anyone who is in need). When he had finished his prayers, Rabbi Leib put on a new pair of shoes which were made of morocco leather. He laced them up tight and then began to dance. One of his disciples who was present said, ''The power of God flowed forth from his dancing. Every step expressed profound mystery, and a strange, unearthly light filled the house where he was. Everyone who was there watching him saw the heavenly host join in his dance."

To be caught up in mystic dance is a deeply religious experience not only for Hasidic Jews but also for Sufi Moslems. Christians, for a variety of cultural reasons, do not usually include dancing among the "inspired" actions of devotion. As we celebrate the feast of Pentecost, we have to wonder about just how we would be affected if we were possessed by God's Spirit. In hundreds, if not thousands, of churches on this feast, Christians sing and pray, "Come, Holy Spirit." But this prayer usually carries an unspoken conditional clause, "but come in acceptable ways!"

If we are unwilling to be "inspired" as was the saintly rabbi in the story, to allow the Spirit to move us as the Spirit desires, then should we really pray, "Come, Holy Spirit"? Each Pentecost we listen to the story of the first Christian Pentecost, when the Spirit of God caused the friends of Jesus to behave in such a manner that the crowds thought them to be drunk. The purpose of this reflection is not to call for mass congregational dancing on Pentecost Sunday; rather it is intended to challenge our awareness of what we are asking when we pray, "Come, Holy Spirit."

God hears the prayers of those who are really serious about what they are requesting. Are we really serious about our petition for the Spirit of God—the Spirit of Fire, Truth and Justice, Love and Divine Madness to come into our well-ordered, respectable and middle-class American lives? If we are dissatisfied with our daily lives, with their lackluster drabness, with their lack of passion and divine flavor, then like Rabbi Moshe Leib, let us pray with devotion to the Spirit of God. But before we begin such a faith-filled prayer, perhaps we should look around and ask ourselves the question, "Am I ready—*really* ready—for the Holy Spirit to respond to my prayers?"

A NEW NAME FOR THE HOLY SPIRIT

On Pentecost, Jesus gave his infant community a rare gift, the gift of the Holy Spirit. But two thousand years removed from that event, it is too common to think about that divine gift of Spirit as something which is the opposite of matter. We might have a better understanding of the Holy Spirit, which each of us has also received, if we would change our name for the Third Person of the Trinity.

Change the name of the Holy Spirit? How unthinkable! Yet when many of us were growing up, we called the Third Person of the Trinity the "Holy Ghost." Within the past twenty-five years, however, that term has fallen from our vocabulary because of the negative connotation of the word "ghost." But now, perhaps, because we have grown accustomed to change, we could make another one. To assist us in understanding the full implications of our gift, I would propose that we do not say "the Holy Spirit" but rather "the Spirit of the Holy." The shift may seem slight, but it is significant.

The Risen Christ continues to give to us, as he imparted to the first disciples, the gift of the Spirit of Holiness. Becoming saintly people, becoming holy, is the real work of our lives. But we often think that our efforts to create a daily prayer life are doomed from the beginning. We feel constricted by our jobs, commitments and the constant lack of time to pray or do spiritual reading. But we **have** been given the gift that helps us make holiness a reality in our lives.

If you see a need to create a nourishing daily prayer life but lack enough desire to carve out time for it, take out that gift of the Spirit of the Holy given to you by the

Risen Christ and use it. Pray to the Spirit for a hunger and thirst for holiness, and you may be surprised at what happens.

When you are caught in one of those dry deserts of prayer, devoid of any emotional nourishment or inspiration, when you are tempted to get up and walk away from what seems to be failure at prayer, that is the time to reach inside your heart for your personal gift of the Spirit of Holiness, the time to pray for perseverance and discipline.

This proposed change in the name of the Third Person of the Holy Trinity will probably never happen in church worship. But as we begin our personal prayer times, we might find it to be of great assistance to make the sign of the cross with these words:

> In the name of the Father,
> and of the Son
> and of the Spirit of the Holy.

ADVENT: THE SEASON TO STAY AWAKE

The season of Advent is ushered in by the words of Jesus: "Be constantly on the watch! Stay awake! You know not when the appointed time will come" (Mk. 13: 33). Perhaps the following story, believed to have been handed down from the Prophet Mohammed himself, will help us to reflect on this theme that initiates Advent.

Once a good man lived a life in which he cultivated all the qualities necessary to reach Paradise. He gave alms to the poor; he cared for the homeless. He had great patience with the unexpected hardships of life. He made pilgrimages to holy shrines. He prayed five times a day and kept busy doing good. He had, however, one fault—he tended to be heedless.

The man thought this to be a small failing since he did so many good things. Yet, on occasion he would be so involved in good works as to miss the needs of the poor person who lived next door. And often he was so eager to complete his morning prayers that he failed to heed the beauty of the sun rising. As his many charitable deeds and numerous prayers left their impression on his soul, so did his fault of being heedless.

When the man died, he awoke to find himself walking toward the great walled garden of Paradise. Up ahead were the tall gates of Paradise, and so he began to examine his conscience to see if he was worthy to enter. After a brief examination, he saw no reason why he should not be admitted to heaven.

But when he arrived, he found that the tall gates were shut tightly. Then a voice addressed him: "Be watchful, for the gates will open only once every hundred years." So the good man settled down to wait, excited at the prospect. But deprived of opportunities to do good to others and to practice his virtues, he found that his capacity for attention was short. After watching for what seemed to him like an eternity, his head nodded in sleep. For an instant—only an instant—his eyelids closed. And in that brief moment the gates of Paradise opened wide. But before his eyes were again fully open, the gates closed with a clang loud enough to wake the dead.

The moral of the story is that even good works, prayer and desire are not sufficient. We need to cultivate a vigilance, a way of life that makes us constantly awake to the Mystery. For as Jesus and Mohammed said, we know not the appointed time.

THE UN-SAINT OF ADVENT

The pre-Christmas season has two feast days honoring Mary, the holy mother: the Immaculate Conception on December 8 and Our Lady of Guadalupe on December 12. I would like to propose that we find room in Advent for a feast day honoring Joseph, the foster father of Jesus and husband of Mary. Without such a feast of Joseph of Nazareth—the carpenter, son of Jacob, the dreamer, the receiver of angelic messages—he easily becomes a silent "stand-in" in the Christmas drama. St. Joseph doesn't need another feast day, but we do. We need to be reminded of the qualities that he possessed, qualities that are especially necessary during these hectic holidays.

It would be no less refreshing a feast day than the soft drink which advertisers have named the un-cola. The celebration for that un-hero—who stands in the Gospel shadows, who stands smiling at the edge of a crowd of admirers flocking around his lover, Mary, and his son, Jesus—could hold prayerful insights for us all. We know little about this man Joseph from an out-of-the-way town in Galilee who nourished the holy family with his affection and tender love. He supported Mary and the Divine Child with the quiet strength of his attentive presence. Thomas Merton, although speaking of the famous Zen scholar, Suzuki, gives us a good picture of St. Joseph:

> He was not compelled to play the complex games by which one jockeys for advantage in the intellectual world. Therefore, of course, he found himself quite naturally and without difficulty in a position of prominence. He spoke with authority, the authority of a simple, clear-sighted man who was aware of human limits and not inclined to improve on them with high artificial structures.

We need more of such saints in our society to offset our passion for the famous, well-known and "titled" people whom we admire so much.

Perhaps the best feast day would be an un-feast day, an un-celebration honoring the saint who stands in the background of every crib, who has no great lines in nativity plays. It is a necessary feast day, for who among us will ever have a special day set aside to commemorate our holiness? We, like Joseph, have an active and central part to play in the drama of redemption. Joseph, the simple but superior man, the hidden but dynamic lover, embodies an essential secret of this spiritual season: the clear, quiet stability necessary for the miracle of the divine birth.

A NEW CHRISTMAS GREETING

The greetings that we usually exchange with one another, such as, "How are you?" "Have a good day" or "Take it easy," are replaced in this season with the ancient and beautiful expression, "Merry Christmas." While I'm a strong believer in traditions, I would like to propose a new holiday greeting that not only sums up the awesome mystery of the incarnation of Jesus Christ, but is also an excellent greeting or farewell for any day of the year.

It's not a new salutation but a very old one, used for centuries by Italians. If you have ever traveled in Italy or even seen European films, you will likely be acquainted with the term "ciao," pronounced "chow." Today it is widely used throughout the world both as a greeting and a farewell between friends. The word comes from the dialect of Veneto, the region of northeast Italy around the area of Venice. It was the habit of the citizens of that city to greet and take leave of their friends with the respectful phrase, "Schiavo vostro." In the local dialect it was pronounced "s-ciao" and eventually shortened to "ciao."

"Schiavo vostro" literally means "I am your slave." While the Gospel writers did not record the first words of the baby Jesus, I can guess what they were. The original utterance of the infant of Bethlehem must have been something like "I am your servant." If the incarnation of Christ means anything, it means that God not only became flesh but also came to serve everyone as humbly as a slave. At his Last Supper, Jesus performed the duties of a slave when he washed his disciples' feet. He told them that he was giving them an example, that they should likewise become slaves to one another. As the message of the Good News spread to Greece and Italy, the term "slave" was often considered to be offensive, and so it was changed to "servant." Today, the title "slave" remains a very negative one, considering that it has been only about 120 years since black people were slaves in this country. And even the title "servant" does not have a ring of nobility for most people. But true service is not the same thing as passive submission to the whims of another—Jesus, in fact, often defied the religious leaders of his day. Rather, it involves seeking what is truly good for another person and being willing to sacrifice toward that end. There is great nobility in that kind of service. Thus, one of the most beautiful names for the bishop of Rome isn't the title of authority, "Pope," but rather "The Servant of the Servants of God."

If we want to make Christmas more than a festival of gift-giving, carol singing and feasting, we might begin to greet our friends and members of our families with the expression, "ciao!" Imagine what would happen to the average home if each person who dwelled there became a slave for the others. And imagine what the world would be like if every disciple of Christ became a true slave for the world. Imagine what changes would occur among the poor, the hungry and the homeless if we greeted them with a genuine "ciao."

But the consequences of taking such a greeting seriously would not only make each of our homes—if not the world—a totally different environment, it would require a radical change in us. So perhaps, considering the high cost of such a true Christmas and Christian greeting, we should stick to "Merry Christmas" or even "Have a nice day." These greetings are safe and neutral, and they do not personally cost us anything. Ciao!

SERVANTS WITHOUT CALENDARS

Christmas has come and gone; a new year awaits us. The echo of the song of the angels, "Peace on earth," still lingers in the winter wind, but after all these centuries there is very little peace on earth. How many more Christmas feasts will it take till we see that prophetic song fulfilled?

A story is told about a young couple who had a child. The father of the infant went to a carpenter known for his fine craftsmanship and asked, "Will you make a cradle for our baby boy?"

The carpenter agreed, saying, "Come next week, I will have it for you."

After a week the young father came to pick up the cradle, but the carpenter wasn't finished. Week after week the father came back; months passed, then years, but the cradle was never completed. Meanwhile, the infant became a child, and finally an adult. In the course of time he was married, and he and his wife had a child. The grandfather told his son, "Go to the carpenter and ask him if he's finished with the cradle I ordered twenty-three years ago." So the young father went and inquired.

"Off with you!" the carpenter shouted. "I refuse to be stampeded in my work just because you and your family are obsessed with your need for this cradle!"

As we prepare to conclude another year, almost the 2,000th since the coming of the Prince of Peace, this story reminds us to be patient with the promise of the Divine Craftsman. One of the duties of those who are servants of God is to be willing to do things God's way. The divine timetable is unlike ours, which looks for success **right now**. Weeks turn into months, years into centuries, and we continue to wait—sometimes in faith, sometimes in frustration. To surrender to such an undefined divine agenda is difficult. We very easily grow tired of doing good, of praying and working for peace. We grow weary of crying out for justice.

But as the old carpenter demanded patience from the family "obsessed" with their desired cradle, so God requires patience from us. As servants of the Timeless, we are to use our time as tireless workers who labor daily with devotion for peace and justice— but without watches, clocks or calendars.

ACKNOWLEDGEMENTS

The author is indebted to the following authors whose books were used as resources in writing this almanac:

A Feast of Days, Paul Jennings, 1982, Maxwell House, London; *Brewer's Dictionary of Phrase & Fable*, Ivor Evans, 1981, Harper & Row, New York; *Catholic Dictionary*, Donald Attwater, 1941, Macmillan, New York; *The Cat's Pajamas*, Tad Tuleja, 1987, Fawcett Columbine, New York; *Chase Annual Events*, 1988, Contemporary Books, New York; *Connections*, James Burke, 1978, Little, Brown & Company, Boston; *Cosmos*, Carl Sagan, 1980, Random House, New York; *Curious Customs*, Tad Tuleja, 1987, Harmony Books, New York; *Dictionary of Christian Lore and Legend*, J.C.J. Metford, 1983, Thames and Hudson, London; *Encyclopaedia Britannica*, 1960, Encyclopaedia Britannica Inc., Chicago, London; *Extraordinary Origins of Everyday Things*, Charles Panati, 1987, Harper & Row, New York; *Familiar Quotations*, John Bartlett, 1980, Little, Brown & Company, Boston; *Famous Last Words & Tombstone Humor*, Gyles Brandreth, 1989, Sterling, New York; *Handbook of Christian Feasts and Customs*, Francis X. Weiser, 1952, Harcourt, Brace & Company, New York; *Harper's Index Book*, Lapham, Pollan, Etheridge, 1987, Henry Holt, New York; *Mammoth Book of Fascinating Information*, Richard Manchester, 1980, A & W Visual Library, New York; *Saint Andrew Bible Missal*, 1962, Biblica, Bruges, Belgium; *Tales of the Dervishes*, Idries Shah, 1970, E.P. Dutton, New York; *Tales of the Hasidim*, Martin Buber, 1948, Schocken, New York; *The Best Book of Trivia*, V. Schei & Jack Griffin, 1958, Gallery, New York; *The Book of Holidays Around the World*, Alice Van Straalen, 1986, E.P. Dutton, New York; *The Cosmic Mind-Boggling Book*, Neil McAleer, 1982, Warner, New York; *The Roman Martyrology*, translated by Raphael Collins, 1952, Newman Press, Westminster, Maryland; *The Timetables of History*, Bernard Grun, 1982, Simon & Schuster, New York; *The Timetables of Science*, Hellemans & Bunch, 1988, Simon & Schuster, New York; *The World Book Encyclopedia*, 1966, Field Enterprises, Chicago; *The World's Religions*, Wm. Ferdmans, 1982, Wm. Ferdmans Company, Grand Rapids; *Thread of Life*, Roger Lewin, 1982, Smithsonian, Washington, D.C.; *Zen Art for Meditation*, Stewart Holmes & Chimyo Horioka, 1973, Charles Tuttle, Rutland, Vermont; *Zen Poems, Prayers, Anecdotes, Interviews*, Lucien Stryk and Takashi Ikemoto, 1965, Doubleday, New York; *Zen to Go*, Jon Winokur, 1989, New American Library, Penguin, New York.